To Natalie a
my very good Sunday lunchtime
drinking friends.

Tony Hackett

Both Sides of the Bar

Both Sides of the Bar

Tony Hackett

CARLOGGAS PUBLISHING

Copyright © C A Hackett 2004
First published in 2004 by Carloggas Publishing
Lower Carloggas Cottage
Newquay Rd, St Columb Major
Cornwall
TR9 6SD

Distributed by Carloggas Publishing

The right of C A Hackett to be identified as the author of the work has been asserted herein in accordance with the Copyright, Designs and Patents Act 1988.

All rights reserved. This book is sold subject to the condition that it shall not, by way of trade or otherwise, be lent, resold, hired out or otherwise circulated without the publisher's prior consent in any form of binding or cover other than that in which it is published and without a similar condition including this condition being imposed on the subsequent purchaser.

British Library Cataloguing in Publication Data
A catalogue record for this book is available from the British Library

ISBN 0-9547853-0-4
Typeset by Amolibros, Milverton, Somerset
This book production has been managed by Amolibros
Printed and bound by T J International Ltd, Padstow, Cornwall, UK

*To Sylvia
my boyhood sweetheart
my wife
my business partner
my best friend
and without whose encouragement
this book would never have been written.*

Contents

The background years 1

Life before 3

Opening time 5

The Crows Nest 15

The Dukes Arms 60

The Brave Old Oak Hotel 137

Bartholomew Arms 209

Reflections 286

Illustrations facing page 184

The Background Years

I first met Sylvia when my parents moved to Foxton, a small village near Market Harborough, in 1948. My mother had taken the tenancy of the Shoulder of Mutton, a public house in the village.

In those days, it was quite common at a lot of rural tenancies for the wife to be the license holder, enabling the husband to follow another occupation. My father, who had retired from the Leicestershire Police Force, was in charge of security at a nearby disused wartime airfield, used by the War Department for storing military vehicles returning from abroad.

Sylvia had lived in Foxton all her life, together with her older brother and younger sister. My father's police service meant that my two older sisters and I had lived in numerous other places before moving here. Our previous residence was a large manor house used as a country club. Neither my younger sister Paddy, nor I, wanted to move to Foxton – she still lives there!

I met Sylvia when I went to the weekly table tennis evening held in the village hall. A dance had been organised for the following week, we danced together and that was that. Sylvia was 16 and I was 14 coming up to 15.

Sylvia worked for a lingerie manufacturing company and I had just started work at a garage, both in Market Harborough. I left the garage after a few months and got a job as a laboratory assistant at a firm in the town making foundry supplies. My ambition was to join the Royal Navy as soon as I was old enough and I achieved this in late 1949 at the age of 15.

I served on two destroyers, HMS *Crossbow* and *Broadsword*, a minesweeper depot ship HMS *Mull of Galloway*, and the cruiser HMS *Superb* on which I spent 18 wonderful months in Canada, USA, West Indies and South America, prior to our marriage.

We were married in the village church in July 1955. I was 21. Shortly afterwards I sailed on HMS *Birmingham*, a county class cruiser, for a three-year commission in the Mediterranean. Sylvia and a few other wives flew out to Malta for a short holiday at Christmas, and while she was there, I obtained a transfer ashore to join the staff of the Commander-in-Chief Mediterranean, Lord Louis Mountbatten. We spent two and a half years marvellous years in Malta during which time our eldest son, Stephen was born.

After our return to the UK, I was posted to submarines at Faslane Naval Base in Scotland, and we stayed there until I returned south for a resettlement course and eventual demob in late 1959.

For many years now, Sylvia, our sons, friends and ex-colleagues, have all said I ought to write a book about our life and experiences as publicans and hoteliers. Now that I have reasonably mastered the intricacies of my computer, I have decided, in the words of Wilfred Pickles, to *"Have a Go!"*

I received a lot of assistance from Betty and Gordon Peck from Woodford, Janet Bull from Towcester and Lee Penny, Ken Vaughan and Douglas Blake at Blakesley in checking facts not covered by Sylvia's diaries and our old business records. I thank them all and apologise for being such a nuisance.

LIFE BEFORE

Whilst serving for ten years in the Royal Navy, I spent the years 1955 – 1958 in Malta, as part of the Commander-in-Chief Mediterranean's staff. During this time, I started a rugby club (The Forts) for Naval personnel serving in shore establishments. For the last two years we rented an empty bar, which we converted to a clubhouse and Sylvia and I acted as honorary Steward and Stewardess. This involved all planning, negotiating with suppliers, stock control and serving behind the bar. We ran the club on the same lines as a civilian rugby club with no rank differential whatsoever. When we left the island, the membership had risen to 150 consisting mainly of RN, RAF and Army personnel, with fixtures against visiting warships swelling the takings. Apart from the obvious pleasure we derived from seeing the venture go from strength to strength, we gained a good insight into the licensed trade.

During the Suez campaign, the island was flooded with service personnel and I played, on average, four games a week, including five games for the Royal Navy versus the Army. Normally the Navy would give the Army, strengthened by the Royal Marines, a thrashing, but amongst the many troops on the island was the Duke of Wellington's Regiment. They had been the Army champions for the last five years, and included National Servicemen Hardy and Shuttleworth, the England half back combination, Rev Robin Rew, Ireland and British Lions captain, a young Mike Campbell-Lamerton who went on to captain Scotland and the 1966 Lions, and Phil Horrocks-Taylor, England and 1959 Lions. In addition, they had a couple of National Service Rugby League International forwards. The Navy had Malcolm Phillips, England, Alf Valentine, Scotland and Andy Mulligan, Ireland. We were pleased the Royal Marines returned to their normal allegiance with the Royal Navy; this gave us Dan Scully, 6' 6" of solid muscle, a Special Boat Squadron Colour Sergeant. The Army won the series 3–2 in which, considering the strength of the opposition, we gave a very good account of ourselves. During this period my boss on C-in-C's staff, Captain Duncan Campbell, apart from giving me lots of time off to play rugby, allowed me to leave the office three times a week to receive beer deliveries to meet the extra demand. I was fortunate in that both him and his deputy, Lt Cdr Brian Pleass used the club.

Before leaving the service, I applied to take a three-month hotel & catering resettlement course as part of the preparation for returning to civilian life. The first month was spent at Westminster Catering College, London where I was given basic tuition in food preparation. This was followed by two months concentrated training in kitchen and bar work at The Castle Hotel, Windsor. On two occasions, I was seconded to assist in the kitchens of Windsor Castle for Royal functions – quite an experience. Those three months gave me a very good basic training and introduction to the licensed trade.

Opening Time

On leaving the Navy in 1959, Sylvia and I applied for the position as managers with: Bass, Ind Coope, Marstons, Charles Wells, Phipps Northampton Brewery Company and Everards. All gave us initial interviews but most intimated they thought we were too young at 25 and 26 respectively. Ind Coope however did offer us the Old White Swan Hotel in Leicester market place. They seemed to think that because my mother had kept a village pub for a number of years, I must have gained some experience helping her. The truth was, I joined the Royal Navy at the age of 15 and in my ten years' service, had spent a considerable time at sea and abroad. Still, I was quite content to let them think otherwise.

The pub was next door to the Corn Exchange, a popular dance hall at that time, particularly with American service personnel from local air bases. We went along at night to view the place and discovered that half the premises had been closed by order of the Watch Committee (then the city's licensing authority) due to fights that had taken, and were still taking place on the premises. Two of the previous managers were still in hospital and a blonde, long-haired, simpering homosexual named Cyril was temporarily in charge. I asked him how he handled the trouble and he said he did not. At the first sign, he locked himself in the wine store and pressed a panic button installed by the local police.

Most of the trouble came from American serviceman and Teddy Boys from the dance hall fighting over local girls, plus the odd prostitute-fighting-prostitute over clients. According to Cyril, it was separating the latter that resulted in the last manager's worst injuries Even with its closed rooms, the Old White Swan was still one of the largest public houses in Leicester. Built around 1750, it was once the premier coaching hotel in the town. The function room, seating 150, had been the venue for annual Fat Stock Dinners and Hunt Balls for many years before the war. This was one of the rooms now closed. There were three bars with six full-time bar staff, twelve part-time and two full-time cellar men. The manager's accommodation consisted of a six-bedroomed flat with lounge, kitchen and bathroom, all very huge. The other bedrooms had been closed due to their dilapidated condition.

We realized we were being offered an excellent opportunity to make our name in the trade by taking on what was obviously a challenge to such a young and comparatively inexperienced couple. We asked the brewery to give us a week to think it over before making a decision. I contacted the Provost Marshals at the two main American air bases and they were equally keen to have it cleaned up. I reasoned that getting it placed out of bounds to the American servicemen would reduce the friction between them and the local lads who were the root cause of the trouble.

I presented my proposals to the brewery and warned them that initially there would be a drop in takings, but was confident I could get back the good class trade it had previously enjoyed. The brewery director said he would study our proposals and contact us in a few days. They were true to their word and, two days later, we presented ourselves for what we hoped was going to be the most important day of our lives.

Mr Hubbard, from the brewery, said he had studied our proposals very carefully and would offer us the following terms of contract; the joint salary would be £9 per week. We were allowed one day off together each week and one week's holiday a year. All catering would be ours. The pub was selling 16 barrels of beer a week (1 barrel = 36 gallons) and 10 gallons of spirits. He said they were prepared to let this drop to 12 barrels for a limited period whilst I eliminated the trouble. When I asked what the brewery considered a "limited period," after some discussion on the telephone Mr Hubbard eventually replied, "One month!"

It was obvious to both of us that the brewery was not serious over wanting the pub "cleaned up". With the departure of the Americans, trade would decrease by at least 50% for a month and maybe much longer. What they really wanted was another manager who would put his head and career on the block, and maintain the volume of trade at its present level. We were very disappointed with the outcome and today still wonder which path our career would have taken had we been allowed to put our ideas into practice.

Some two years later, we learned the pub had closed following the closure of the American air bases. It stayed closed for three years and reopened later as the first and largest Bernie Inn in the Midlands

Before leaving the Navy, I had decided on the licensed trade as my number one choice for a future career. Other possibilities were the Police Force, Customs Service and Prison Service. All offered what was most needed in the late 1950s, a place in which to live. All service personnel were encouraged to put their names down on council house waiting lists two years before leaving the service. In 1956 I put my name down with Market Harborough RDC, and at that time was 3,500th on the list. A points system was operated and with just one child, we did not score very highly. When I left the service the council informed me I was number 4,800, hence the need for a career that provided housing.

While still serving in the Navy I sat and passed the entrance exams for the Police and Customs Service, so after our disappointment with Ind Coope I attended a selection board with a view to joining the Derbyshire Police Force. Derby was my choice because the Chief Constable at that time was an ex-Welsh Rugby International and it was generally understood that if you played for the county force, promotion would be a lot easier. This was apart from the pleasure of being able to once again play rugby twice a week, as I had in the Navy – when not at sea.

About a week later, we received a letter from Charles Wells Brewery at Bedford, offering us the Fox Inn at Carlton a village in Bedfordshire, as assisted tenants. This was a scheme operated by some breweries making it easier for tenants to take small pubs whereby the brewery owned the fixtures, fittings and furniture and rented them to the tenant. It was ideal for couples with insufficient capital to take a full tenancy. That same day we made an appointment to view within 24 hours.

The Fox Inn exterior was straight off the lid of a chocolate box. It stood by the village green with a thatched roof you could touch from the ground. It looked like an old-fashioned bread loaf. The inside was a complete dream – flag stoned floor, twisted oak beams, window shutters, and a magnificent fireplace. At a time when pub interiors were being vandalised by brewery architects, it was good to see its character was still intact. Unfortunately there was just the one room, which at the very most, would have held only 30 or so customers if they all stood up.

The one other pub in the village was at least four times larger. It was the HQ of the village cricket and football teams and with its darts and skittle teams was the hub of village life. I discovered the main clientele of The Fox were officers from a reformatory school on the outskirts of the village. A good class trade but insufficient to warrant our both being employed full-time at the pub. I did not want to be a part-time publican but we had fallen in love with The Fox and so told the brewery we would take it. The total capital involved was a brewery deposit of £25 and a combined business and ingoing rent of £20 per year. Stock cost would have been minimal and the total would have been well inside our £95 savings.

We viewed The Fox on a Tuesday and were to obtain the licence and move in a week the following Monday. On the Friday before, we had a visit from a Mr Perratt of Phipps Northampton Brewery Co. (PNBC) who informed us he had a manager's job for us at the Crows Nest in Irthlingborough, a small town in Northamptonshire. We told him about our proposed tenancy of

The Fox and he strongly advised against taking it saying, "I know the pub well and it has a long history of disasters. The last tenant hung himself in the bar two weeks before you viewed it, and the tenant before that had been bankrupted." Charles Wells brewery later confirmed this. He went on to say, "I am confident that once you see the Crows Nest you will quickly forget The Fox." We never did, and for many years afterwards, we still waxed lyrical about its charm.

When we went to view the Crows Nest, we had great difficulty finding it. The pub was situated on a new council housing estate, up a very steep hill, about a mile outside the town; we later discovered the reason for this. The main employer in the town, Richard, Thomas & Baldwin was an iron ore mining company, and their mine workings ran under most of the surrounding area. Evidence of mine subsidence was apparent in fields adjacent to the estate. The Crow Hill estate composed of some 900 houses, four shops and a large Co-operative Society laundry employing 300 people, mainly women. .

The Crows Nest was situated on the end of the housing, the intention being to extend the development later, when council funds were available, making the pub the centre point of the estate. Our first reaction on sighting the pub was one of awe. It was not yet a year old and its sparkling new red brick facade, surrounded on three sides by car parks, with a very large sunken lawn to the rear, made a very impressive picture. We stood outside for an age, hardly daring to enter and announce ourselves, in case we had come to the wrong Crows Nest.

We entered through large light oak doors into a lobby with gents and ladies toilets to the left, lounge and stairs to manager's flat dead ahead and bar to the right. The bar was a long room with quarry-tiled floor, large windows and furnished with "Ercol" ultra-contemporary light oak upholstered furniture – very "with it" and expensive at the time. The bar servery was fitted with flexi mirror glass on the back fitting and, with the subdued down-lighting, looked very "swish". All woodwork including the bar counter was finished in light oak, making it light and airy. A large walk-in wine store was situated to one side of the bar, with a door to the off licence shop opposite. A further door at the back of the bar led to the cavernous refrigerated ground-floor cellar. The walls and ceiling were lined in thick Formica-covered insulation. The floor and thralls were finished with white glazed bricks; making it look and feel like an operating theatre! In those days, all beer came in wooden barrels and these were fitted with gleaming white plastic covers.

The lounge bar servery led off the bar, the only difference being the counter, which was covered with burnished copper. We had never seen a bar covered with copper before (1959) and thought it looked very glamorous. Though the pub was new, the lounge had large floor-to-ceiling Portland stone mullioned leaded glass windows looking out on a flagstoned patio with steps leading down to the lawn. A large fireplace, also in Portland stone, complemented the windows perfectly. With a bright predominately orange and brown patterned Wilton carpet and matching curtains, dark brown velvet covered tub chairs and low copper topped tables, the effect was rather stunning.

The pub lawn, the largest I had ever seen, contained 40 folding tables with four chairs per table. Moving the furniture, mowing the lawn and disposing of cuttings was almost a day's work. The manager's enclosed vegetable garden, three large wooden portable sheds used as bottle sheds, garden furniture storage, and a two-car garage completed the outside facilities. The sign at the front of the car park showed a tree with a crow in its nest on one side and a sailor in a crow's nest on the other (very appropriate for me). Six futuristic floodlights on top of very high poles illuminated the building, lawn and car park at night.

The living accommodation was vast, lounge, dining room, kitchen, bathroom, extra toilet and three bedrooms. Considering our furniture consisted of just a bed, dressing table and chest of drawers, all of which I had made myself while on leave, we would have a lot of empty space. We later learned that the Crows Nest had been PNBC's showplace pub and the first one designed by non-brewery architects. In the late '50s, building materials were still in short supply and very few adventurously designed houses and buildings had been built.

You have probably guessed by now, we were completely overawed with the size, and grandeur of it all. There and then we decided this was the place for us. It must be said, going back many years later, it never seemed quite so large as it did then in 1958. We telephoned Charles Wells and explained the position; they were very understanding. They said we were probably making the right decision and released us from any obligation to them. We made an appointment to see the Managed House director at PNBC to be interviewed as suitable managers for the Crows Nest

Phipps Northampton Brewery Company was a long established brewery with imposing Victorian premises. The offices were situated at the top of the building and reached by a wooden stairway straight out of a Charles Dickens novel. We both commented on the wonderful smell of floor polish and dried hops as we ascended the stairs at the appointed hour.

Mr R O Baillon, the Managed House director had played over 100 games for Northampton RFC during the period 1932-1945, and in turn had been secretary, chairman and president. Quite early in the interview he said, "I see you play rugby; would you be interested in playing at Northampton?" I said I would but later events were to prove this impossible. Whether or not that influenced him to short-list us, I shall never know. I do know the brewery interviewed ten couples for the position; six were already managers within the group. They had a long waiting list for positions as managers, and an even longer list for tenancies. He started by saying, "We would not normally consider couples under the age of 40, and with new managers it is our standard practice to employ them first as assistant managers, then for a period as relief managers." He said he had been influenced by my references from running the rugby club in Malta. I had obtained references from the Fleet Sports Officer, Commander Jock Aitkin who had been a Scottish rugby international in the 40s, my long-suffering boss on C-in-C's Staff, Captain Duncan Campbell and Group Captain Bob Weighill, England 1947 and future secretary of the Rugby Football Union. Quite an array of influence!

He asked us numerous questions about the Forts Rugby Club and about my time in the service, but very little about much else, apart from one question that has stayed in our minds ever since, and one that we always ask couples who tell us they would like to run a pub: "How strong is your marriage?" At the time we thought it rather impertinent but experience since has shown this is probably the most significant factor in running a pub successfully. In later years, we witnessed the break-up of numerous marriages amongst friends and colleagues within a very short time of entering the trade.

We both have our own views as to what causes these break-ups. Sylvia thinks it's always the man's fault, triggered off by working often for the first time in close proximity to young women. It is a fact that the majority of publicans leave their wives for a barmaid. I tend to think it is the wives' fault. So many couples today take a public house after one or the other is made redundant. Often the wife, middle 40s, has brought up a family and considers herself "over the hill". They move into a pub, she is soon chatted up by male customers and realizes she is still attractive to men, tidies herself up, new hairdo, uses a bit more make up, suddenly she is the centre of attention.

Most red-blooded males after a few drinks fancy "pulling" the landlady! However unattractive she might be, after a few pints, she is the most sensuous, seductive beautiful creature he has ever set eyes on. Knowing that the male customers lust after her, what a feather in his cap it would be if he were the one who scored! The landlady, if she is a professional, plays up to this but keeps it within safe limits. It is when her head is completely turned that the damage is done. In our younger days, I was regularly asked, "Do you mind Sylvia being chatted up?" My reply was always the same: "I shall start to worry when she's not."

Anyway, I digress. Mr Baillon told us, the terms of employment were as follows: – each to work six days a week *with* separate days off, this had to be taken as a complete day, not two halves, and one of us had to be on the premises at all times, day off to be taken on Tuesday, Wednesday or Thursday, one week's holiday a year or two weeks salary in lieu, stock taken each month, two bad ones (with a discrepancy over £5) in succession and you risked dismissal. Plucking up courage I asked what the salary was and at that Mr Baillon bent below his desk and mumbled what I thought was six pounds seven shillings and sixpence a week joint salary. I was certain I had misheard but didn't like to ask him to repeat it, thinking Sylvia probably heard the true sum. As soon as we left the room, I turned to Sylvia and asked her what she thought it was. She confirmed my worst suspicions; she had heard the same amount.

When I left the Navy I was earning approx. £11 per week and for the last 18 months while at Faslane submarine base in Scotland had paid £1.10 shillings (£1.50) weekly rent to share a house. I had various perks and whilst at sea spent very little, so we managed quite well on my naval salary. To live on half that amount made us think long and hard whether the Police Force offered a better alternative. As managers, benefits would include free accommodation, rent and rates, free electricity, water and gas, free disposables, e.g. cleaning materials, light bulbs etc. Although it was difficult to put an accurate figure on these perks, £3 a week was probably not far off. Many hours were spent discussing the pros and cons, pub versus police force, but when the brewery offered us the position the following week, we accepted, confident that we had made the correct decision. .

We spent the weekend before taking over on the Monday with the outgoing managers, Bert and Beulah Angel. Bert had been a full-time official for the Co-operative Workers Trade Union before entering the trade. On occasions, he had stayed at a hotel owned by Beulah's parents in Rushden when in the area on union business. Despite a 20-year age difference, they fell in love and married. Bert was quite a character, very small, with a broad cockney accent and not a hair on his head. Both of them were very kind and taught us much in such a short time. They were the first licensees at the Crows Nest and would be moving to the Abington Park Hotel, a large rambling Victorian edifice in Northampton.

The Crows Nest

On Monday, Bert and I, together with the brewery District Manager, Mr Frank Sellars, attended the Magistrates Court at Wellingborough for the transfer of the licence from Bert to me. It wasn't a full transfer session so I would be granted a temporary Protection Order. The Chairman of the Bench asked Mr Sellars if the brewery were happy with my being so young. He said he couldn't remember granting a licence to anyone so young before. For one dreadful moment I thought he was going to refuse my application until Mr Sellars pointed out that I had served 10 years in the Royal Navy and had excellent references.

On granting me the licence he asked the police inspector present to ensure that extra supervision was applied to the Crows Nest until the next Brewster Sessions, when, if still of "unblemished character" he would grant me a licence proper. The police diligently visited the premises every night for a month then twice weekly afterwards, much to my discomfort. Thankfully, no opposition was offered when two months later I was granted a full licence and my name went over the door. *"Charles Anthony Hackett Esq., licensed to sell Intoxicating Liquor on or off the Premises"*. I liked the esquire bit!

After the granting of the Protection Order, we all went back to the Crows Nest for the transfer, the stock had been taken, inventory checked and eventually the keys were handed over with handshakes all round. On Mr Sellars' instruction I went behind the bar and served drinks to him, Bert, Beulah, Sylvia and myself and we toasted our future success. That evening I received a telephone call from Mr Sellars, during the ensuing conversation he suddenly said, "By the way, Mr Hackett, I didn't see you pay for the drinks you served to us." He paused and then went on, "I hope you paid for them later." The future pattern of attrition had already started to emerge.

We had a very busy evening session, which is quite normal with everyone wanting to get a look at the new landlords. There was no shortage of advice on whom to trust, whom to be friends with, whom to discourage, how to keep beer properly, who would be my best customers. It was endless. At one stage it felt as though everyone in the room had more experience at being publicans than we had.

That night, in bed, we studied carefully the Brewery Managers Handbook – the bible. After ten years in the Navy I was accustomed to reading "Queen's Rules & Admiralty Instructions" but had never experienced anything as trifling as the *Northampton Brewery Company's Instructions and Guidance to Managers*, (1938 edition).

"Managers should at all times be clean and presentable whilst on duty, with neat and tidy hair, clean fingernails and sober clothing. Managers may accept occasional drinks from customers but this should not be taken in excess. Toilet pipes, if bright metal, should be polished after each session. Glasses should always be polished after washing in two changes of water. Beer in drip trays to be returned to the barrel at the first opportunity. If it has to be left overnight in a bucket, it should be covered over with a clean cloth. Managers and staff are to remove cigarettes from their mouths before serving customers. Managers should purchase an approved daily newspaper for their customers' perusal. If the house has a music licence and piano, it should only be played by an accomplished pianist. The law visits with severity the licence holder who harbours in his house certain classes, such as thieves or reputed thieves, vagabonds, policemen on duty, prostitutes for an unreasonable time, and for allowing their house to be used for betting. The practice of managers entertaining "friends" on the premises after licensing hours is prohibited. Should any manager be found on his premises, during licensing hours, in a state of drunkenness, he will be dismissed forthwith and be liable to prosecution. Managers should not allow any bad language or disorderly conduct on their premises. It is illegal to pay wages in a public house, or any place for the sale of liquor, except by the licensee for his own staff. Staff, whilst on duty in the bar, should not have any money whatever on any part of their person. Any manager found guilty of grogging shall be dismissed forthwith." Most modern-day licensees regularly risk dismissal for the breach of at least four rules!

Grogging was a process common when spirits were delivered in wooden barrels. After emptying the barrel you poured in a small amount of water, and by constantly swilling the water round and turning the cask daily, bringing the water into contact with the whole of the interior of the cask. After a couple of weeks you had a slightly lower strength spirit than that which the cask originally contained. I have heard old publicans say that you could get a gallon from an 18-gallon cask. About the only thing the 50-page booklet didn't threaten was transportation to Australia!

Some 15 years later, the National Association of Licensed House Managers NALHM was formed to give managers protection from exploitation by breweries. Today they are extremely well paid with a five-day week and four weeks' holidays amongst other things. However, I do have to say that when entering managed houses today, some of the old brewery rules wouldn't go amiss.

Quite recently I had reason to write a letter of complaint to Greene Kings brewery concerning one of their houses in Rugby.

Last summer Sylvia and I visited the pub at 7 p.m., just wanting a quick drink. We stood at the bar for five minutes before the barman broke off his conversation with a girl seated at the bar, long enough to enquire if we wanted serving. There appeared to be four staff on duty; two girls were playing pool and another barman sat at a table reading a paper. We took our drinks and sat down; I then noticed on our table was a completed application form for a barman's job. Shortly afterwards I went to the gents toilet which was flooded; some enterprising person had wrenched a door from the washbasin unit to stand on clear of the water. While I was there, the newspaper-reading barman came in and announced, "The drain's blocked again" – as if I needed him to tell me.

When I returned to our table, the form was still lying there, so on leaving we took it with us as proof of its existence The four-page form contained the personal details of a 22-year-old youth, who we were sure would not have wanted them left on a table for all to read. I duly wrote to the brewery enclosing the form and after some five weeks received a letter of apology, which stated that their 23-year-old manageress was newly appointed and had been under pressure! And to think I was considered too young and inexperienced at 25. Mr Frank Sellars, wartime Staff Sergeant in the Royal Leicestershire Regiment, would have had a field day if it had been one of his pubs.

The customers at the Crows Nest were employed in a variety of trades, mainly mining, leather dressing, boot and shoe operatives and building trades. Most were young with young families. Some were natives of Irthlingborough but many came from surrounding towns, Rushden, Higham Ferrers, Burton Latimer and Finedon. A few had married local girls but most were there because council houses in Irthlingborough were easier to obtain than in their own towns. Very few people had cars in 1958 and, with the estate being a mile from the town, it wasn't the most convenient area in which to live. The steep hill made cycling impossible for most of the journey to the estate, and pushing a pram up the hill was a major feat. Consequently, when houses became available in the town and surrounding areas, the Crow Hill residents eagerly sought them.

Couples willingly exchanged a modern house on the estate for a 1930s style house or even a 1940s pre-fab. This had the effect of making it a transitional residence for a lot of the estate couples. They were reluctant to involve themselves in any community activities, or to establish relationships with their neighbours. We were made very aware of this in our first few weeks when delivery drivers, tallymen, debt collectors etc all asking in the pub if anyone knew where a Mr So-and-So lived. Often no one replied but it sometimes later transpired that his neighbours were there in the bar. If it was a known debt collector – and they called daily – you could understand the reluctance to divulge information, but not for a doctor or postman as sometimes was the case.

Darts and a game of table skittles (mainly played in Leicestershire, Northamptonshire, Warwickshire and Bedfordshire) were very popular in the area, but the Crows Nest had neither. A pub of its size should have had at least one team in each pastime, which helps to create friendships amongst customers. We installed a dartboard during the first week for which I had to obtain special dispensation from the brewery, as my games allowance (for the purchase of cards, dominoes, darts etc) of £4 per year had already been spent by Bert when he first opened the pub. The dartboard, purchased from the brewery, cost £2. 15s, three sets of darts £1 and a darts mat was a further £1.10s. In authorising the expenditure Mr Sellars informed me he expected an increase in takings to justify this expense. We were allowed to spend £1 on any item for the pub, without brewery permission, provided it was considered necessary and of a competitive price. I put up a notice inviting customers to enter a darts competition with a £1 prize that I supplied myself. In no time, we had some 50 entrants and the first steps had been taken to form a team.

When the winter dart leagues started, we had two teams entered in different men's leagues and a ladies team playing friendlies. The friendships I had hoped for were being formed amongst the players and supporters; it always existed below the surface and just wanted bringing out. It wasn't long before I formed an angling section (the River Nene ran at the bottom of the estate) and was organising coach outings to watch Northampton and Peterborough football matches. Our enthusiasm knew no bounds

When we took over the pub, the takings averaged £130 a week. Beer was 1/1d a pint and spirits 1s 3d (5p and 6p). The weekly barrelage was seven barrels (36 gallon each), spirit sales were negligible, about a bottle a week. Large off sales of cigarettes boosted the takings (no machines in those days). At the end of the first year we had increased the takings to £210 per week, the weekly barrelage to eight barrels, with spirits just two bottles. The small spirit sales reflected the standard of the clientele at the Crows Nest. In those days, only the wealthy drank spirits. Women customers tended to drink shandy, lemonade or fruit juice. Babycham and similar drinks had not yet entered the market. On special occasions, wedding and birthday celebrations and Christmas, they would drink port, sherry and the occasional liqueur. During the year the price of beer had increased to 1s 2d and spirits to 1s 4d a tot (6p and 7p).

Our staff wage allowance was based on a brewery formula of no staff for the first £50 takings then one staff hour for each £5 taken. For example, takings of £90 entitled us to 16 staff hours. This could be one person for 16 hours or four people for four hours each. The biggest problem with this system was you never knew what your full allowance would be until the end of the week, which went from Monday to Sunday. As most staff was needed on Friday, Saturday and Sundays, if you over-estimated your weekend takings and employed too many staff, you were in trouble. My cash float was £20 and by the time I had obtained change for the three tills, there was very little cash in hand remaining. Under- or over-spend could not be carried forward to the next week. It was a ludicrous situation. The only solution if you over-staffed, was either to pay them out of your own pocket or make them wait a week for their money which understandably was not popular.

Until our second son Timothy was born (December 1960) we worked the bar ourselves Monday to Thursday, to have the maximum money for staff at the weekend. One big advantage then, over now, was you didn't have to enter the actual names of staff on the wages sheet, or stop tax and National Insurance. This enabled us to do the cleaning and claim the badly needed money ourselves. The weekly takings and expenses sheet had to be completed, takings banked and sheet posted to the brewery by noon on Mondays. Woe betide any manager who was late posting his return.

The licensing hours were 10 a.m.–2.30 p.m. and 6 till 10.30 p.m. Sunday was 12 noon to 2 p.m., and 7 till 10 p.m. One afternoon a week and Sunday mornings were spent cleaning beer pipes. A laborious time-consuming job involving mixing caustic soda with water, drawing it through 1" diameter monel metal (a corrosion-resistant alloy of nickel, copper, iron and manganese) pipes, then pulling through copious amounts of salt water followed by equal amounts of fresh water. There were six hand pumps in the bar and three in the lounge with a total pipe run of some 250 feet, consequently when I had finished my arm felt as though it was dropping off.

One day a week in the summer my day's routine would be; 8 a.m. clean bar and toilets – Sylvia did the lounge – stack furniture, start mowing grass, 12 noon – 2.30 p.m. serve in the bar, then complete the mowing and replace chairs and tables. 6 p.m. back in bar until closing. The lawn furniture had to be put away each night otherwise it went missing.

Our first Christmas as mine hosts

Sylvia was required to spend a lot of time serving in the bars so it was fortunate that Stephen, our eldest son, was a contented baby and didn't require a lot of attention. He was just two years old when we moved to the pub and with our accommodation being upstairs; it was just as well. Timothy was born on the 7th December 1960; on learning of his birth, Mr Sellars remarked, "It's a good job it wasn't any later otherwise Mrs Hackett would have been struggling to work over Christmas."

By then, trade had really taken off so we shipped the children to Sylvia's parents the day before Christmas Eve, and Sylvia was able to work flat out over the holiday. Her parents couldn't stay at the pub as we could only furnish one bedroom. There was no such thing as closing on Christmas night; in fact it was often the busiest evening over the period. Very few families had television so the men would leave the women and children to play with their presents, and go to the pub for a bit of peace.

Birds Eye frozen turkey dinners appeared on the market for the first time that year and we experienced their tasteless texture for our Christmas lunch. How we would have loved a customer to invite us to their house for lunch. It seemed like no sooner had we sat down to eat our offering than it was time to open again.

The brewery sent us a standard letter each Christmas stating, "You have been allocated the sum of five shillings (25p) for the purchase of Christmas decorations. Whilst this may not seem a lot, it must be remembered that greenery best captures the true spirit of Christmas. This can be obtained free from local hedge rows." We always had an illuminated Christmas tree standing on a flat roof, at the front of the pub. That alone costs us five shillings!

In September I started a club for customers to save money for Christmas drink. The money was banked each week and accounts kept by an appointed Treasurer. The first Christmas club order I placed with the brewery was for 120 cases of mixed wine and spirits. As soon as they received the order I had a visit from Mr Sellars

– the brewery thought I had gone mad. I asked him if the brewery could give a cash discount for such a large order, and I would pay it into the Pub Community Fund, which I had started to pay for, amongst other things, a Christmas party for customers' children. He said he would get back to me, which he did after Christmas.

His proposal was that the money should be banked each week into the brewery account. All goods would be "brewery own" brands and for this they would give a discount of 1 per cent. When I said I had expected a better deal than that, he said, "The company does not wish to encourage Christmas clubs to operate from managed houses, we prefer customers to patronise our own off licence shops."

It must be remembered that this was before supermarkets arrived, the only outlets for the sale of intoxicating drink were pubs and off licenses. This was just one of many instances where we found our entrepreneurial talents being frustrated by the brewery, when all we were trying to do was make a name for ourselves, and money for them.

"You cannot be a sportsman and a licensee"

I had been asked to play cricket for the town cricket club but a senior pub manager in the group who was my mentor, warned me that the brewery would take a dim view of my being absent from the pub for part of a Saturday evening. He suggested I considered playing for Rushden Town Thursday XI, as did a couple of other managers. This I did on my day off and thoroughly enjoyed myself. I also played in a match for the brewery in the annual fixture against the County Police, and for the Tenants and Managers against the brewery.

With the rugby season coming up, I reflected on Mr Baillon's comments about my joining Northampton RFC. I failed to see how I could travel to Northampton and further afield to play, and be back in Irthligborough for opening time. I had thought about approaching Mr Baillon on the subject but didn't think it wise to go over Mr Sellars's head. I couldn't ask permission from him as I was certain what his answer would be.

One of my customers was on the committee of Irthlingborough Diamonds FC; I had mentioned to him that I had played a fair bit of soccer in the navy, as on destroyers it was difficult to form a rugby team. He asked me to go along to the pre-season Saturday afternoon trial, which I promptly did. To my surprise, I was selected for the 2nd XI for a home game. I must have played well as I was selected again for the following week, away at Wolverton, some 30 miles away.

It was my experience that unlike rugby teams, soccer teams didn't involve themselves in post match festivities. This was correct, but by the time the coach had gone all-round the houses dropping people off it was 6 p.m. before I arrived at the pub. To this day, I cannot believe it was an accident, but when I walked in I was astonished to see Mr Sellars standing at the bar! He had never been there on a Saturday before, so I could only deduce someone had tipped him off. My suspicions centred on the manager of a pub in town, which was the HQ of the football club. We had crossed swords once or twice at LVA meetings.

Anyway Sellars in his normal sarcastic manner said, "Have you been gardening, Mr Hackett?" – no showers in those days so I still had mud in my hair from the football. I told him the truth and he reminded me that it was my responsibility to be on duty at all permitted hours. I said, "You may not be aware, but as a result of playing football for the town, I have gained a lot of extra customers." His reply was so typical of the man, "I think, Mr Hackett, you need to decide whether you want to be a publican or a professional sportsman, you cannot be both." I reluctantly told the football club I was only available for home games, and, as this would not be fair on my deputy, I would understand it if I wasn't selected again. During the remainder of the season, I did play a few home games for the reserves. It was the first time since I was 12 years old that I hadn't played a season of rugby.

Banquets and balls

In the November of our first year, the LVA held their Annual Banquet and Ball and a banquet it really was, with an hors d' oeuvre, soup, fish course, sorbet, main course, pudding, biscuits & cheese, petites bouchées and coffee. The cost of a ticket was three guineas (£3. 3s.) and the dress was white or black tie for the men with evening dress for the ladies. I didn't own a dinner jacket and I don't think there was anywhere in those days where you could hire one. Anyway, the cost of the meal was sufficient to ensure we wouldn't be attending.

Apart from the meal the evening was spent raising money for trade and local charities and for this reason alone, all licensees were expected to attend with guests. I could not face telling committee members we were too hard up to go and tried desperately to think of an excuse. I confided to a fellow manager and he offered me the loan of his son's dinner jacket and his wife a dress for Sylvia but we still had the problem of finding £8 for our two tickets. Our salvation came from a most unlikely source.

Each year a director of a brewery took the Presidency of the LVA and the high point of his year was the Annual Banquet. At this event he was responsible for providing gifts for the ladies, paying for the printing of menus and supplying and presenting bouquets for VIP and committee men's wives. He also supplied the star prize for the draw and gave the main speech of the evening. It was customary for a brewery representative to sit at each table usually occupied by his area tenants or managers. This particular year Colonel David Jones a director of PNBC Brewery, had taken the Presidency.

On his weekly visit, Mr Sellars – who after inspecting the cleanliness of my toilet pipes and cellar – mentioned the banquet to me. I told him Sylvia and I wouldn't be attending, as we couldn't afford it on the low wage the company paid us. This practically produced in him a state of apoplexy. "Mr Hackett," he said, "don't you realize you have an obligation to attend as Colonel Jones is this year's President?" He went on to explain that all tenants and managers from the President's Company were expected to attend as a show of support and respect for him during his year of office. I told him, "If the President or company cared to buy us tickets, we would be more than prepared to give him our support and respect in every way, otherwise, if anyone asks us why we were not attending, I will have to tell them we can't afford it on our salary." I reminded him that the cost of two tickets was equal to a week's pay for us.

He said he would talk it over with our area manager – his boss- to try and resolve the problem. He visited us a few days later and said the company was prepared to let us borrow the money from our float and pay it back at £1 per week. I told him if he made it 10/- we would go, this he agreed. He told us this was to be treated as an exceptional one-off and never to be repeated. A few minutes later he returned to tell us the car park needed sweeping.

Glad rags

It was our first ever evening dress function. Sylvia had decided not to wear the borrowed long green taffeta dress; it made her look too much like a saloon owner in a Wild West film. Instead she wore a long silk tight Chinese dress with slits to her knees, which I had bought for her when in the Navy. I wore my borrowed dinner jacket that was a size too big and stank of mothballs but I felt like Humphrey Bogart in it.

The event was held at the Overstone Solarium, a 1930s' complex built in the grounds of Overstone Hall. It was a perfect setting for such an occasion, built and decorated in the Palladian Style with ornate ceilings, marble staircases and Venetian glass chandeliers. I drove up to the steps leading to the main entrance in our old Morris Minor for Sylvia to get out and almost immediately, a Rolls Royce pulled in behind us bringing the Mayor & Mayoress of Wellingborough. The doorman, who was about to open our car door to let Sylvia out, suddenly changed course and attended to the mayor. At least Sylvia had the privilege of leading the dignitaries to the Ball.

We must have been the only licensees attending the Ball without guests. We had kept our attendance secret from as many customers as possible; we didn't want them to think we were "flash" and wealthy. Burt and Beulah had warned us how important it was not to let the customers on the estate think we were better off than they were, the customers would accept us more if they thought they were our equals. We certainly didn't have to put on an act; most of them had far more money than we had! The other reason for not having guests was because we were doubtful if any of our customers had either the clothes or money to attend, and we certainly couldn't afford to pay for their tickets.

We were both amazed at the amount of jewellery the landladies adorned themselves with and the elaborate dresses they wore. It wouldn't have been too unkind to say some of them looked like decorated carnival elephants with their jewels and bright colours. It seemed as though there was a competition to see who could dress the most garishly, I thought at the time they looked like a lot of pantomime dames. I clearly remember Sylvia saying to me, "I hope I am not in the trade long enough to dress and look like them." I was so pleased Sylvia had changed her choice of dress; although a colourful red, it stood out against the others with its plain lines and showed off her slim figure perfectly. She looked beautiful! Without any doubt, it was certainly the cheapest dress on display but I felt so proud of her. During the evening Colonel Jones came over, spoke to us, and asked which public house our parents kept! It was the first but not the last time I was to meet with the great white chief.

My sporting interests pay off

All managers were entitled to 10 per cent of the net profit from any bar they operated away from their pubs, and the organisers received 15 per cent. As a result of my Rushden Town cricket connections, in 1961 I was offered the opportunity to operate the bars at the County Cricket match held annually in May on their ground. I was asked to supply and operate four beer tents and run a bar in the pavilion. It must be said that most licensees were in the main getting on in years and had little need or energy to involve themselves in what was a very involved and energetic undertaking. The brewery had a large outside catering department that supplied marquees counters, back fittings, chairs, tables, glassware etc. in fact everything needed to operate a licensed bar successfully. The draymen erected the marquees and, in the case of this particular event, four men spent a whole day assembling them. For Saturday's first day's play, I employed sixteen bar staff and together with washers up, glass collectors, etc. had a total staff of twenty-four.

The match, against Nottinghamshire, was not one of the more attractive fixtures, Notts being around the bottom of the league. Northants had Frank (Typhoon) Tyson playing for them, but not even his presence could raise the attendance above 800 on an overcast day. I had been led to expect at least 3,000! Numerous showers throughout the day drove spectators into the beer tents which helped to swell the takings, but overall they were disappointingly modest, hardly enough to pay the staff.

On Monday (no Sunday cricket in those days) I reduced the staff needed for each marquee to two, ran the pavilion bar myself and dispersed with all other staff. Tuesday I operated with just one beer tent and the pavilion bar. With rain falling after lunch, the match finished early for the day. Heavy rain again throughout Wednesday made play impossible and mercifully brought a disaster for me to an early end. After paying all expenses there was nothing left for me and all my hours spent planning, organising and working went unrewarded. However, all was not lost.

While serving in the pavilion bar I had been introduced to the Secretary of the Northants County Cricket Club, Mr Ken Turner. A week later I received a telephone call from him asking me if I would go and see him at the County Ground. He said he was impressed with my organisation at the Rushden match, and asked if I would be interested in operating the bars at a forthcoming barbecue organised partly to welcome the Australian touring team prior to their fixture at Northampton, and as a fund-raising occasion for George Tribe's benefit year. When he told me an attendance of 5,000 was expected my knees went weak. I would have just a month to organise everything, marquees, staff, drink etc. When I informed the brewery they wanted me to hand over the event to a more experienced manager; they didn't consider I had sufficient experience to handle it myself. I told them (tongue in cheek) I believed if I didn't run it the opportunity would go to another brewery.

All stops were pulled out to give me all the help and assistance I requested. The event was held in the grounds of Billing Aquadrome, a popular Northants holiday park. The brewery's three largest marquees were joined together to form a main area of approx. 240ft x 60ft with 4 smaller marquees leading off to act as bars. I advertised and recruited a staff of 40, many of them brewery employees needing a bit of extra cash. The event, on one of the hottest nights of the year exceeded all expectations; the official attendance was 5,800. In all something like 30 barrels of beer were sold including a whole brewery dray loaded with bottled beers. I had the opportunity to meet and talk to members of the Australian Team that included captain Richie Benaud, Neil Harvey, Wally Grout, Bill Lawry, Graham McKenzie, Bobby Simpson and Alan Davidson, plus ex-players Keith Miller, Ray Lindwall and Lindsey Hassett, all heroes of mine.

I cannot remember exactly how much our 10% came to but I do remember we were able to trade in our faithful old 1949 Morris Minor reg. no. ODR 328, brought back from Malta on HMS *Eagle*, and buy a new Ford 6 cwt van, from Ward's of Wellingborough. This was the only new vehicle we have ever owned to this day. We bought a van for two reasons, we needed more carrying capacity for the outside catering we were doing, and in those days there was 25 per cent purchase tax on cars but not on vehicles without rear side windows. Sylvia shed a few tears at the departure of "Oder" – we had many happy memories of time spent driving her, both in Malta and Scotland. Sylvia taught me to drive in her and with the help of a £1 note inside my licence, I used her to pass my driving test in Malta.

Two months before arriving back in the UK, I adopted the recommended unofficial naval dodge and applied to the London County Council to be issued with an International Driving Licence, saying I was returning to the UK to undergo a course and on completion would return to Malta. This entitled me to drive in the UK for a year. When it was about to expire, I wrote again to the LCC and said I had returned to the UK for a further course, etc.

I did this for four years until I was stopped one night at a roadblock in Kettering and was asked to produce my licence by a policeman I had played cricket with. He looked at the licence, winked at me, and said, "Thank you, sir, I hope you enjoy the rest of your stay in this country."

I thought I had pushed my luck long enough and applied to take a driving test. I duly reported for the test at Northampton where the examiner asked me where my "L" plates were. I told him I was a visitor to this country driving on an International Licence and didn't need any plates. He asked me why I wanted a UK licence and I said I liked to collect them for every country I had lived in. He failed me. I subsequently applied for a provisional licence, applied for a test and passed, five years after first legally driving unaccompanied in this country.

With the unparalleled success of the cricket barbecue I undertook every type of outside function possible, Dances, Weddings, Point-to-Points, Car Hill Climbs, Auction Sales and more County Cricket matches at Rushden and Wellingborough. Some were very good money earners and some not so good, but we almost doubled our yearly salary by doing them. I was extremely fortunate in having an excellent head barman in Herbie Wesley, and our success in taking on so many outside functions was due in no small part to his efficiency. I would attend court most weeks and apply for so many occasional licences; I was on Christian name terms with the court officials and even some of the bench.

It was very hard work and put a lot of strain on Sylvia, as I would often be away from the Crows Nest for most of the day and evening. I would make numerous journeys to the event taking supplies, and afterwards, all part-empty bottles of wines and spirits, part cases of bottled beers and minerals had to be taken back to the pub and into the Crows Nest stock. Carting these goods plus ferrying staff often meant I wouldn't return home from an event until the early hours of the morning, when I would unload the van and count the takings before going to bed. I would have to return to the venue the next day to organise the collection of empties, etc. by the brewery.

Attached to The Working Men's Club premises in Irthlingborough was a hall with the evocative title of The Harmonic Hall. This was the only room in the town large enough to hold 400 for a function. The Diamonds Football Club held dances there at regular intervals and I was invited to run the bars. The WMC had a licence but as a members' club they were not allowed to sell alcohol to the general public.

The dances were very well supported though few arrived before the pubs closed. Before 10 p.m. there would be the odd smattering of young girls and older people, but from then onwards the masses would queue to get in. Fights were a recognised part of the evening's festivities, often involving a quarter of those present. I had no problem with this but what did concern me was the amount of glasses broken in the ensuing mêlées. This would eat into the evening's profit and mean less for the organisers and myself. The club officials were mostly the wrong side of 50 and the players were busy joining in the fracas as part of their evening's entertainment. It was therefore left to me to attempt to protect my interests.

After a few functions, I pinpointed the instigator of most fights down to one person, a chap named Ray Denton. He was a James

Cagney type, small, snappy dresser, aggressive with a penchant for causing mayhem. I had noticed that once he started a fight, and it was well established, he would walk up to tables and tip them over breaking all the glasses in the process. I started tracking him during the evening; never letting him out of my sight. He was aware of my presence and would try and dodge me without success. This led to a few skirmishes between us, but after a few drops of blood had been spilt, we built up quite a rapport between us. I would make comments such as, "It's quiet tonight Ray," and he would reply, "Yes, I thought the same, perhaps its because Jesus Christ has got his eye on me." (In those days I had a very long beard.) Anyway my persistence paid off with fights and breakages reduced to a minimum.

Three decades later, I met Ray at a Civic Dinner in Northampton. He said he had a furniture restoration business in the town, which I thought was rather ironic for a man who in the past preferred wrecking furniture to restoring it. We had a long chat about old times at the Harmonic Hall and he left me with the remark, "At least you and I fought cleanly, not like they do today."

After I had run the bars at the Hall for four years the magistrates, following complaints from the police, imposed a 10.30 p.m. deadline for bars at dances there. This had the effect of reducing attendances to such a low they were no longer a viable proposition. There was always an eight-piece band to pay for plus the hire of the hall. It was a big blow to the Diamonds Football Club as it was their main fundraiser. They took a good amount on the door and I gave them 15 per cent of the bar profit which, although just for two hours, was a very busy period, keeping four barmen going non stop. It was a big setback for the football club, just when their teams were achieving great success in the leagues.

The view from the Crow's Nest gets better

For some time it had concerned me we were not making full use of the pub lawn. In those days, very few men ever took their families out to the pub for a drink; it just wasn't the done thing, a sign of a man's weakness some might say. Consequently, the lawn was very rarely full.

After the success of the County Cricket barbecue, I had toyed with the idea of holding a similar event on a smaller scale, on the lawn. I put a proposition to David Knighton, who by this time had become our very good friend and worked for us (unpaid) behind the bar. He served on the Diamonds committee and was very enthusiastic about my plan. I told him I would organise a barbecue for the football club, providing they assisted me in the preparations. He sounded out the other committee members but their response was not encouraging. Half of them had no idea what a barbecue was and when it was explained to them they thought the idea of people paying to stand out in the open eating semi incinerated food was hilarious. I must admit I didn't agree with them then, however, after many years attending barbecues myself; I tend to agree with them now!

I asked to be allowed to attend the next committee meeting to explain the benefits of my proposal, and as a form of blackmail I put it to them that (1) their reserve team played most of its fixtures on the recreation ground behind the Crows Nest. They and the opposition changed in my bar, and, at my own expense, I had installed showers in the gents' toilet for their use. I intimated that in the future not only may I have to consider charging them for these facilities, but also if no other way was found to raise funds they were in danger of folding up, so they really had nothing to lose.

The secretary of the club, Tony Jones, was younger than most of the committee; he worked in sales for a local leather firm. He was sympathetic towards my scheme and could see the potential of staging a barbecue and raising considerable funds for the club. Eventually he and David Knighton persuaded the rest of the committee to support my plan.

My first problem was what to do about food. At Northampton a local blacksmith had constructed the barbecues to a design supplied by the Australian Embassy in London. The embassy, through the Australian Meat Council, had also arranged for the supply of steaks, which were served in rolls. I enquired from the blacksmith about the cost of making a barbecue but the quote received was prohibitive. I also had doubts whether Irthlingborough people would be able to afford to buy steaks.

It was at that stage that someone suggested I should contact the American air base at Chelveston, near Rushden. What a brain wave, not only did they offer to supply the barbecue equipment but also men to help operate it and chicken to cook.

A 5ft chain link fence attached to concrete posts surrounded the Crows Nest lawn. This obviously wasn't going to be high enough to keep out gatecrashers so Tony Jones arranged for his firm to supply rolls of 8ft wide hessian, used to wrap bales of leather. It was suspended on wires stretched from scaffolding poles to form a perfect barrier and windbreak. On the side adjacent to the recreation ground, we dropped the fence, and the brewery erected two large marquees on the field butting up to the lawn. A stage for the band was constructed on the patio above the lawn and with floodlights lighting the pub and marquees, coloured lighting on top of the hessian, all courtesy of the US Air Force, the arena looked magnificent.

I had booked a band appropriately called the "Double Diamonds" from Market Harborough who had a very good following in the Northants/Leics area. They based their style on "The Shadows", then all the rage, and, though not knowing when I booked them, their lead singer was at school with me. I arranged for a local farmer to let us have a field opposite the pub as an overflow car park and with posters and tickets printed, we were ready to go.

To a lot of people in 1960 a barbecue was something that took place on beaches in films. Chicken was a food you had at Christmas or on special occasions. Barbecued chicken, especially cooked the American way, was new fare for most English people. Our problem therefore was to try and sell the event to a very sceptical public.

With all this in mind and a large degree of uncertainty, we hoped to attract an attendance of 400.

The event, on a Friday evening, was scheduled to start at 8 p.m. At 7 p.m. the pub car park was full and cars were streaming into the overflow car park. At 7.30 p.m. the local police arrived to direct traffic off the main A6 road following traffic chaos. At 8.30 p.m. we had to ask the police to stop any more cars from trying to get to the event. The lawn and pub was bursting at the seams, and the police had to call out reinforcements to stop people from scaling the fences.

The chicken ran out at 9 p.m. and the Americans sent to the base for more supplies. Beer ran out in the marquees at 10 p.m. – the licence was granted till 11.30 p.m. Keg beers had not yet made an appearance and cask beer needed at least 24 hours to clear, so I couldn't give them draught beer from the pub. Bottled beer was popular in the '60s and I always carried a large stock. I started loading sack barrows with cases of beer but they were sold before they reached the marquees. People were buying them by the case. The event was a chaotic, resounding, financial success.

At a post mortem that took place after the event, the official attendance from tickets sold and people paying at the door was 800. The police estimated that 150 cars were parked in the overflow car park. The Americans said 1,000 chicken portions were sold, I sold 10 x 36 gallons of beer and 100 dozen bottles of beer in the marquee alone.

We last visited the pub fifteen years ago and the most common thing people said to us was, "Do you remember that barbecue?" It put the Crows Nest on the map. The Diamonds FC made more money from that one event than they had previously made in four years holding dances at the Harmonic Hall. During the remainder of our time at the Crows Nest, another two barbecues were held which, though making good profits, never offered me the challenge of the first. No attempts were made to hold any more after we left!

In the 1960s the popularity of wrestling was at its peak

particularly in Northamptonshire. Doug and Ken Joyce from Rushden were both world champions at their respective weights, though it has to be said that all countries seemed to have their own world champions. I had a very good friend on the estate named Arthur Farey, an ex-Royal Naval shipwright who had been awarded the Distinguished Service Medal for bravery during his time serving on Russian convoys, Arthur would never talk about what he did to deserve his award, but he had a framed photograph in his house showing him being presented with his medal by King George VI.

Arthur served in the navy with Dick and Jacky Turpin, brothers of World Middleweight Boxing Champion Randolph. All three had been British boxing champions. They lived at Leamington Spa and paid frequent visits to my pub while staying with Arthur. Dick and Jacky had taken up wrestling and Dick was trying to break into the promotion side of the "sport". I asked Dick if he would be interested in staging an event on the lawn at the pub. Dick told me that unofficially staging bouts in the area came under the control of one promoter, and they operated a closed shop for staging events throughout their "territory". Dick said he would give it a go but warned me he wouldn't be able to obtain the services of any star wrestlers as they were scared of being blacklisted by the sole promoters. However, he had formed an amateur wrestling club in Leamington and we had a thriving one in Rushden, so he was certain he would be able to stage an event with members from the two clubs participating. Once again, I received considerable assistance from the Diamonds FC and the evening was a complete success with over 400 people attending.

With the profit made from the barbecues and wrestling event, Irthlingborough Diamonds Football Club were solvent and went from strength to strength. They started life in 1947 as a schoolboy soccer team (bright as Diamonds) and after becoming a senior club, progressed through various leagues until in 2001, having merged with Rushden Town FC to form Rushden & Diamonds FC, they were promoted to the Football League Division 3. They now have a magnificent stadium and function complex at

Irthlingborough. Sylvia and I derive great pleasure in knowing that we assisted in some small way in their success.

It gives us even greater pleasure to know that the function suite at the ground is named after our very good friend, David Knighton, who was such a help in our early years. Many years later, Stephen, our eldest son, went back to Irthlingborough with David Knighton and recorded a match on video for the club, the first time they ever had a game recorded on this new medium. David will feature a lot in my story.

Irthlingborough was well catered for with shops, virtually all of them were on one side of the main street and Co-operative Society owned; chemist, ladies & gents outfitters, furniture shop, carpet shop, television shop, ladies & gents hairdressers, ironmongers, butchers, fishmongers, bakers, undertakers, bank, coal merchant, paint shop, etc., etc. all Co-op. The dividend received on purchases, 10d in the £1, went a long way towards paying for people's annual holiday.

The town needed to raise money for a mini van to take OAPs to Kettering Hospital, the nearest place for medical treatment. There was a doctors' surgery in the town but health centres had not yet been invented. The organisers asked me if I could organise an event to help them raise more funds.

Irthlingborough was well provided with drinking establishments: The Bull, Sow & Pigs, White Horse, British Arms, Drum & Monkey, Railway and The Sun public houses and in addition there was a British Legion Club, Band Club, Conservative Club and Working Men's Club. The clubs were a bit of a joke: I used to say, "The Legion Club's chairman was a conscientious objector, the Cons Club chairman was the Socialist chairman of the Town Council. If you pulled out an instrument and played it in the Band Club, you would be thrown out for making a noise, and the Working Men's Club was next to the Labour Exchange and full of unemployed layabouts every lunch time."

I studied the distances between each pub and came up with the idea of holding an inter-pub relay race.

The first leg of 100 yards from the British Arms to the Sow and Pigs had to be run by a grandparent; the next leg of 150 yards from the Sow & Pigs to the Sun by a female. From there the 200 yards to the Drum & Monkey by a person over 65. The 75 yards from the Drum & Monkey to the Bull, the Bull, up hill for one and a quarter miles to the Crows Nest, the return one mile down hill to the Railway, and the half a mile back to the Bull in the town square for the finish could be run by anyone.

When arriving at each pub the incoming and outgoing runner had to drink a pint of beer each, ladies half a pint. Only when both runners had finished their beer could the next runner set off.

All the pubs entered two teams and the event was held on the Sunday before St Swithan's Day. Television was still a novelty with regional programmes just starting. I put the word round that television cameras would be there to record the event and so as not to disappoint people, I painted the letters BBC TV with blanco on the side of my van, mounted a wooden tripod, with a dummy camera attached made from a cornflake box, on the roof, and parked it in the square early in the morning.

About an hour before the race started, up rolled a real BBC television camera van, which proceeded to film the whole event from start to finish. This was the first time Irthlingborough had ever appeared on television and was the talking point that weekend. Whether or not this was the main attraction I shall never know, but the pavements through the town were packed solid with spectators and I wasn't the least bit concerned exactly what brought them there – TV or the race. With street bucket collections and entry fees, £120 was raised towards the £300 needed for the bus. Rumour had it that the local bookmaker had a field day. On the Monday evening, houses with a television set were packed with viewers, as was the pavement in front of the Co-op television shop, for the showing of the event. The Crows Nest winning team composed of Ken Read, Sylvia, Stan Lloyd, Jack Whittaker, Frank Hale and Graham Mutton.

Apart from the overwhelming success of the day, an added

pleasure for me was when, having taken over in fourth place on the second leg, Sylvia running with all the determination she puts into anything she does, overtook the other ladies and gave us a lead which we never lost. When she stepped onto the dais to receive her trophy from Bob Taylor, the mayor, she received the loudest cheer of the day. On Monday morning, when she banked as usual, even our bank manager, Mr Kerry, a Captain Mainwaring stereotype, was moved to say, "Well run, Mrs Hackett, you ran like an Amazonian." The only previous occasion when he praised us was when I once handed in a dud half crown piece. Had I known he wouldn't replace it with a good one I would have kept quiet about it.

"Mum says, can she pay you at the end of the week?"

In the mid 1960s, trade had increased to such an extent that the Crows Nest customers presented a 100-signature petition to the brewery asking for the public bar to be extended to give more space and allow table skittles to be played. For table skittles you needed a minimum space of 16ft x 8ft with a cage surrounding the table to protect drinkers from the cheeses (4" diameter, 2" thick box-wood discs that you throw) ricocheting off the table. This was duly built later that year, giving us a bar area extended by a third and a new off sales shop.

Off sales was a very important part of our trade. The pub "slate" (credit) quite often formed 25 per cent of our weekly takings although it was strictly against brewery rules. At each monthly stock take I had to say how much cash was outstanding "from account customers". This was really a huge joke as the only accounts my customers ever had were with the bookmaker! At times, it seemed the whole estate existed on credit. We were inundated with requests from women wanting goods on tick, the most popular items being cigarettes and crisps, and, on many occasions, they sent their children with begging notes. It was all too common for a child to come to the off sales with a note for four bottles of lemonade on the slate, and return with the empties five minutes later. It was perfectly obvious that their parents wanted a shilling for the gas or electric meter, and having no money would pour the drink into a jug and immediately return the empty bottles for the three pence deposit charged on each bottle.

It annoyed us intensely to see their husbands losing money gambling, when we knew their wives were desperate for money. The men on the estate were big gamblers, they bet on horses, greyhounds, pigeon racing, fishing matches, in fact anything that moved, plus cards.

We reluctantly inherited Saturday and Sunday lunchtime card schools. Apart from being illegal, it meant that if a man lost his week's beer money, the winner was more than likely to spend it on something else. This way I ran the risk of prosecution if they were caught playing, and losing a customer until his next payday. All my attempts to stamp out these card schools failed. All pubs in the town had the same problem; the biggest culprits were the mineworkers. Often they played at work and continued playing in the same school at weekends.

I also inherited the honorary position of bookies' runner. Bert Angel had been recruited, and supplied by the local bookie with a leather bag with a clock device on top for the purpose of taking bets; I was expected to continue with this arrangement although again it was highly illegal. On Saturday mornings, customers gave me their betting slips and stake money, which I placed in the bag. At 1 p.m. I would lock the clock to the bag, which sealed it and recorded the time this was in place. Bets in the bag for a race-taking place before this time were invalid, as the punter could well know the result when completing his slip.

Betting on horses was a completely new experience for me; in the past I occasionally had the odd flutter on the Grand National and Derby sweepstakes but never placed a bet with a bookmaker. However, it wasn't long before I knew what doubles, trebles and yankees were as I had to check each ticket and stake money before placing them in the bag. Some customers had difficulty in filling in their tickets so Sylvia and I were often called upon to do it for them, all part of the service. One customer, a butcher, did have a sizeable win and rewarded us with a joint of beef, which I suppose was better than a joint of horsemeat. Usually we were treated to the odd drink by winning customers and at Christmas the bookmaker generously gave us a calendar and diary.

I started a football pools syndicate at the pub, which 40 customers joined. I had great difficulty getting people to pay their share of the stake money on time and after six months with quite a large sum owing I put the word around that we had a win. Between the Sunday morning when I started the rumour and Wednesday when we would have received the winning cheque, all outstanding monies had been paid in; I then disbanded the syndicate: a great relief.

In the early '60s, the Mods and Rocker era, trouble was never very far away especially with families on the estate drawn from such a wide area. I would go for a whole week without any trouble at all, and then suddenly I could be involved in numerous scuffles in one evening. One particular family was a constant menace.

Old Jack, the father, was one of the most harmless characters you could hope to come across, as long as he had his pipe, a tin of snuff and a pint in his hand he was the picture of contentment. He had six children of whom three were boys, who I shall just call Tom, Dick and Harry. Dick had just completed his National Service in the Army, Tom and Harry failed National Service selection on practically every test from eyes, and feet to an IQ of minus 100. Harry worked on a building site and Tom was a porter at a hospital.

Individually they were good lads, but if for any reason I had cause to eject one of them, the others would think it a Roman holiday and all join in without stopping to find out the reason why.

Those were the days of drip feed paraffin heaters, a gallon glass bottle filled with paraffin suspended over a wick. During one altercation I was having with Tom and Harry, Dick picked up a heater and threw it over the bar, the bottle narrowly missing a barmaid, smashed against the back fitting, showering the whole area with burning paraffin. Fortunately, there were two fire extinguishers behind the bar so the fire was quickly put out without too much damage. However, typical of the boys, the next morning Dick saunters into the bar, puts a new glass paraffin bottle on the counter with the words, "I think I broke yours last night, giz a pint please!!"

If for any reason I was having trouble with strangers the brothers would be the first to ask if I needed any assistance. I never encouraged them though, my big fear being if I was getting the better of the fight, they might change loyalties and decide to gang up on me. Despite their many faults, looking back we were fortunate in having a good bunch of customers, most with hearts of gold, drawn together by the isolation of the Crow Hill estate from the rest of civilization.

We had our share of con men, petty crooks, oodles of adulterers and wife beaters but no serious criminals. Children sometimes stole my lawn furniture if left out overnight; they once broke into my empties shed and took over 100 cases of bottles, which, over a period, they then returned to the off sales shop for the deposit money back. On another occasion they set my garden fence alight and, if I left any empty barrels outside, would have great fun rolling them down the hill at the back of the pub and into the river.

Boot and Shoe Trade holiday fortnight took place at the same time each year, when it seemed as though the whole of Northamptonshire would decamp to Great Yarmouth for the duration. On Saturday the men were in the pub while their wives packed the cases and got the children ready. The coaches stopped outside the pub at noon to pick up the men (they always kept them waiting) and then set off for the Ponderosa Caravan Camp site at Hopton-on-Sea, on the outskirts of Yarmouth.

Most families occupied caravans next door to their Crow Hill neighbours so a row of caravans would replicate their street on the estate. Customers usually asked to borrow all my spare dominoes, pegboards, playing cards spare darts and the same groups who played these games in the pub would be in the camp site clubhouse, morning and evening, playing with the same people they played with the rest of the year. I don't think most of the men ever saw the sea.

A customer once told me if it had been possible for them to sit at corresponding tables in the club as they normally occupied at the pub, they would have done so. They hated having a change in their routine. It was common for us to receive hundreds of seaside cards from them, which we were reluctantly obliged to display until Christmas. Woe betide us if we failed to display someone's card.

In the five years we were at the Crows Nest we never took our week's holiday. The brewery made it difficult for us to do so. As junior managers we were not offered official brewery relief managers so had we wanted to take a holiday, it would have been necessary for us to supply our own reliefs. They would have to be vetted by the company, a daunting process. The alternative was to be paid two weeks salary in lieu of a holiday, which we gratefully received. Sylvia's parents took Stephen and Timothy on holiday to the seaside each year, for which we were very thankful. They were good boys and seemed to accept that we couldn't go with them; it was going to be some years before we could afford both time and money to take them ourselves.

I become involved in trade politics

It was compulsory for managers to join their local Licensed Victuallers Association; for me this meant joining the Wellingborough & District branch. Managers were the poor relations of the association and were made to feel like it. Tenants and free house owners formed the majority of the membership, most of them over 60 and most of them inheriting their pubs, both tenanted and free, from their parents. It was quite common in those days for pubs to remain in the same family for two or three generations.

With a small brewery, the directors treated tenants as part of the company family; they would often personally visit their tenancies to collect rents and check if they had any problems. Directors would be known as Mr John or Mr William as the case may be. A tenant would have to do something seriously wrong to have his tenancy terminated, whereas managers lived in permanent fear of losing both their home and livelihood.

With this status division, it was hardly any wonder relations between managers and tenants were tenuous. Very few trade problems were discussed at monthly meetings, most of the time was taken up with social matters. Far more time was spent discussing which fish course to have at the Annual Banquet than items affecting the trade generally.

When the question of price rises came up, we were told it didn't apply to us and we were not expected to join in the debate. The same applied to discussions regarding staff wages, bar prices, subscriptions, etc.

The way the LVA branch was organised, on a committee of 12 the managers had just one representative. In the branch the total number of members was 127 of which 28 were managers; therefore our representation on the committee was wholly disproportionate. Eventually I got rather fed up being treated like a second-class citizen so I organised a meeting for my fellow managers to discuss the problem and decide what to do about it. It was agreed at the meeting that we obtain brewery permission to form our own association. The brewery raised no objection provided we remained affiliated to our local LVA branch, ensuring that licensing hour extensions for holidays and all legal matters were handled by the LVA. We notified Fred Thornton the secretary of the branch and asked him to call an Extraordinary General Meeting informing the other members of our intentions.

The managers attended in force and I informed the meeting what we proposed doing and the reasons for it. There were some very strong opinions voiced and I was accused of being a rabble-rouser, young upstart and of having too high an opinion of myself. However to stave off the breakaway, it was agreed that managers had received a raw deal in the past and in future the office of vice chairman of the association would always be held by a manager, and there would be an addition of two further managers on the committee making four managers in all.

This went a long way to meeting our grievances, and following a recess at which we agreed the changes, we dropped our breakaway proposals. Much to my amazement, the managers proposed me for the position of vice chairman. I said I had so little experience of trade affairs and thought a more senior person with greater knowledge of the trade would fill the role better. No other manager was prepared to stand for the position so I was duly elected as vice chairman of the Wellingborough & District Branch of the Northamptonshire Licensed Trade's Association. What a grand title! This automatically made me a committee member of the East Midland Society of Licensed Victuallers, a body representing over 3,000 licensees, and at 27 I was by far the youngest member.

In my new role, it was necessary for me to attend monthly meetings of the Grand Council of the NLTA at Northampton, which was made up of Brewers and Licensees, and quarterly meetings of the East Midlands Society of LVs at Birmingham. I enjoyed a slap up lunch at the former and generous expenses for attending the latter which was much appreciated.

Our first introduction to the local Licensed Victuallers Association came shortly after taking over the Crows Nest. We were asked if we would like to go on an outing to the Guinness Brewery at Park Royal, London. As only one of us could be absent from the pub at a time, I told Sylvia to go.

She took £1 to pay for her day out and, not knowing what was involved, I gave her a further £1 from the till to buy any items for the pub that may be on sale at the brewery. Before the coach left for the journey to London the seat numbers, 1-40 were chalked around the sidewall of a tyre and a mark was put on the wheel arch. 2/6d (12p) was collected from everyone and when the coach stopped, the person whose seat number was nearest to the mark took the money. During the journey, the coach stopped at five pubs and each time a further 2/6d was collected for the next game. By the time they arrived at the brewery, with having a drink at each pub, Sylvia had already spent 15/- (75p).

She enjoyed her tour of the brewery and the hospitality afterwards all provided free. Fortunately there was nothing on sale at the brewery, for on the journey home they stopped at a further four pubs and an extra three times for the men to relieve themselves. Each time they stopped another 2/6d was collected for the wheel, which left her with just 10/- to pay for the coach and driver's tip. It was fortunate other landlords on the coach generously bought her drinks at the stops. The whole day out cost £2, almost a third of our weekly wage.

This was the pattern for all LVA outings, Brewery trips, race meetings, London theatre trips; the money some publicans and their wives spent was beyond our comprehension.

When Babycham first came on the market, Showerings, the producers, invited us for a day out at their works in Shepton Mallet. Again, Sylvia represented us and this time the coach was paid for by Showerings. The usual pattern was followed i.e. numbers on the wheel, numerous pub stops, etc. newspaper on every seat and a slip to have a 5/- horse racing bet with the compliments of Babycham.

After a tour round the plant, they were treated to a scrumptious lunch with any amount of drinks concocted around Babycham, e.g. Brandy & Babycham, Advocaat and Babycham, Port & Babycham and many others. After all this, they were taken to Wincanton Races where they were again plied with drink and a cold buffet. Ralph Showering, with his brother joint owner of the company, had a horse running which Sylvia used her 5/- free bet to back. It won at 8-1, which was just as well for what was to come.

After all the food and drink they had consumed at Showerings' expense, dinner had been booked for the journey back at the Royalist Hotel, Stow-on-the-Wold. The menu, pre ordered, was for five courses at a cost of £1. 17s 6d. Was it any wonder that most publicans, and more so their wives in those days, tended to be on the large size if not just plain fat. Had it not been for her winnings, Sylvia would once again have been embarrassed by her shortage of money. Needless to say, our attendance on LVA outings was extremely limited.

Changes for the better

Colonel Jones had been the Chairman of Campbell Praeds, a small but popular brewery in Wellingborough. In 1956 they were taken over by Phipps Brewery and he became chairman. In 1958 Phipps merged with their main competitor, Northampton Brewery, to form Phipps Northampton Brewery Company, and Colonel Jones became an ordinary director of the new company.

In 1960 PNBC were taken over by the mighty Watney Mann & Crossman brewery from London, and Colonel Jones was appointed Chairman of Watney Mann (Midlands).

During the war, he had been Colonel of the Northamptonshire Regiment and had been decorated for bravery. A tall and very imposing figure, he was a good sportsman, and a man noted for his directness, standing no nonsense.

One result of his being back in charge was that most of the old Praeds staff were promoted and had the ready ear of the chairman. Mr Sellars was moved from his post as District Manager to the stocktakers' department. His replacement was a Mr Ronald Loomes, a true gentleman and sportsman.

Ron's father had been Head Brewer at Praeds (God, in the brewing profession) and he himself was Assistant Head Brewer before they merged with Phipps. Praeds Brewery was closed down following the merger and Phipps' own brewers, being the larger partner, carried out all future brewing at Northampton.

Praeds staff were found alternative employment within the group, and Ron was given the post of Off Sales Department Manager. He was educated at Wellingborough School, noted for its sporting facilities, and had been captain of soccer and cricket. At age 45 he was too old for soccer but still played and loved cricket.

As my new District Manager I had at last found an ally and his encouragement enabled us to take the Crows Nest trade to heights never envisaged by the brewery. His good friend and ex-Praeds colleague, Herbert Drage, was promoted to Tied House Manager.

Bert Drage had been at school with Ron and, on leaving, both of them joined Praeds Brewery. He was an excellent cricketer, some say he ought to have turned professional but I suppose he had better prospects in the brewery trade. (Professional cricketers were poorly paid and only for the summer season. They relied heavily on having a good benefit year to boost their finances.)

The outcome of all these changes was that suddenly life as a manager was becoming more tolerable. Under Watneys we had an increase in salary, given an extra half day off each week, and generally were treated less like serfs.

With the replacement of Mr Sellars with Ron Loomes, I was able to resume my sporting activities. In the winter I was playing home rugby matches for Rushden & Higham RFC and occasional games in goal for Irthlingborough Diamonds, even making the first XI on two occasions where I played with Peter Martin and Trevor Roberts who were to become good friends. I still couldn't play in away rugby games due to the late cessation of the after-game festivities but at least I was enjoying my sport once again. During the summer, I played cricket every week on my day off for Rushden Thursday XI and occasionally for Irthlingborough Town.

We had spent almost five years at the Crows Nest when Ron Loomes said we deserved promotion to a larger house, in those days, unlike now, most landlords stayed in the same pub for life. The house he had in mind for us was The Red Earl on the outskirts of Northampton. It was named after the 6th Earl Spencer (an ancestor of Princess Diana) who, having a bright ginger beard, was known as the Red Earl.

A large gilt-framed oil painting of him dominated the lounge bar and when I looked at it, it was like looking into a mirror. I still had my beard very long then. The Red Earl was much larger than the Crows Nest although similar in age, style, and again positioned on a new estate. It had a very large staff, four of them full-time. It had a weekly barrelage of 15 and takings of £500 per week. It was a good offer and would have increased our salary from £9. 10s to £11.17s 6d. – big money in those days.

By now, we had increased our takings at the Crows Nest to over £350 a week and weekly barrelage to 10. With budget duty increases and a brewery price rise, a pint of beer had increased to 1/5d (8p) and spirits 1/6d per tot. The drinks pattern had changed a lot with drinks such as Babycham, CherryB, Cherrypear, Golden Godwin and Snowball now available for women and bottled and draught lager together with Watneys Red Barrel keg beer had appeared on the scene though, as yet, were not proving very popular. Dark Mild, 3xxx Bitter and IPA Bitter were still the most popular draught beers with Manns Brown, Jumbo Stout, Stingo and IPA being the popular bottled beers.

On a couple of occasions that year, I had played cricket for the brewery with Bert Drage as captain, and had told him it was our ambition eventually to become tenants if and when we could afford it. As Tied House Manager, it was Bert's responsibility to select tenants for vacant pubs within the company's estate

Ernie Goodman – landlord extraordinaire

One evening, wanting a quiet drink with a friend, I went to a pub in a village about four miles away. The Dukes Arms at Woodford was indeed a quiet pub; it was kept by an 84-year-old landlord and had the appearance of having been cocooned for 50 years. Ernie Goodman the landlord and his 82-year-old wife Ida, had kept the pub for the last 52 years and, before that, his parents.

Although the pub had the most magnificent set of pump handles, beer was drawn straight from the tap which involved the landlord and wife shuffling down a passage way and bending down to place the glass under the barrel tap, just a foot above the floor. Ernie and Ida would carry the glass on a beer tray and prior to giving it to you, tip the spillage, flies and all, from the tray back into the glass. It was as well he only had a few customers most evenings. Modern 20-year-old female Public Health Inspectors would throw their hands up in horror at such a practice.

I became very friendly with Ernie, often spending my night off in his pub, listening to his tales about life as a publican in the 1930s and during the war. My one regret is I never recorded his experiences for posterity; regretfully these are now lost for ever. He was a very large imposing man with the most disgusting nose I have ever seen, like a plump purple aubergine with more cavities than a gruyere cheese, cultivated no doubt, through many years of drinking port wine and taking snuff! When he straightened up he was much taller than the six foot I was, his chest was like a barrel and he had the most enormous hands and tattooed arms. On week days he always wore a white collarless shirt and red and white spotted neckerchief but on Sundays wore a stiff collar, tie and waistcoat, though I never ever saw him with his sleeves rolled down. His trousers were always held up by braces and a broad leather belt with a brass buckle.

He could be extremely cantankerous, which partly explained why the pub was usually very quiet, and he rarely had a good word to say for anyone. He blamed the brewery for letting his pub deteriorate, the police for the vandalism he suffered, the parson for not going to see him and his wife, the government for closing local American air bases, the bank for charging him for supplying change. He never had a bank account as he didn't trust them, but once a month collected change from them. He cursed the auctioneer for the low price he got for his last lot of pigs, the village for not buying his eggs, the vet for charging him to put his horse down, the doctor for not doing anything to relieve his and his wife's arthritis (although the village surgery was held in the front room of his daughter's house,) the village bone setter (osteopath) for not setting his broken ankle properly and, most of all, the villagers for not using his pub.

He told me he used to visit St Neots market to buy vegetables for sale in the pub before his gammy ankle stopped him driving his 1936 Ford pick up which still stood in a shed out the back. I was fascinated by the stories he told me about all the pubs he used to stop at on the way there, and again on the way back, and how friendly he was with the landlords and how they must miss his visits. I told him I would pick him up the following week and take him to St Neots.

Our first stop was at a pub in Kimbolton. As we entered the bar the landlord said, "Good God, you still alive, bugger off." I asked the landlord what my "father" had done to upset him. It appeared the hostile greeting was due to Ernie's last visit some ten years ago when Ernie, having had a bad day at the market, arrived the worse for drink and had been refused service. He proceeded to smash all the glasses on the bar with a sweep of his hand. I sheepishly offered to pay for any damage he had done but was told, "Just get him out of here and don't ever bring him back." We had made a good start on our trip to market.

The next stop was at the Fox at Catworth, a famous old staging inn on the A14 road. Ernie told me he used to sell them eggs on his way to market and vegetables on the way back. We bought a drink and Ernie asked the barmaid if the landlord was about saying he was an old friend and wanted a word with him. The girl said he had gone into Thrapston and was expected back shortly. It was at this stage that an old man came up to me and asked, "Is that man with you Ernie Goodman?" I said he was and I was driving him round his old haunts. The man replied, "If I were you I would get him out before the landlord returns, the last time he was in, he tore the front door off its hinges after being refused service for being so rowdy." I told Ernie we had to go otherwise we would be late for the market, and I promised him we would call to see his friend on the way home. I avoided stopping at any other pubs by using the same excuse.

St Neots market was the main selling place for all the market gardeners and small holders in a wide area. A cattle market was held in the morning, Ernie told me he went to the cattle market first where he would meet up with old friends, have a few drinks with them before going on to buy his produce. I quickly discovered there was no such thing as a few drinks with Ernie. In his huge hand a pint glass and its contents disappeared in record time. I had always prided myself on having a good beer input, but, as in most things with Ernie, I was an apprentice on a learning curve. My only saving grace that day was whilst Ernie could still down his beer in record time and consume large amounts, with age, the alcohol effect registered much more quickly.

We bought lots of produce at ridiculously low prices; the auctioneers all remembered Ernie and said how nice it was to see him again, although one winked at me knowingly as he said it. Opposite the market was The Cannon pub, and Ernie, saying his ankle was playing him up, left me to go and have a sit down. After some 30 minutes the auctioneer announced over the loud speakers, "Would the person with a Mr Goodman from Woodford, go to the Cannon pub."

The sight that greeted me was not completely unexpected after what I had been told that morning. Ernie had blood down his shirt and the landlady was wiping more blood from his head. Apparently, he had met a gypsy horse dealer who had sold him a gold ring the last time they met. The gold turned out to be of inferior quality and ever since Ernie had tried to trace the man without success. A row had ensued and Ernie had ended up hitting the man with his fist and knocking him out. An accomplice of the gypsy, in turn, had hit Ernie with a beer bottle. The only effect this had had on him was to make him go berserk and have to be restrained by customers.

Worry about his condition and age had led the landlord to give

Ernie goodness knows how many brandies, but fortunately this and the beer he had drunk earlier took effect and after getting him into my car with lots of assistance, I drove all the way back to Woodford with Ernie fast asleep in the back seat.

When I woke him up he wanted to know which pub we were at and when I told him his own, he said how sorry he was for falling asleep, because he wanted to introduce me to "more of my friends at pubs on the way home". I said, "Next time, Ernie," thankful for my early escape, I drove home with my produce.

I went to St Neots market many times after that, but never took Ernie again. From the numerous pubs I called at in time, I learnt that Ernie Goodman was the most famous, or infamous whichever way you considered him, publican ever to travel the 24 miles from Woodford to St Neots. He had left many scars on people's memories and bodies along the route.

I was often told stories about when Ernie went to Thrapston in his pony and trap and, at an appointed hour, his horse would stand in the doorway indicating it was time for him to go home. The landlord and Ernie's cronies would load him in the back of the trap, and the horse would find its own way back to Woodford. I heard, from witnesses, stories about Ernie's displays of strength, and how he would take part in bare fistfights at the back of the Swan Hotel for large wagers. I was told that many Thrapston businessmen owed their success to winning money on Ernie's fights.

During the war, he had narrowly escaped being sent to prison for assaulting and injuring four American servicemen in a fracas at a village dance. It was said that no constables had ever entered the Dukes Arms unless Ernie invited them. He was indeed a larger than life character and a true throwback to a bygone age.

A change of direction – decision time

I had, on occasions, asked Ernie if he ever thought about retiring. His answer was always the same: "We have nowhere to live boy, and no money to retire on, if the brewery wants me out they will have to pay for us to go into a home." I had said to Bert Drage that if ever Ernie retired I would be interested in his pub. Over the years many rumours had circulated that Ernie Goodman was retiring but both Ernie and the brewery had denied all.

For some time our thoughts had turned towards the possibility of having a tenancy, but we were restricted in our choice by long waiting lists for tenanted pubs and the small amount of savings we had. We thoroughly enjoyed our time at the Crows Nest, achieved a tremendous amount of success, made a lot of good friends, a lot of money for the brewery but not a lot for ourselves.

We earned a fair amount of money from our percentage share of the profits from the outside bars we ran, but as this was our first home, we had to start from scratch. Although most of our furniture had been bought second-hand from Wilfords furniture auctions in Wellingborough; we had to buy carpets, soft furnishings, and all the numerous items needed to set up a home for two small children and ourselves. We constantly found we had to buy things for the pub that the brewery in their parsimonious manner would not pay for.

One especially measly sum was a gardening allowance of £3 a year from which I had to buy petrol for the mower and pay for mower repairs, cut flowers for inside the pub and plants for baskets, troughs, and flowerbeds outside. The soil on the estate was terrible and a lot of fertilizer was needed before anything grew. I never received anything for all the car journeys I carried out in the brewery's interest.

Another major expenditure was clothing for Sylvia and me. Those were the days when you expected to see a clean, smartly dressed couple behind the bar, not wearing a scruffy "T" shirt, jeans and trainer aberrations you are accustomed to see today. In the winter I would wear a blazer, suit or sports jacket and in the summer a lightweight linen jacket, always with a shirt and tie. Sylvia made a lot of her clothes but still had to buy more than the average woman. With all the beer spillage that happened behind the bar, a pair of shoes would rot in a matter of weeks. These days beer is served so far from the top of the glass, it's almost impossible to spill it.

My allowance to buy drinks for our games teams was spent in the first few weeks and I continually had to supplement it from my own pocket, When it comes to free beer, customers do not differentiate between tenants and managers, they think the first pint, bought by landlords at all away matches, is their just reward for representing the pub!

When we left, the Crows Nest had two men's winter league dart teams, two summer league dart teams, and the same with skittles, dominoes and cribbage. We also had ladies dart and skittle teams competing in both winter and summer leagues and playing numerous friendlies. We entered teams in various angling competitions with great success, and played regular friendly football matches on the estate Recreation Ground. We entered and won on four occasions the town cricket club's k.o. competition. We also won the inter-pub relay event that I had organised. Not a bad achievement when you consider none of these teams existed when we took over.

One hazardous side of entering teams for angling competitions was my cellar being used to keep the team's maggot bait cold overnight. Maggots if not kept cool will quickly develop into chrysalises that are useless as fishing bait. They would be stored in empty Smith's crisp tins minus their lids to enable the maggots to breathe. For one particularly big Sunday competition, six tins each containing half a gallon of maggots were left in the cellar overnight. The following morning I heard Sylvia screaming and rushed to find her pointing to the cellar where the floor, walls and ceiling was covered with maggots.

What had happened was that the sawdust, in which the maggots are kept, must have been warm when the tins were put in the cellar, this had caused condensation to form inside the tins enabling the maggots to scale the sides and escape. Luckily being Sunday,

I had until 12 noon to clear away the maggots before the pub opened. I continuously hosed down the cellar and kept clearing the maggots from the drain. I needed all the extra time that a Sunday gave me, but for many weeks afterwards maggots and chrysalis would mysteriously appear each morning. I knew they shouldn't be able to get into a barrel, or if they did, to get past the hop filters. However, for many days when the customers held their beer up to check the clarity – a ritual always carried out by so called beer "experts" – I would be ready to explain how a maggot came to be in their beer, "I think it must be the larvae of a hop fly which just goes to prove, in spite of your doubts, that they still use hops for brewing beer!"

I had heard on the grapevine that a tenancy was coming vacant in a village not far from the Crows Nest. We had by then decided that although the offer of management of the Red Earl was an attractive proposition, we didn't relish starting again on another council estate. In addition, the idea of being our own bosses, benefiting fully from our ideas and hard work, appealed to us. We realized the financial limitations that management presented us with would make our dream of one day owning a Free house difficult to achieve.

I telephoned Bert Drage and asked him if he would consider us as prospective tenants for the Axe and Compass at Ringstead. Bert's answer was, "So you are no longer interested in the Dukes Arms then?" I said I couldn't continue waiting for Ernie Goodman to call it a day, to which Bert replied, "I have his notice, received today, on my desk in front of me." Apparently, Ernie had blacked out lifting a barrel of beer and was discovered lying on the floor by his daughter Grace, at whose house the doctor had his surgery. She fetched the doctor and the outcome was, between them, they persuaded Ernie and Ida to call it a day and go and live with her.

I suffered mixed emotions on hearing the news, I badly wanted a tenancy and, with the dilapidated condition of the Dukes Arms, I knew the cost of the ingoing wouldn't be too high, and as trade was practically non-existent, the challenge to pull it round was just what we wanted. At the same time I felt a great sadness that Ernie was going to leave the pub that had been his home and life for so many years without the fanfare he deserved. It was like a boxing champion retiring from the sport with flu, just before his biggest fight. Ideally, I would have liked him to have died behind the bar. It would have been a fitting end to the career of a man who was a legend in his lifetime. I told Bert I was indeed more than interested in the Dukes Arms and the next day I received the details in the post.

The rent was £16 per year; in return the brewery decorated the inside of the premises every three years and the outside every four. The rates were £32 a year which considering the size of the pub and grounds was reasonable. The estimated value of the fixtures and fittings was £58 and stock £36. There would be a brewery deposit of £25; this was in case you failed to pay your monthly bill on time, and £10 for a Justices Licence, making a total of £167, which was £47 more than our savings.

In addition to this, I would have to pay for the services of a valuer. I gambled on not having to pay the rent until the end of the first month, and then in quarterly instalments, and the same with the rates. I asked Ernie to reduce his stock to the minimum, as I would receive a month's credit on new supplies. From what I had seen on the premises, I thought the estimation of the value of the fixtures & fittings was rather high, so with a bit of luck we might get away with having sufficient funds. To be on the safe side I had arranged with Abbott's Garage at Irthlingborough to purchase our van for £85 if necessary, though doing business without a vehicle would be an inconvenience. I did, however, sell my Zeiss camera, which I had bought overseas in the Navy, for £7 just in case we were short.

We told Bert we could meet the financial qualifications, and then went through the formalities of an interview, so different from our previous one. We had to give the Managed House Department a month's notice enabling them to appoint new managers, but as they had long waiting lists, this was soon concluded. Ron Loomes, a good friend as ever, hurried this along.

Before concluding this account of our career at the Crows Nest, it would be remiss of me not to list some of the many good friends there, who gave us such splendid support and encouragement when we most needed it.

Herbie Wesley our bar manager at outside functions, Jean Meakins our No 1 barmaid, Arthur Farey, Peter & Mary Martin, Ebbie Seckington, Len & Kath Smith & their friends George & Mary? Alan (Spider) Kelly our No.1 barman, Maurice & Jean Kelly, "Big" John Underwood, Alan Moss, John & Daphne Pratt, Bertie Hudson, Peter Fox, Rex Cowper, Arthur Tyler, Ginger Burton, Gordon York, Bill, Ken & Dougie Bland, Major Reg. Bland, Joe O'Toole, Frank Britchford, Charlie Lowe, Ken Read (schoolmaster and ex-Chindit Captain), Frank and Margery Houghton, Dennis Adams, Bruiser Knighton (David's father), Jack Garley who became a publican himself, George Slawson, Barry Postlewaite, Arthur Fairlie, Ernie Peck, John Adams, Wag Parsons, Keith Parsons, Jack Brown & Tony Bilson – farmers, Peter the Pigeon (a Lithuanian refugee), Karl Monkelt who had been a German POW, Frank Hale, Freddie Goodwin gamekeeper, Frank & Val Douglas, Graham Mutton, Jack, Roy, David and Gordon Carpenter, Alan and Jim LeMarquand, Jack Whittaker, Stan Lloyd, Roy Waterfield, Capt Parker, solicitor – a regular lunchtime customer, our local bobby PC Bert Ireland who became a good friend and so many others whose faces I remember clearly but whose names escape me. It was a wrench to leave them all but they understood we had to move on up the ladder. Our heartfelt thanks to them for making our stay so happy.

My Licensed Victualler colleagues also deserve a mention.

Dick Tyldesley from the Golden Lion, Wellingborough. I once asked Dick, "How do you know when you are successful in the trade?" His reply given as a typical blunt Yorkshire man was, "When you can say to your best customer, you are a boring old sod, I'm sick of having to listen to your same old repetitive jokes, do me a favour and bugger off." Many times in years to come I wanted to utter those words, but it was to be a long time before our finances allowed me that pleasure.

Len (Fanny) Fancote Wing Cdr rtd, Leslie Eves, Cyril Plowman whose busiest night at The Bull, was on his day off. The pub packed with customers waiting to see what antics Cyril would be getting up to on his return, which was always at 9 p.m. Always worst for drink, he would berate his customers for their past sins and lack of patronage, often finishing with the words, "Clear off the lot of you, I am inebriated and your unwelcome presence offends me, I am going to bed and putting an end to my worthless life and deny the world the benefit of my genius any longer!" With a flourish he would usher them all out and lock the door. The last we heard of Cyril he had become a father for the first time at the age of 60.

Arthur Handscombe, with the physique of a blacksmith and the looks to go with it, whose son was a top London brain surgeon, Lennie Talbot, Val Randolph who spent many years on the stage with a Music Hall act, an accomplished pianist who also played the musical saw, George Elliott, Cyril Pickering, neither he nor his wife were ever seen behind the bar without a cigarette in their mouths, she had a compulsive cough which guaranteed a generous coating of ash in your pint, Ernie Tipler and Bill Oatridge both fine hoteliers of the old school.

The average age of licensees then was around 60-plus. Quite a few had inherited their pubs but a majority of the remainder were retired servicemen, policemen, sportsmen and a fair smattering from the entertainment profession. We were never short of pianists and artists on social occasions. Gentlemen and characters all, I owe them a great deal for all the support and encouragement they gave to a bolshy, angry young mess deck lawyer. Thanks, chaps.

THE DUKES ARMS

Although I had visited the Dukes Arms many times I had never looked at the living accommodation very closely. I was familiar with the layout and I knew that Ernie and his wife lived downstairs, but I thought the latter was purely for convenience. I also knew that Ernie and his wife suffered from severe arthritis but what I hadn't realised was neither of them had set foot upstairs for 18 years! They slept in what should have been the smoke room and used the saloon bar as their kitchen/dining/sitting room. We were in for a considerable shock when we first inspected the premises and so was John Nelson, my Tied House (tenancy) District Manager. He had last visited the pub some nine months previously when, because he hadn't made an appointment, was told by Ernie to clear off.

On entering the front door, a passageway ran straight through to the rear door leading to the outside toilets. The public bar was to the left with varnished wooden fixed seating on three sides and the bar counter across the other wall. There was a wooden seat against the bar and a trestle table in front of it. This just left a small area at the end for serving drinks. As their regular trade consisted of just four or five elderly village residents who had their beer brought to them, this arrangement worked satisfactorily. Six magnificent beer pump handles dominated the bar counter, they were alternate green and red fluted porcelain columns with hop leaves encrusted on the bases and lots of gold highlights. I had never seen handles like them before nor have I seen any since.

A large glass case containing a stuffed cock and hen pheasant, woodcock and grouse, filled one wall behind the bar, and a serving hatch through to the tap room was at the rear of the servery. A passageway behind the bar contained a wooden thrall with the two firkins (nine gallons each) that constituted their weekly draught beer sales. A door at the end led to a very large room, where during the war Ernie kept chickens.

It was built over a large disused cellar and had a wooden floor, which was perforated with rat holes. To the right of the entrance door was the saloon bar, further down the passageway a door to the right led to the smoke room and a door on the left to the tap room. A large larder/scullery was reached down a flight of steps by the back door. Behind another door, a flight of stairs led up to the first floor.

The largest room upstairs was approximately 45 by 20 feet and had been a billiard room. Ernie told me that before the war, some of the directors of Praeds Brewery whose house it previously was, had a large pheasant shoot in the area and after shooting would return to the Dukes Arms for dinner and to play billiards until the late hours. Ernie said that a Mr Downing, who was the company chairman, had the table brought from the Hind Hotel, Wellingborough when the hotel was damaged by fire. He told tales about the riotous evenings in that room, some with ladies of rather "loose morals", other times when large sums of money changed hands at cards.

During the war the shoot parties ceased and Ernie let American servicemen from nearby camps, play on the table. The ceiling bore evidence of this with numerous holes, which they had poked through with billiard cues. After the war, the table deteriorated through damp and misuse and in the end Ernie sold the slate base to a gravestone mason and chopped up the woodwork for firewood. It was obvious from stains on the floor that the roof leaked.

The bathroom contained an old rusty cast iron bath that also leaked. There was no washbasin and the toilet was cracked and badly stained. There were four bedrooms altogether on the first floor and an attic room was reached by a rickety flight of steps. I asked Ernie when the upstairs was last decorated and he said before the war. As this was now 1962 that would have been at least 22 years!

The area outside the pub was surrounded by a high stonewall with a gate to the side of the building and another at the bottom of a path. The ladies' and gents' toilets were down that path and consisted of one ladies' w.c. back to back with a gents' w.c; these were brick built, windowless with tin roofs. The gents urinal had no such luxury: that was just as well as flushing only took place during a rainstorm! The concrete floor was badly cracked; in the summer the aroma was a trifle over-powering. There was a detached building that had once been a blacksmiths shop and still had the forge and bellows inside. Three stables, four pigsties and a covered area surrounded a cobbled yard and alongside the perimeter wall was a substantial kitchen garden. The pub overlooked a large village green, one of the largest in the county, the site for a visiting fairground during the annual Woodford Feast Week.

Woodford was situated on the A604 between Kettering and Thrapston, the lower end of the village fronting the River Nene. With a population then of around 1,500, it was a large village and supported three public houses, The Dukes Arms, Prince of Wales, White Horse, and a large Working Men's Club. Three other pubs, Bakers Arms, Engine and Coach & Horses, closed just after the war

There was a Co-operative store and butchers' shop, two general stores, one kept by a nice Mr Pitts whose nickname was Zasu, after the actress! These were the days before supermarkets: post office, a fish and chip shop, a ladies' and gents' hairdressers, a market garden and a garage. There was once a shoemaker's shop where the owner, Mr Wilson, made boots for the furnace workers.

There was ironstone mining and limestone pits on the outskirts of the village, and up until the late '40s, the village had an iron foundry that, together with the nearby quarries, employed a third of the village men. Horses were used for many jobs down the pits and quarries and one of the perks the men had was to grow mushrooms on the manure. These were sent twice a week to Covent Garden and the money divided between the men.

A part of the village called Newtown along with a terrace of houses was built circa 1880 to accommodate the ironworkers. At this time, 30 families moved into the village from Wiltshire. The furnaces were eventually taken over by Stewart & Lloyds and closed down with the workers being offered jobs at their huge plant at Corby, some eight miles away. For the ladies there were two clothing factories: Wallis and Linnell opened in 1887, and employed 50 women and later on, Ideal Clothiers from Wellingborough opened a factory. In addition, quite a lot took in work at home for the shoe trade. Prior to the Beeching cuts, the village had its own railway station.

The village had two chapels, Baptist and Methodist. A 12th century church stood majestically by the river. It was famous for its medieval brasses and, in a glazed recess set into a pillar, the embalmed heart of a Lord of the Manor who died in the Holy Land. His heart was brought back to the village by a faithful follower. The church later became famous for a series of photographs taken inside, which, when developed, clearly showed the presence of a ghostly figure.

There were five main families in the village, the Coulsons, Clipstons, Warrens, Allans and Bosworths; all were to have an influence on our years at The Duke.

The day for moving arrived and we enlisted the services of my mother to help us. She looked after the bar whilst I attended to the valuer and licensing matters and Sylvia supervised the removal men and our children. It is normal practice for both in and outgoing tenants to have their own valuer, but with so few fixtures, fittings, furniture and stock and the need for me to save money, I agreed to our sharing the same valuer and with it the cost. Peter Stiles of Merry Bros. & Cowling, who was to become a good friend, carried out the valuation. The fixtures & fittings were valued at £16 and the furniture at £12, this low figure reduced Ida to tears, and Ernie to a state of disbelief. If only we had been wealthier, I would have asked the valuer to be more generous with his valuation, but, after all he was neutral to both parties and within a few weeks, we threw most of it out.

When it came to the stock, we were astonished at the items Ernie owned. Peter Stiles opened a cupboard and inside was four dozen mixed bottles of elderberry, cowslip and ginger wine. When Peter asked Ernie why he had so much of this wine in stock, Ernie said he had bought it off the ration during the war for sale to the Americans who loved it and would willingly pay 2/- (10p) for a bottle. Spirits and imported wine was rationed to retailers during the war but apparently not British wines. When John Nelson reminded Ernie that the war had been over for 20 years, Ernie blurted out, "The way the world is going, it won't be long before there is another one." Ernie's dismay at the furniture valuation had left him rather tetchy, and, with his volatile reputation, no one dare ask him whether he thought the Americans would return to drink his cowslip wine.

Three nicotine-stained and fly blown cards behind the bar contained stuck-on packets of breath sweeteners, aspirin and indigestion tablets. According to the price changes crossed out on the cards, the items had increased in stages over the years, from an original farthing to a penny ha'penny a packet. For your money you got ten tablets wrapped in paper. The empty spaces where sold packets had once been, varied in shades from dark brown to almost white, the latter indicating that a packet had been sold recently,

The only spirits in stock were those on the optics, whisky, rum, gin and brandy. The half empty brandy bottle was a brand that had ceased production in 1950. The "spirit" that remained had a furry growth in it, which clearly indicated the contents were not as pure as they should have been. Sylvia used it for cleaning stains off the counter. A glass sweet jar behind the bar contained four small packets of biscuits of very doubtful age and manufacture.

The total value of stock was £20: a large part of that was the British wine and a considerable amount of empties discovered in an outhouse. Fortunately, it was standard practice for the brewery to deliver new stock on the day a changeover took place, which meant we had fresh supplies and a month's credit to pay for it.

John Nelson, Ernie and myself attended the Magistrates Court in Thrapston for the change of licence. The Chairman of the Bench, Colonel Nigel Stopford-Sackville, the clerk of the court, Colonel Vincent Sykes MC, and the police inspector all paid glowing tributes to Ernie. Colonel S-S told the court, "I remember going with my father to the Dukes Arms in a pony and trap, the horse shied and if Mr Goodman hadn't restrained it with his massive strength, I may not be here today." Poor Ernie was overcome with the tributes paid to him and for the second time that day I saw tears run down his monstrous nose. Also on the bench that day was Commander Carey Wilson RNSR, who lived in Woodford.

A week before we had opened an account with the Westminster Bank in Thrapston after supplying them with four character references. Wouldn't it be sensible if youngsters today had to meet the same strict standards that were applied then? The final bill for the ingoing of the Dukes Arms and associated fees came to £84, well within our capability, and with due ceremony the first cheque either of us had ever written, was handed over. The draymen had, by that time, delivered our first order and we were in business.

We had forgotten to obtain change for the till (or rather drawer) so a quick dash to the bank for £3 worth of change was necessary. Our hopes of sudden wealth were somewhat dashed when John Nelson informed us it was customary for the first drink served to each customer to be on the house. We need not have really worried as customers didn't exactly flock in and most who did were friends from the Crows Nest calling to wish us luck. At the end of the day, we had taken £3 18 6d, which Sylvia made up to £4, and I went to Thrapston the next day and banked. We banked every day that week and at the end, our takings totalled £36.

During our first week I remarked to my mother that trade was a little disappointing, I fully expected villagers coming in, if for nothing else to see what we looked like. Mother said it was not helping trade with Ernie encamped inside the door each session. Ernie was our first customer each morning and evening, he sat just inside the bar with a battered old exercise book in front of him. He told mother he was waiting for people who owed him money and had stayed away from the pub to avoid paying him. He hoped that with a new landlord the people would now use the pub and he could collect the money owing.

I spoke to Ernie about this and it transpired that some of these debts went back before the war, in fact the oldest entry was 1937 – nearly 30 years ago! Some people had died and he was hoping to collect off their relatives. It was obvious the word had got round the village about Ernie's presence and this was keeping customers away. Woodford people were very stubborn, as was Ernie, and some of the debts were more about self-respect than finance. There was no doubt a lot of the people could afford to repay his money, but, as I later discovered, it was a matter of principle to most of them, because of Ernie's bombastic manner. I asked Ernie what was the total of the money owed to him and was staggered when he said £78. Not all was for drinks over the bar, some was for bacon obtained from his pigs, taxi journeys, rent for his stables but most from outstanding loans.

I couldn't let this situation continue any longer, I asked Ernie if he would let me try and collect the money for him, but it was obvious he wanted the pleasure of extracting his due from the debtors himself. I spoke to his daughter Grace about his attitude and the problem. She said she was powerless to make her father back off. He had looked forward to this moment for months. I had one last attempt to get him to see reason but with no avail, I therefore had no other option than to tell him if he continued with his actions I would have to ban him from the pub.

It was a dreadful moment for me, I shall never forget the look of incredulity on his face as he stared straight at me, and for a moment I really thought I was going to be on the wrong end of the famous Ernie Goodman right hook. His mouth opened but no words came out, he just got to his feet and walked out. I went after him to tell him it would only be a temporary measure, but he just carried on walking down the path without stopping or turning round. As he neared the gate, I saw his handkerchief come out and I realized a tear was being shed. Without a doubt, it was the most poignant moment in my life, I felt powerless to do anything to ease his sadness and humiliation.

For some months afterwards, Ernie would look over the gate and pass the time of day with me, but he never set foot inside that gate again.

Ida died a few years after they left the pub and Ernie followed her a month later.

"I'm prepared to meet my Maker, Whether my Maker is prepared for the ordeal of meeting me is another matter"

Winston Churchill

We are tenants

The shock we had on seeing the dilapidated living accommodation upstairs was soon matched by daily discoveries. The cracks in the flagstones behind the bar had weeds growing from them. Because of the leaking bath and broken washbasin, the only place we could wash ourselves, the children, cooking pots and dishes was in the sink behind the bar. Fortunately it was a large Belfast sink so we could sit the children in it. After I partly sealed the crack in the bath with filler, as long as we regularly emptied a bowl placed underneath to catch the drips, it was possible for Sylvia and myself to have a quick bath together. After the first heavy rain, we discovered the children's beds were wet so I had to buy a tarpaulin to suspend over it in wet weather. Holes in the roof above the billiard room necessitated placing numerous receptacles to catch the water coming through the ceiling. I painted marks on the floor so I could quickly put the containers in place when a storm threatened.

We moved the beer barrels from the passageway behind the bar; it wasn't large enough for the extra barrels we were selling, so I had the large larder converted into a cellar. The beer engines – last used in 1949 –were reconditioned, and new beer pipes laid underground connecting the larder to the bar. The cooker that had previously been sited in the larder was now moved to the passageway behind the bar. The main drawback with its new position was that cooking could not take place during opening hours, the passage was windowless and any fumes wafted into the bar.

The brewery's Estates Department had said they didn't want to do repairs in a piece-meal fashion, and, if we would bear with them, they would send a surveyor out to list all the work needed, including decorating inside and out, and then get estimates for an outside contractor to do the work. This alarmed me, as it didn't fit in at all with my plans. Having some knowledge of how the brewery worked, I knew that if they carried out minor works to make the place habitable, nothing else would happen for a long time, and I wanted *major* alterations.

We had moved in the early summer and the brewery allocated money for major works in April each year. I asked Bert Drage to give us time to show just how much we could increase the trade, then for the brewery to make the decision on how much money to spend on revamping the pub. Bert asked Sylvia how she thought she could possibly manage to bring up two small children in the conditions that existed. Sylvia said as long as she thought it would eventually lead to her "dream pub" she could put up with the hardship. Bert said he had confidence in our making the Estates Department sit up and take notice and supported our "scheming".

For so many years The Dukes Arms had ceased to figure on their maintenance chart due to Ernie's intransigence. He was worried his rent would increase from the £12 a year he was paying, and, when they sent their surveyors to the pub, he ordered them off the premises. They could have demanded access but it suited them to spend Ernie's allocation elsewhere. Therefore, we had nine months to prove our point and determine the future destiny of the Dukes Arms.

Sylvia and I decided that, with the premises in its present dilapidated state, we weren't going to increase our trade sufficiently with mature customers. We agreed the answer lay in the clubroom and the younger trade who, by this time, had become liberated by teenage heroes such as Cliff Richards, Marty Wilde and James Dean. The age of the modern, individualistic teenager beckoned. They had ample money to spend, and, apart from clothes, not a lot to spend it on. McDonalds, KFC and Pizza Parlours had not yet been "invented", Indian and Chinese restaurants were to be found only in London and major cities. Coffee bars had opened but again only in towns and were mainly used as meeting points.

I remember when Peter & Mary Martin, very good friends of ours from Irthlingborough, were emigrating to Australia, we took them to London for a day out and went to Veeraswamey's Indian Restaurant in Regents Street for dinner. It was such a novelty that none of us ever forgot our visit there. A towering tall turbaned Sikh, resplendent in the uniform of an Indian Army Lancer, opened the door for us. All the male staff wore Indian servants' uniform and the female staff wore saris. The restaurant opened in 1927 and was the oldest established Indian restaurant in the country. The food was genuinely Indian, not as today, an Anglicised version. If you asked for a Balti or Chicken Masala they would soon show you the door.

The few discos that had opened were situated in major towns and cities. To the best of my knowledge – and for our sins – we operated the first disco in Northamptonshire. Going back to the youngsters' lifestyles, it is a fact that in the late '50s and '60s youngsters paid a lot of attention to their appearance; jeans and T-shirts had not arrived. A young man wouldn't dream of going out at night without wearing a smart suit, drainpipe trousers and short jackets maybe, but polished shoes and shirt and tie were the order of the day. The same standards applied to older men as well. To see a man in the pub during the evening without a jacket, collar and tie was the exception.

So we set to and cleaned out the large clubroom, which involved carting away barrow loads of vintage chicken and rat droppings. I nailed old flattened crisp tins over the rat holes, after putting down copious amounts of rat poison. The room was approximately 45 by 15 feet. It had an old iron upright coke stove with a piped chimney going through the eaves as its main form of heating. Ernie had used the stove for boiling up his pigswill. The walls and ceiling were lined with tongued and grooved timber and wooden seating was fixed round the walls.

I bought a load of furniture very cheaply from a pub that was closing down; not brilliant but it served a purpose. I built a bar counter, canopy and back fitting across one end, covered the ceiling in the room with string garden netting and hung coloured lights between this and the eaves. I obtained advertising posters from a travel agent, and pasted these round the walls, and with candles in Chianti bottles on the tables, the whole effect was of a Parisian basement bar, or so I thought. Whatever it represented, it was extremely popular with the younger element.

After a few months, I installed a Rock-Ola Juke box and trade really took off. I shall always remember the most played records were Bobby Vee's "Rubber Ball", "Telstar" by The Tornados and Susan Maughan singing "Bobby's Girl". We were getting trade from Irthlingborogh, Finedon, Burton Latimer and Kettering. The larder-turned cellar quickly became too small to hold enough barrels (36 gallons) so I started having hogsheads (54 gallons), still in wooden casks, and on a good Saturday night I could easily sell two of them in addition to loads of bottle beer.

One disadvantage with this type of trade – and there's always one – was the fights that took place. Some were caused by inter-town rivalry among the lads, but the main instigators were the girls. Mini skirts and tights had just arrived on the fashion scene, and I have to say that as the skirts got shorter so did the boys' tempers. I stopped wearing a collar and tie behind the bar and started wearing roll necked sweaters, which came off more easily in a brawl.

We had our own resident village policeman named PC Dowdy. Ron Dowdy was a very nice person and a good community village bobby. If you were an OAP requiring help, he was your man. If your dog was caught worrying sheep, watch out he could be merciless! However, when faced with a bunch of drunken yobbos, Ron was not at his best. If on duty on a Saturday night, Ron would conveniently decide to visit a quiet neighbouring village to investigate an alleged report of poachers.

My policy then and in the future, was never to call the police to a disturbance that took place at any pub kept by me. My father, who spent 22 years in the Leicestershire Police Force, once told me that he would never willingly attend a disturbance at a pub. His opinion was that if a landlord was ready to take a customer's money for alcoholic drink, knowing that it may lead to that person becoming troublesome, he should personally be prepared to sort out the consequences of any trouble.

On numerous occasions, I found myself going to Ron's assistance when he was on duty at village dances. He was once set upon by a bunch of yobbos who picked him up and threw him into the village horse trough. Ron's only comment was to say, "Now then lads, that's not playing the game." A colleague of his, PC Mick Millward from Titchmarsh, was a much tougher proposition. His philosophy was to hit them first and face the consequence afterwards. Mick was usually to be found on duty at most village dances in the area.

One Saturday evening I broke up a fight involving a group of youths from Finedon who were fighting a group from Kettering. After sorting it out, one of the Kettering youths, known as "FF", (on advice I have not written his full name) pulled out a knife and said, 'I'm going to stick you!' I had no experience in tackling a person with a knife but had seen men in films wrap a coat round their arms, which I did with my sweater. After circling round each other a few times, "F" lunged at me and slashed my sweater nicking my arm in the process.

Just as I was beginning to think things were getting rather nasty, round the corner walked Mick Millward. I had never been so pleased to see a copper in all my life. A neighbour, whose house overlooked the pub yard had seen what was happening and dialled 999. Without saying a word Mick walked up behind "F" and hit him over the head with his truncheon, knocking him unconscious. At the court case that followed "F", who had previous convictions for assault, was found guilty of causing GBH and sent to prison for three years. As he left the court he looked at me and drew his hand across his throat. The gesture was well understood but I need not have worried, "F" was stabbed to death during a fight in Bedford prison nine months later.

Woodford Feast Week

During the first Saturday evening in July the sound of numerous large heavy lorries pulling onto the village green, heralded the arrival of Thurston's Fun Fair, an important part of Woodford Feast Week. The feast was a traditional event going back hundreds of years. Having spent the previous week at Kettering and before that Northampton, the showmen looked upon Woodford as an enjoyable break after the rigours of operating at these two larger events. The showmen's families went back many generations and in the main were good, clean-living hard working people. Their expensive traditional caravans were spotlessly clean and they loved to show you round them. Each showman owned his attraction or stall, often handed down from father to son. They paid a fee to the owner of the Fair, which covered his cost of renting the site, advertising and generally organising the event.

The fair's owner provided the main attractions and at Woodford this was the dodgems and cakewalk. In charge of their erection was the "Bossman", who was also responsible for driving the huge Diamond T prime mover that contained the generator, which supplied all the fair's electricity, and towed a trailer with the heavy attractions onboard.

Barry was the "Bossman", a Norfolk man with the broadest accent, tremendously strong he ran his team of roustabouts with a rod of iron, and they needed it. They were the labourers, who did all the heavy dirty work erecting and dismantling the large attractions. They slept under the vehicles or in anyone's bed who would have them. It was said, but I could not possibly comment, that many individuals in Woodford owed their being to the fairground men! An idea of how true this was could be measured by the amount of inhabitants whose birthdays happened to fall in the same month. I had it on good authority that the local shop sold more birthday cards in March than any month, but there again, this could possibly be pure coincidence.

When it was first known we were leaving the Crows Nest to live in Woodford, Mr Kerry, the bank manager was very concerned and said to Sylvia, "I do hope you will be all right, Mrs Hackett, Woodford is not known as Wicked Woodford for nothing. Over the years, many a tomcat had gone up the wrong entry." (*An old country saying!*)

In the days when steam engines pulled the trailers, they filled their boilers with water from the Dukes Arms' cellar, which was permanently flooded. With the increased trade we were doing, it became necessary to have the cellar drained, fitted with an automatic sump pump and renovated so it could once again be used as a beer cellar. The pantry, even with hogsheads could not hold the amount of beer we were selling.

During Feast Week trade was phenomenal. What with the 30 odd fair men popping in and out for a drink, tradition had it that anyone who had ever lived or had relations in the village, returned for Feast Sunday. After church the fair was officially opened and from then to the following Saturday evening crowds flocked to the village and into the pubs. Being the pub nearest to the fair, we gained most of the trade.

Village fairs were traditionally places where old grievances would be sorted out and Woodford was no exception. All the fairground men kept pick axe handles behind their stalls and, at a given signal, would rush to the point of trouble. Together with the roustabouts they made a formidable team and when you included the women, no sober person would ever think about causing trouble. A few did though; I once saw Barry lay three men out in as many minutes.

When the fair "pulled down" the owner and Barry toured all the pubs and shops, asking if any of the fairground people owed any money or had caused any trouble. Was it any wonder there was always a welcome for them in the village? When we eventually left Woodford for Towcester, at least 20 of the showmen called to see us during Northampton Fair week. This happened every year we were there, which shows how much they appreciated our friendship and we theirs.

Sylvia's misery ends – or so we thought

After our first Christmas was over, we received a visit from Colonel David Jones, and his wife, he said they just happened to be passing, which could have been the case. However, he seemed to know an extraordinary amount about the Dukes Arms and, although a supposed unofficial visit, asked Sylvia if they could look upstairs.

Both he and his wife were shocked at the condition of the premises although we had splashed a bit of paint around, the roof had been repaired and we had a new bath, washbasin and toilet. I explained to him that we had been prepared to put up with its state in the hope extensive alterations would be carried out in the new financial year. He said we couldn't possibly continue to work and live in the conditions that existed, and he would instruct the Estates Department to treat the matter with a degree of urgency. True to his word, the brewery's head surveyor arrived the next day with a young architect named John Reed.

John had recently joined Watneys (Midlands) from the head office in London and, as yet, had not been responsible for any alterations; ours was to be his first. He returned after two weeks with preliminary drawings for our comments, this in itself was unheard of. Normally the Estates Department treated tenants and managers like a bunch of morons, it was rare to be consulted even about wallpaper.

John's scheme was to redesign the interior of the pub completely, knocking down walls to form larger rooms. The existing passageway would become the area behind the bars with a counter running the length of the new bar, formed from the existing bar, tap room and passageway to the clubroom. An archway would connect the saloon bar and smoke room to form a lounge and the two serveries would be linked to that of the bar. The result would be to provide a large public bar, a lounge bar with a snug recess, new inside toilets, and part of the clubroom would form a games area.

This final alteration meant doing away with the clubroom but it had served its purpose, namely in enabling us to increase the trade to such an extent that the large sums proposed would be justifiably spent. We had used the youngsters to attain our aims and having achieved that, would then part company with them. Cruel? Maybe, but the thought that the skin would be allowed to re-grow on my knuckles was an experience that couldn't come soon enough.

Final plans were drawn up and the work was put out to tender.

Chalk and cheese

Woodford had its fair share of characters amongst the village elders. One who arrived shortly after our arrival was "Gentleman" Jack Smith. Jack was one of the top leather reps in the country. He had been an accomplished horseman of some renown, horse breeder and breaker well known in hunting circles throughout the country. One of his proudest boasts was that he had provided horses for three kings, a queen, ten generals and British Army regiments across the world.

In his day he had been a proper ladies' man, what you would call today, "a smoothie", some might say a Gigolo or even male escort. This had nothing to do with his looks because he resembled W C Field, it was his way with horses. He had an expression: "You tell a good horse and woman the same way. They both have a strong back and good hindquarters which they spread readily on command."

He had married a very wealthy woman from Oundle who worshipped him but, after a few turbulent years together, threw him out because of his womanising and drinking. She gave him a generous monthly allowance on the understanding he would not embarrass her by having affairs with any of her friends. Jack went to her house for tea once a month to collect his allowance and mow the lawn, although she had a gardener.

He was very friendly with a man named Dick Chamberlain who had a leather and shoe factory in Higham Ferrers that, if my memory serves me right, made "John White" shoes. When the horse business petered out after the war, Dick Chamberlain gave Jack a job as a leather representative, and he soon rose to be one of the best in the country. Jack stayed in the very best hotels throughout the world, seducing the very best women in the process.

This all came to an abrupt end when the company was sold to the British Shoe Corporation and Jack was made redundant. Good though he was, the shoe industry was going through a bad time, and rather than seek further employment at the age of 68 he called it a day.

For a while he lived in hotels throughout the county but when his money was running low, he obtained lodgings in Woodford. This was akin to skid row as far as Jack was concerned. Although Aggie Cumly's lodging house was very clean and respectable, a hotel it was not. Jack had only ever been used to the very best, women, horses, wine, cigars, food and travel – he was a connoisseur. He had his own room at Aggies, which at least placed him in a class above the other "guests" who shared rooms. He paid a fellow boarder to clean and polish his car, a Rover P4 given to him when he left his job, another was paid to clean his shoes and take him tea and papers in the morning. Not for nothing was he known as "Gentleman Jack".

When he first started patronizing The Dukes Arms, he drank nothing but large brandy and sodas, smoked Players Perfectos, which were very expensive and had his name printed on individual cigarettes. A very generous man, he treated any elderly person who happened to be in the pub. Many waited until they saw his car drive down the road before going out for their morning refreshment. Most of the time he wore a camel overcoat over a smart tweed or pinstriped suit. His shirts were the best quality, shoes or boots matched the finest, and he topped it all off with a brown trilby. In a sentence, he was a picture of sartorial elegance.

It was therefore with sadness that over the years we witnessed Jack's decline. It started gradually at first with his tipple changing from brandy and soda to nips of barley wine, still more expensive than ordinary beer, and his cigarettes changed to Capstan Full Strength. We noticed his clothing becoming very threadbare, his shirt cuffs and collars were frayed and his coat and Trilby hat developed a shine. He still bought people drinks but with not quite the old enthusiasm. Dents and scratches on his car were left unattended and his journeys reduced.

When the alterations were well underway I decided to get Sylvia away from all the mess. It was beginning to get her down. I asked Jack if he could recommend a hotel I could take her to for a few days. Jack, in his booming voice, said, "Dear boy, there is only one hotel in the country worthy of Sylvia's patronage, The Lygon Arms at Broadway, when you make the booking, tell the owner Dick Lygon or his Manager Douglas Barrington, that Jack Smith of Oundle recommended you to stay there." I told the receptionist, and, low and behold, when we were shown to our room, a bottle of champagne, compliments of the management, awaited us. We had a wonderful few days and when I came to pay the bill the receptionist said, "Dinner on your first evening was with the compliments of Mr Jack Smith." Typical of Jack's generosity.

Incidentally, I still have a 1955 copy of Ashley Courtenay's guide *Let's Halt Awhile* that Jack gave me. In its day the "bible" for well-heeled travellers.

Tommy Abbot was another of the village characters and one of life's gentlemen. He first served in the army as a boy soldier during the Boer War and continued in the regular army, seeing service throughout the First World War as a groom in a cavalry regiment. In the 1920s, having served his time, he left with a small pension and joined the Fire Service. He served 20 years in this role until eventually retiring with another pension in 1940.

Among his many attributes, Tommy was an old soldier through and through, from his service style haircut to his highly polished brown boots and brown leather gaiters. Although quite small, with his smart appearance and military bearing he stood out from most of the other villagers of his age group. During the day Tommy was often seen wearing a brown service apron doing his household chores and always in his brown boots and gaiters. I have difficulty in trying to remember an occasion when he didn't wear his boots and gaiters; they were definitely his trademarks.

Once a week he came across the road to the pub with his handcart, collected all our families' shoes and brought them back an hour later highly polished. If anything could be polished, Tommy was the man. On his weekly trip to Thrapston market he put on his best brown three-piece tweed suit, wore his gold watch chain hanging from his waistcoat pocket, and obligatory gaiters and boots. He always wore a '20s' style stiff rounded collar with his shirt, and folded his raincoat into a neat roll, carrying it over his shoulder. A flat cap and walking stick completed his outfit. In his market day attire, he always reminded me of men in old W.W.1 photographs marching off to join the army.

Tommy and Jack Smith had a common interest: their love of horses. Tommy was one of the last people in the village to use a pony and trap, his horse, Captain, was much loved by the village children. That is where any similarity between them ended. They were continually verbally sparring with each other, Jack the more intelligent and Tommy the more independently minded.

He had his own house which he kept immaculately, and did everything for himself, Jack, on the other hand, lived in lodgings and couldn't wash a handkerchief let alone wash and iron a shirt. Jack was extremely generous, even in later years when his financial position deteriorated. Tommy was very careful with his money almost to the point of being called a skinflint. This dissimilarity was a major factor in their many differences of opinion. Tommy would taunt Jack about him living in a lodging house and Jack would call him a "mean little bugger" saying, "When are you going to give us back some of that pension we have been giving you for 30 years?" At times they were like a music hall act.

Tommy had a rather squeaky voice which Jack could take off perfectly. Often when Tommy walked into the bar, Jack in his best Tommy voice, would say, "Would you care for a drink with me, Jack?" He would then add in his own voice, "That's very kind of you, Tommy, I'll have a large brandy & soda." Tommy would walk threateningly towards Jack waving his walking stick and say, "I earned my money fighting for my country to protect sops like you!" No real harm was ever meant; indeed Jack often took Tommy to market in his car.

After we had been in the village for four years, Tommy applied and was accepted as a Chelsea Pensioner. We often wondered if they let him wear his brown boots and gaiters. He was greatly missed in the village.

Will it ever be finished?

An old family firm from Thrapston won the contract for the alterations, Loakes & Son. The tender was won with a quoted price of £4,000, the price at the time of a new three-bedroomed house was in the region of £1,800. Reg Loakes, the son part of the name, was a 60-year-old man about town. He had inherited the business from his father and appeared to play no active part in running it.

He had a good clerk of works and an experienced but aged work force; most had been with the firm all their lives and had been engaged by and worked with his late father.

His sister was a joint director of the firm although she worked as private secretary to Tom Bletsoe, the owner of Messrs Bletsoes, Auctioneers. Had it not been for his sister, I think Reg would have sold the business years ago, and frittered the money away on drink, women and horses, not necessarily in that order. His nose was bettered only by Ernie Goodman's and had been acquired from his daily drinking sessions in the many hotels and public houses of Thrapston. These were the halcyon days before the breathalyser, when a man could have a good drink and then be helped into his car by the local PC. That happened daily to Reg. A senior freemason in his local lodge, some said he was untouchable by the law in the Thrapston Area.

Anyway, his firm was given the contract and we suffered the delays, waiting for materials, men being taken away for other jobs and no work taking place after midday on Friday when Reg arrived with the wages and then spent the rest of the day drinking with his workmen.

Because Reg was incapable of giving an order for fear of upsetting his men, they worked at a speed matched only in my experience, by dockyard mateys. John Reed did his utmost to speed up the work but, despite his efforts and threats that they would never be given another contract, it took from early April until late October 1964 to complete the work, a period in time forever etched in our minds. Public houses could not close in those days for any reason other than complete destruction or severe damage, e.g. by fire. Failure to open could lead to the loss of a Justices Licence.

Having experienced the alterations at the Crows Nest, we thought we knew just what to expect, but the walls there were of modern brick construction and not very thick. The walls at The Dukes Arms were, in places four feet thick, with the centre filled with rubble and dust. The day they broke up for the Easter weekend, they knocked a large hole through an outside wall and then went off and left it. It blew a gale every day that holiday and the dust was unbelievable. Sylvia's anger at their lack of consideration lasted for the duration of the work.

Nevertheless, I have to say the work they did was of the highest standard, especially the bar fittings. They employed three carpenter/shop fitters who made joints by hand, not with machines. Whilst the work was progressing slowly inside, the outside was completely restructured in the space of a week. The pigsties were demolished, as was the covered area once used for storing hay. Two of the stables were converted into a garage and the remaining one to a store. The cobbled yard and large kitchen garden were covered in tarmac providing a car park for some 30 cars. We were left with a small area that was turfed to make a lawn and flowerbed. The blacksmith's shop was retained as a bottle store.

A bit of luck money

One worthwhile contact that came about as a result of meeting Reg Loakes was our being invited to run the Market Bar.

Reg's sister was secretary to Tom Bletsoe whose firm were the main Auctioneers at Thrapston Cattle Market, held every Tuesday. The market was situated very conveniently just off the main street in the centre of the town. Through Reg. we learnt that Bletsoes were looking for someone to open a bar and restaurant in a new building at the market. I went and saw Miss Loakes and she gave me the details which involved tendering for providing breakfasts, lunches and on-going snacks from 6.30 a.m. until 4.30 p.m. and running a bar from 10.30 a.m. till 4 p.m. Thrapston pubs and hotels had a special market day extension. I knew the two hotels in the town would not be interested in tendering, as they were very busy on Market Day.

Pubs supplying food, apart from the odd sandwich, were unheard of, whereas we had big plans to do full-scale catering once the alterations at the pub were completed.

I provided them with sample menus and a bar price list. On the question of rent, I said I would do it on the understanding it was rent-free for six months, then negotiable after that. My terms were accepted and we invested in cooking appliances, utensils, crockery, cutlery and all the paraphernalia needed to serve 60 breakfasts, 80 lunches and snacks to hungry farmers, buyers and drovers. A good kitchen and bar area had been incorporated into the new building and only needed minor alterations to suit us.

By this time, although the alterations had not been completed, we were employing our first staff. Betty Peck, a pocket automaton whose accent was a curious combination of Corby Scottish and East Northamptonshire was the first to join us. During the evening Mary Pendered, whose daytime job was running the PX at an American air base, did bar work and the one and only Kath Forscutt, a very sprite and energetic over-60-year-old completed the early team.

We had traded in our Ford van for a secondhand Commer Express delivery van that, for those days, went like the proverbial pooh-off-a-shovel. This wasn't going to be large enough for carrying all the supplies needed for the market, so in addition we bought an old Bedford side loading van. I took Sylvia and all the supplies for the catering at 5.45 a.m. then returned to the pub. She soon took on a woman from Thrapston to assist her but it was extremely hard going to keep up with the demand for food which tended to come in waves. Betty looked after the Dukes Arms and I would return to the market with the bar supplies at 10 a.m.

It was a long tiring day for us both but more so for Sylvia, and in the winter it was very cold in the room. There was just one small fireplace to heat a very large area. The farmers were well wrapped up and being outside workers, never seemed to notice the cold. After we finished, everything had to be loaded into the van and we then cleaned the room before leaving. We would usually get back to Woodford at about 6 p.m., just in time to open the pub. However, it was a very good money earner and helped to provide the money needed later on for carpets, furniture and the thousands of items needed to replenish the pub. I regularly sold four 10-gall kegs of Red Barrel and never less than 15 bottles of Haig whisky. Farmers and buyers wouldn't drink any whisky other than Haig. When I asked why; I never received a conclusive answer. Maybe all farmers have shares in Haig?

My best customer was a buyer named Victor Bunker. Vic was one of the biggest cattle buyers in the country. Amongst his clients were Baxter's butchers, the London Meat Company and Dewhurst butchers. His main rival was Phil Johnson who bought for the Co-operative Wholesale Society. Between them they would buy at least three-quarters of the whisky sold, treating the farmers, who being very experienced recipients of handouts, went from one to the other with their empty glasses. This presented me with problems, after serving a farmer, he might say, "Mr Bunker is paying for this." When Vic came to settle his bill he often said, "Have I spent that amount? I've no money, governor, I shall have to go and ask Tom Bletsoe for a bit of luck money." This I took to be a commission from the auctioneers for his attending the market, whatever it was, he always paid his bill.

Victor lived in Oxfordshire on a very large estate. He once told me that before the war, he and his brother reached the semi-finals of the doubles at Wimbledon. He always travelled in a chauffeur-driven Bentley, which was just as well for often he would be incapable of driving himself. We once had reason to be grateful for this arrangement.

During the school holidays, Sylvia took Timothy, our youngest son with her to keep him out of mischief – always a difficult proposition. At her busiest period, he was carried into the restaurant having fallen off a wall, breaking his arm, and suffering possible concussion. Immediately Victor told his chauffeur to take Sylvia and Tim to Kettering hospital where he waited for them and brought them back three hours later. That was just one of many of Timothy's escapades at Woodford.

One day while Sylvia was at the market a farmer asked her if she was interested in having two cade lambs (lambs whose mother had died); he warned her that they would need a lot of looking after. She brought them home and her troubles really started.

Pinky and Perky followed her everywhere, in the pub, up the stairs; they even tried to get in the car with her. One day a lamb was off colour and Sylvia rang the farmer to ask what she should do to make it better. He told her, "Give it a teaspoonful of brandy," but Sylvia, who never does anything in half measures, gave it couple of tots. After a few minutes the lamb started staggering around, laid on its back with its legs in the air, gave a big sigh and died. Sylvia was heartbroken but when she told the people at the market, they fell about laughing. Thereafter, every time farmer's wanted a tot of brandy, they asked for "lamb sauce".

With the death of its twin, the other became even more possessive; chasing any dog or cat that came anywhere near Sylvia. Eventually it became impossible for her to leave the lamb without it becoming very aggressive, it kept banging its head against the back door until she attended to it. When it was three months old she gave it back to the farmer and we all breathed a huge sigh of relief.

That year I organised a pumpkin growing competition, and I sowed my seeds on top of the lamb's grave. I easily won the trophy with an 88lb monster; some said it was due to the lamb's carcase but others said it was due to the brandy in its body.

A New Duke is born

In the autumn the alterations were coming to an end. Whilst the work progressed so slowly for most of the time, during the last month everything started to take shape. The counters, back fittings and all internal woodwork made from light oak were superb, the light fittings were the best available at the time, recessed electric fan heaters were fitted low down in walls. Two "Hole in the Wall" fireplaces were fitted in the lounge bar, and the sanitary fittings and vanity units in the toilets were of the best quality. The saloon bar and lounge were carpeted in very expensive Wilton, which together with the curtains and fitted tapestry-covered deep upholstered seating were supplied by Jeffrey's of Northampton, the local Harrods.

The bar furniture consisted of beech wood Formica topped tables with matching beech wood upholstered chairs and barstools. All walls had fixed fitted seating. At the time it was a showplace, John Reed and the pub were featured in colour in the Watney house magazine, and an article on its design appeared in the *Morning Advertiser*, the trade daily newspaper. We were delighted and thought it represented everything that was good in modern pub interiors. Looking back, it represented everything that I now detest in pubs, Plexiglas mirrors behind the bar, down lighting, Formica counters and tables, flecked walls and even a photomural of a lakeland scene over the chimney breast – dreadfully garish and bad taste but in 1964 it was innovative.

We visited the Hotel & Catering exhibition at Olympia that year and came away with many ideas for introducing pub food to the county. We saw a piece of equipment called "Flavourfare" which was a large griddle and fryer, both having built-in turbo extraction fans. The cooking fumes were drawn into a slot at the rear of the appliance, trunking carried them away to an outside grille. The compact nature of the equipment and its revolutionary extraction system meant it could be fitted under a staircase recess, behind the bar.

During a visit to the officers' mess at Chelveston American Air Force base, we saw some green cloverleaf shaped rubber place mats which looked very attractive especially when combined with rosewood handled steak knives and forks. We also liked their large tomato-shaped plastic sauce bottles. From the Crows Nest barbecue days, I was friendly with the mess manager, an American civilian. I asked him if he could get us a supply of the mats, cutlery and sauce bottles and he said, "No problem." He also showed us some bright orange oval steak plates that he had just bought for the mess, again I asked and he agreed to sell us some.

All these items came from America and had never been seen

before by the British public. Naff they may be now but then customers were continually asking us where we had bought them; and could we get them some. Altogether we bought 20 place settings, plenty we thought but nothing like enough as it turned out.

The alterations were finally completed in October; I don't know who was most pleased to see the back of the other. We had a big official opening night attended by Col Jones who was shortly to retire; we presented an inscribed silver tankard to John Reed who had done a splendid job in pressurising the builders to the end. It was noted by all that the builders were not represented though they had been invited.

By this time racked beer, i.e. beer that had been filtered prior to filling the casks, had gradually replaced traditional draught beer. All of us welcomed this transformation. Changing a barrel was made easier by not having to worry about disturbing the sludge below the tap; barrels could be tapped and served up in a much quicker time, and the beer had a longer life as no air entered the barrel.

CO_2 was fed into the barrel via a spline screwed into the top, this low-pressure gas replaced air that entered the barrel under the old system. Most of all, spillage on the floor was reduced, so at last, decent shoes could be worn behind the bar. Beer could still be drawn up by traditional beer pumps but at the Dukes Arms we were to be used as a test bed for new systems.

The cellar had been fitted out to a high standard, better even than the Crows Nest. The walls and ceiling were insulated and lined with stainless steel sheeting. A cellar cooling system had been installed and a fan that blew cold air up and along the beer pipe ducting.

First of all the brewery fitted what was known as the Hudson & Dobsworth system. The beer after leaving the barrel was pumped up to dispense points using compressed air supplied by a compressor in the cellar. The dispense point was a clear plastic cube mounted on the counter. Inside was a round cavity that filled with a measured half a pint of beer. When a lever was moved a diaphragm pushed the beer out, down a spout into the glass, and beer flowed in behind the diaphragm to refill the cavity. Thus for a pint you first moved the lever one way and then moved it back again. The customer could see the beer flowing into the cavity. The problem with this system was that air would also force the diaphragm across and that meant a measured pint was often short.

This system was quickly replaced by the Porter Lancastrian system. Although similar in principle to the H & D, this used an electric pump to force the beer up to a dispense point which consisted of a stainless steel horizontal tube to replace the round cavity. Again, you moved a handle one-way for a half and back again for a pint. The advantage of this system over H & D was that the diaphragm was replaced by a piston that had a valve to allow air but no beer to escape. The dispense points needed to be stripped down each week for cleaning which was a lengthy job when you had ten of them, and often the piston would jam. With both systems, I noticed that in spite of the ducting fan, the beer was often quite warm.

The man responsible for installing these systems was a newly appointed cellar inspector, ex-Chief Engine Room Artificer Ken Anderson.

After leaving the Navy, he had done a crash course at Watneys Brewery at Mortlake, London and emerged two weeks later as an expert on beer systems. I took an instant dislike to him and he to me. It had nothing to do with the fact that I had been in the Electrical Branch and he in the Engineering Branch of the Royal Navy, nor that his port division had been Portsmouth and mine was Chatham. It was more due to his thinking he was an authority on all things to do with beer keeping and dispensing after a two-week course. The ducting wafting fan was his idea and when I told him the beer was too warm, he accused me of switching off the cellar cooling system at night to save money.

The Head Brewer and Brewing Department were gods in the brewing industry; as far as they were concerned publicans were people, who undid in a few moments, what they had spent weeks in producing i.e. beer. Their motto was, "There is no such thing as bad beer, only bad publicans."

Ex-Chief ERA Anderson's department came under the control of the Brewing Department and any complaint I may have made against him would have fallen on deaf ears. In his presence I fitted a blanking plate in place of the cooling unit switch, which I left on permanently. I then taped the plate and its fuse and got him to sign both tapes so that if any attempt were made to cut off the power, he would know. I told him to come back two days later to check the beer temperature.

I arranged for my District Manager, John Nelson, to be present when he returned. A thermometer in a glass of beer confirmed the beer was too warm. The cellar was at the correct temperature and the wafting fan was on. I could see that Anderson was at a complete loss to explain the reason for the high temperature. After a few minutes I put him out of his misery, I told him to take the room temperature, then to take the temperature in the ducting, there was very little difference. I then took him down the cellar and asked him to check the ducting wafting fan. To his great embarrassment, he discovered he had fitted it with the impeller reversed, causing the fan to suck warm air from the bar into the ducting. I didn't tell him that my brother-in-law, who had also been an electrician in the navy – and a better one than me – had discovered the fault the previous day. Surprisingly, Mr Anderson never came to see me again.

We persevered with the Porter Lancastrian system but eventually it was replaced with Alumasc taps, which, although they didn't measure the beer, were simpler, more efficient, by far.

The drinking population of Woodford were a strange breed. Very few Working Men's Club regulars dreamt of using a pub. The members owned the club and all profits were ploughed back into it. Most WMCs obtained their beer from the Co-operative Clubs & Institutes Brewery which tended to be cheaper, and clubs received a bonus cheque each year based on sales. At Christmas, all members received ten free pints, which were mainly paid for from this bonus or profits from the fruit machine. The Club had the dubious advantage of being able to permit children on the premises, which appealed to a few hen-pecked fathers but not to more serious drinkers, thank goodness. Children, in my opinion, should never be allowed anywhere near a pub. When the law was changed to allow children into pubs the character of the traditional pub and all it stood for came to a sad end.

The village pub customers were much more flexible with their drinking habits and would patronise all of the village pubs from time to time. However, the WMC. had some 40 per cent of the drinking population and to make the Dukes Arms a success I had to tap into this potential trade. To this end in 1963 I was initiated as a member of the Royal Antediluvian Order of Buffaloes, Lord St John Lodge No.7619 that met every Monday evening at the WMC. In a short time I progressed through the ranks to become a Primo, which qualified me to take charge of a Lodge.

The entertainments room in which the lodge was held was always extremely cold. One freezing November evening, the brothers asked me if I could provide them with a more welcoming room. I had the ex-billiard room which was unused and although not yet redecorated, was better than anything the club could offer. I cut an obligatory peephole in the door, installed electric panel heating, bought a piano and the Lodge moved to the Dukes Arms with great ceremony on the first evening. I supported the Lodge both financially and in many other ways for nearly two years, but in time it became more and more obvious to me that some brothers were doing a lot more taking than giving to the Lodge, and I became disillusioned with their actions and wound down my involvement.

Halfway through the building work, trade had dropped by half due in the main to closure of the clubroom and the awful mess we were in though a lot of drinkers called in just for one pint to see how the alterations were coming along. After all, it was the biggest project in the village for years.

With the alterations finished, trade increased weekly. We were soon back to the previous figures, but this time with a more mature type of person. That is not to say we didn't encourage the village youth from aged 21 upwards. Because their fathers and grandfathers probably also used the pub, most youngsters were very well behaved, and if working at Stewart & Lloyds, very well paid. By the time Christmas arrived, I was back to having hogsheads (54 gallons) and selling five a week.

Iris Clipston had joined our staff and husband, Peter, helped out when we got very busy.

Woodford men always had a reputation for being hard drinkers, going back to the Ironworks days when the hot working conditions required vast quantities of liquid to replace the moisture lost at work. The average drinker would be in the pub by 8 p.m. seven days a week. If a regular wasn't there by that time, people would ask friends if he was ill! None of this modern tendency of going out for a drink at 9.30 p.m. or even later. The average consumption for a regular would be eight pints a night. If he had come straight from a shift at the Ironworks, this could easily increase to twelve.

In all the time we were at the Dukes Arms, I cannot remember ever using one of our five half-pint glasses. No self respecting man would be seen dead drinking from a half-pint glass. Tales were told about when the village Ironworks was in operation, boys would run ahead of the workers to warn the village publicans the men were coming up the hill and for them to start pulling pints. Another tale told of a ritual in the past when at closing time men would club together, buy a barrel of beer, empty the horse trough on the village green, fill it with beer and dip their glasses in. There must have been a lot of very cloudy beer drunk on these occasions.

Pub games such as skittles, darts, cribbage and dominoes were very popular in the village, dominoes in particular. I put up a notice for pairs to enter a domino league to be played in the pub every Tuesday evening. 12 teams entered and quite a few were WMC. regulars, which was very pleasing. We entered darts teams in various leagues and had an extremely good and successful skittle team that won the Hinwick Home Summer Skittle league, the most prestigious competition in the county.

We had a piano in the bar and one Saturday evening a very striking looking lady asked me if she could play it, I told her by all means if she was a good player. She was, and I asked Rita, who came from Wellingborough, if she would play for us on Saturday evenings on a regular basis. She agreed and I had a small stage constructed, the piano tuned, and we then had another feature, attracting even more customers. Rita, apart from being a very good pianist, was also a good singer and we quickly discovered other singers of varying talent among our customers. It became so popular on Saturdays that if you hadn't got a seat by 7.30 p.m. it was standing room only and very little of that. There was an added bonus with Rita playing the piano, her husband Geoff was a good barman.

We started serving food on a small scale as soon as the alterations were completed. The menu consisted mainly of steaks, "T" bone, porterhouse, fillet, sirloin and gammon. A very popular dish was a cowboy's breakfast – 12oz gammon steak with two fried eggs, baked beans and chips. With the siting of the griddle and fryer behind the bar, all staff were taught to cook. Whoever took a food order would then cook the meal, a very convenient arrangement for us but highly illegal today. However, although this system would break every rule in today's Food Inspectors' rule book, from the thousands of meals we served, no report was ever received of a customer suffering from food poisoning.

It was completely unknown for pubs to serve meals in 1964 Northamptonshire. If a man wanted to take his wife out for a meal, his choice was restricted to a café, restaurant, hotel or transport café; some of the latter were excellent. There were no fast food outlets – other than fish & chip shops – outside of large towns and cities. We would regularly receive telephone calls from sceptical people asking us to confirm that we did indeed serve food, and menu details. With the ever-increasing demand, we made the decision to turn the old billiard room into a dining room. It had been redecorated to a good standard, carpeted and fitted with wall lights. We still cooked the steak and chips behind the bar, but having converted the bedroom next to the dining room to a kitchen, prepared starters, additional vegetables and sweets from there. At the same time, we increased the scope of our menu by providing other dishes.

We were fortunate in having a very good man to do our butchery. Fred Roberts who lived in the village, was a retired butcher of the old school, he only had to look at a cut of meat and could tell how well it would eat. As the demand for food increased, we had our meat delivered twice weekly by Harry Johnson, a top class wholesale butcher from Peterborough 25 miles away. He was recommended to me by Vic Bunker as a person who bought only the best quality cattle and pigs at the market. As good a supplier as Harry was, Fred would always check deliveries and on occasions reject cuts for not being of a sufficient quality for us. He taught me how to cure hams, a skill I put to use many times over the years. I had accumulated six old salting leads in my outside store. We started making our own sausages from a recipe of Fred's, which proved very popular. At one time, together with our own brawn, we were selling them uncooked to customers but the demand got out of hand and we were spending too much time producing them, though we continued making them for sale on the menu.

With the food explosion, we had taken on three extra staff, Doreen Allan, Margaret Cockings and Joyce Payne, all excellent hard working girls, as were all our staff. Doreen was a bit of a chatterbox and I often had to tell her, in jest, to stop gossiping and get a move on. One evening when she was working in the dining room I shouted up the stairs for her to hurry up. Unbeknown to me she was about to walk down the stairs carrying a tray filled with plates. In her anger she went to stamp her foot, missed her footing and slid down the stairs on her bottom, ending up going through the door into the ladies toilet, still with the tray in her hands and food scraps sticking to her hair. If you ever read this Doreen, Sylvia insisted I include that incident!

In December, we were fully booked every night with works and office Christmas parties, which proved very profitable. We bought our turkeys very cheaply from the son of a large breeder in a neighbouring village whom I shall just refer to as DW. They were so cheap that at times I had my suspicions all was not above board.

This was confirmed one evening when DW asked if I was interested in buying any cheap beef. I asked if it was fresh and he said it couldn't be fresher and he would be back with it in a few minutes. True to his word, he pulled into the pub yard with a Rice Trailer and there in the back was a steaming dead bullock, which had obviously just been shot, DW and the trailer were covered in blood. I told him I wanted nothing to do with it and he left. Weeks later he and his brother had a head on collision in a field with two combine harvesters, writing both of them off. Shortly after this incident, his father's Dutch barn mysteriously went up in flames. The outcome was DW was packed off to relatives in New Zealand and I lost my source for cheap turkeys.

Fresh turkeys

On the opposite side of the village green was a large house that once was a pub. It had an archway under which carriages once drove to the stable yard at the rear. Here lived Riley Smith and his housekeeper Mabel. Riley was a gypsy and proud of it. He had given up the life of a traveller and settled down in the village during the middle 1950s. There was a scrap yard adjacent to his house, but, thankfully, a high stone wall ensured nothing was visible from the road. Many tales were put about regarding the source of Riley's obvious wealth. Some said he got it from Mabel; others said it came from crime or scrap metal. I thought it was just plain wheeler dealing. Anyway he had money – lots of it – and Riley liked nothing better than showing it off on occasions.

He had a Rolls Royce that was brought out for special events and a large black Mercedes straight out of a gangster movie. Heavy gold rings on his fingers matched the gold chain he always wore round his neck, which, in turn, matched his gold teeth. Riley would often describe himself as a showman – as in the fairground – a description that fitted him perfectly. Most of the time he walked around in just a string vest, greasy trousers and cap in even the coldest weather, but when he wanted to dress up out came the snazzy suits and fedora hat. Sylvia always thought he looked just like Anthony Quinn the actor.

Riley had a relation who was connected with a circus that had its winter quarters in a village near Thrapston; I think it was Chipperfields. One night he came to the off sales window and asked if we allowed animals in the pub. I said we did as long as they were well behaved. He returned a few minutes later leading an enormous grizzly bear; it had to stoop to get through the door. Although Riley firmly held a chain fixed round the bear's neck customers scattered in all directions. Riley asked for a pint for himself and some honey for the bear! Another time on a busy night, he walked into the pub with a boa constrictor wrapped round his body; he was indeed a showman. However, he was noted for his generosity, a soft touch for any worthy cause.

During November and December, we ran a draw to provide OAPs with a Christmas hamper. I asked Riley to donate a prize and he gave two turkeys as the star prizes. A few days later, a rumour circulated that the turkeys weren't very fresh. The following year he said he would donate two turkeys again. On the night of the draw, the turkeys hadn't arrived but we went ahead knowing that Riley wouldn't let us down. Halfway through the draw, the door burst open and in walked Riley and Mabel each with a live turkey under their arms. Without any warning Riley pulled the heads off both turkeys letting them flutter round the room splattering people with blood, and shouted, "Now tell me they're not fresh this year!"

He was once taken to court for not filling in his Scrap Dealers register. He told the magistrates he was just an ignorant gypsy who had never learned to read or write and therefore could not keep a proper register. After being fined £25 and while still in the dock, he threw a bag of gold sovereigns down onto the Clerk of the Court's desk, saying, "You will have to count them yourself 'mush', that's another thing I can't do."

His relationship with Mabel, his housekeeper, was always a mystery to the villagers. You never saw a lot of her but she was very well spoken and always well dressed. She kept the house spotless and did all Riley's bookkeeping, at least that which it suited him to keep. Although Riley was a real womaniser and had his share of affairs, if any one enquired about his relationship with Mabel, Riley would get very uptight and tell people it was none of their business.

At times he told the most outrageous stories, but it often transpired that the more unbelievable the tale, the more likely it was to be true. I once discussed with him how much the value of old coins had increased in recent years. I said that even old farthings that ceased to be legal tender in 1961 were worth more than their face value. He said he wished he had known as he recently used three full bank sacks of them as ballast when filling in an old well. I told him to "pull the other one" but he assured me it was true. The next day he asked me to go across to his house and there stood a compressor and air hammer which he had hired. After a short while chipping away at the concrete, he exposed three blue bank sacks, which on closer examination were all, filled with farthings! When I asked him why use farthings in the first place, he gave a typical Riley smile and said, "Think of the surprise someone will have in years to come when they find them, they'll keep on digging, hoping for more." He could be very mischievous.

Riley's son was in prison, for whatever reason I never knew, but Riley told me he was due out within a few days and showed me a Vauxhall Wyvern car he had bought him as a welcome home gift. The car was not new but in reasonably good condition. He also said he had decided to take his son into the business with him.

On the morning his son was due to be released, Riley came into the pub, dressed in his finest with the car, freshly washed and polished outside. Every time he heard a car approaching he jumped up to see if it was the taxi with his son. Eventually this enormous open-topped American car pulled up, inside was a man in a smart suit and very flashy girl. It was his son and girlfriend. Riley showed him the car he had bought but his son said he wouldn't be seen dead in a heap like that. He asked Riley if he had any money for him and they went across to his house.

The son and his girl left in the American car an hour later and Riley came back into the pub, put his head on my shoulder and sobbed his heart out. For a man so strong and proud as Riley, it was a very sad, humiliating experience for him. Knowing how much he had looked forward to that day, my heart went out to him. More about that Vauxhall car later.

"No, but I've got seven donkeys!"

Although by now we were employing ten staff that worked either on a regular basis or just peak periods, Sylvia said she would like a couple of girls who could live in as full-time staff. The idea also appealed to me – and not for the obvious reasons. In those days, it wasn't possible to recruit staff from the continent but you could from Southern Ireland. With the amount of Irish girls who were working in hospitals and hotels in this country, we were of the opinion that Ireland was bursting with girls just waiting to be offered jobs in England.

I was a keen angler and rough shooter as were three friends of mine, Bob Britton who had a market garden business in the village, Tony Gent a builder, and John Dunmore an RAF corporal stationed at RAF Whittering. Thinking I could combine a staff recruitment exercise with a badly needed holiday, at my instigation we organised a two-week fishing and shooting holiday in Ireland staying at a hotel in Strokestown, Co. Roscommon.

By this time, we had changed the Commer van for a Ford Cortina Estate, which was an ideal vehicle to carry four passengers, their guns and fishing kit. Between us we took six 12 bore shotguns and four .22 rifles, quite an armoury. We drove through the night and caught the morning ferry from Heysham to Dun Laoghaire. On arrival, we were asked by the Irish Customs to open up the back of the estate for inspection. On lifting the tailgate out spewed all our guns that we had jammed in last of all. At first, the officers looked at them with some surprise but fortunately, it was reasonably common for parties of Englishmen to travel to Ireland for a shooting holiday. In fact it was so common there was no longer anything left to shoot.

We eventually arrived at our hotel in the picturesque large village of Strokestown. We enquired about the shooting availability in the area and were somewhat dismayed to learn that, apart from wild duck, the area had been shot to pieces and was completely devoid of game. We were later to discover that due to the absence of any closed season, the coarse fishing was in an even worse state. We were perhaps fortunate to discover that the third thing we had all come for was served in perfect condition.

We set up our headquarters in a small bar named "Geraghtys" opposite our hotel. George, the owner, was the most obliging chap; his bar also served as a shop where residents obtained their bacon supplies. Consequently, we found our shoes permanently stained white with the salt liquid that oozed from the sides of bacon stacked in a corner. The liquid ran into a drain in the middle of the bar that, for most of our stay, was always partly blocked. Fortunately the smell was quite enjoyable.

George fixed us up with a ghillie who promised us the best duck shooting in Roscommon, provided we got up at 4 o'clock in the morning which, in our case, meant we didn't go to bed. At the appointed hour, we drove with Thomas the ghillie to one of the many lakes surrounding the town. We took up our allocated positions on the edge of a lake, sat, and waited for the duck to fly in.

After a cold wet hour the duck, as if to order, started to fly in, though somewhat unfortunately for us, not where we were hiding.

After changing our position numerous times, and the duck changing theirs, we gave it up as a bad job and sought solace in George's Bar. We repeated the exercise at different sites over the next few days but as always we were in one place and the duck in another. Our ghillie only had one saying; apart from "thank you, sur" when we paid him, and that was "they'll be there tomorrow!"

One day, desperate to produce something for the hotel chef to cook for us, we set a dozen snares; at least Tony Gent, a self-professed experienced poacher of some renown did. The net result was a ginger cat we had seen about the town which we hastily buried down a rabbit hole.

Every afternoon was spent pike fishing. Before we left, Bob Britton had produced an old copy of the *Angling Times* which showed a picture of an angler with a gigantic pike caught in a lake at Roscommon, this had attracted us to the area. We used herring from the fishmonger as dead bait, and every type of lure and spinner we possessed in our well-stocked tackle baskets, trying to tempt a record breaking pike to our hooks, but with no success. Without a closed season, and the Irish not believing in returning hooked fish to the water, was it any wonder no one had caught a fish of any size in the last three years?

One night a customer in the bar told us of a place where he said he could guarantee us shooting some geese. We set off before dawn in misty conditions and drove to the spot he had indicated on our map. We put out our baited fishing rods in the hope that the last remaining fish in Ireland would be in that bit of water. At first light we heard the sound of whirring wings but because of the mist couldn't see higher than 15 feet. Not to be daunted we put up a barrage of shot from every ready loaded gun we had with us, in the hope the geese may fly into our shot. In our desperation for a kill, we couldn't care less whether our actions could be deemed sporting or not, but we soon knew we were successful when we heard a splash as a goose hit the water. We couldn't see where it was because of the mist but we calculated it wouldn't sink so we lay back waiting for it to get lighter and the mist to clear.

The first we knew something had gone wrong was when we heard the sound of a woman's voice calling out in the distant mist behind us. We then heard the sound of geese squawking and it dawned on us that what we had in fact shot was a tame goose. We quickly packed up our gear and keeping close to the ground, slid away. Back at George's Bar later that morning, our informant asked us if we had any success with the geese. We told him we'd had no luck at all to which he replied, "I'm not surprised, them albino geese take a bit of downing!" at which point both he and George started to laugh. We realised we had been had. It turned out that George had put this chap up to it.

By the end of the first week we were beginning to get fed up with the weather; the fishing and shooting and the food at the hotel were all very disappointing. We were baffled why, in a country like Ireland renowned for its dairy products we were presented with foil-wrapped New Zealand butter portions. The meat served to us was fat and tough, the vegetables, mainly carrots and turnips, had not been peeled properly and were served with the tail intact. Potatoes were always boiled with the eyes left in, and the bacon at breakfast was all fat with bristles still on the rind.

The hotel was owned and run by an English couple and the members of the staff were all nationalities other than Irish. When I asked the owner about my chances of engaging local girls, he said had there been any he would have employed them years ago. He also said that most young girls from the area were already working in England and those too young would join their sisters as soon as they were old enough. I had seen girls about the town but he said they were left behind to look after their fathers and brothers, and others were probably waiting to become nuns. Feeling thoroughly fed up we went to Galway for the weekend, which disappointingly turned out to be just like any large town in England.

The following Tuesday George said there was a horse fair at a town called Ballaghaderreen about 15 miles away. We thought it would be something different to do so piled into the car and off we went. As was to be expected, the town was full of horses and donkeys in all shapes and sizes. We found a good bar overlooking the square and settled down to drink away our woes and take in the local scene. Opposite where we were sitting was a grey donkey and her foal tied to a drainpipe, and at regular intervals, men would walk up behind the donkey and give her a kick. Each time the donkey's head would move forward and hit the drainpipe.

After watching this for a while I asked the barman why they kept kicking her and he said, "It's the only way to tell if a donkey has a good temperament, if she kicks back she will be no good for children." At least that was the thinking behind the exercise. After watching the poor donkey being kicked on five or six occasions, in which time almost the same amount of Guinness had disappeared down my throat, I walked over and asked the man with her how much he wanted for the pair of them, "£9" was the reply. I came back and told Bob who, apart from his market garden, had a vegetable stall on Kettering market and considered himself to be a bit of a dealer. Bob went over and after a few minutes I saw him spitting on his hand and slapping the Irish chap's hand. I thought perhaps they were both Freemasons, but Bob returned and said they were both mine for £6. For an extra £1, I arranged for the man to deliver them both to George Geraghty's Bar in Strokestown.

When we returned that evening, I told George what I had done and asked him if he could find out the best way for me to get them back to England. George rang the B & I shipping line in the morning and informed me that I would need to hire a pen on the boat. The pen would cost me £15 and, apart from a small extra handling charge, this would be the same cost if I had 12 donkeys. I told him to put the word out that I was in the market for buying donkeys and I left George and went to bed that night, happy in the knowledge that I had saved two of God's creatures from a life of sore bums.

I was sharing a room with Bob and the next morning he woke me and told me to go and look out of the window. The scene outside was just like the show ring of a donkey Grand National. Some 30 owners and donkeys were assembled in the small square opposite the hotel. I wondered how much George stood to make out of commission from the owners.

It was all too much for me to cope with so I asked Bob to go downstairs, pick out the best five donkeys at around £5 each, tell the owners I would meet them in George's bar in an hour, and tell the rest to go home. How I wished I had Jack Smith with me, or even Tommy Abbot, both connoisseurs of horseflesh; I presumed donkeys were not much different. Bob, with help from John, did an excellent selection job, whittling them down to eight and leaving the final selection to me. For the purpose of maintaining the strain, I finally settled on three females and one Jack, giving me five females in total and one soon to be a very contented and busy Jack. By midday, I was the proud owner of six donkeys in the middle of Ireland, and I had got to get them to the middle of England. After paying the owners for their animals, the full seriousness of what I had done hit me, but after a few pints of Guinness I felt like John Wayne at round-up time.

A further phone call to the shipping line confirmed my pen was booked, and then they asked me for the name of my agent. This threw me and I asked what was an agent and why did I need one. I was told the agent saw to all the paperwork, would see the animals were passed fit by the Ministry vet, and arrange for them to be taken aboard the ferry. They gave me the phone numbers of five agents and I picked the first one, rang him and discovered he would charge me a £15 fee and I still had to get them from Strokestown to Dun Laoghaire. George came to my rescue and arranged for the donkeys to be put in a paddock just outside the town, and a man and vehicle to take them to the docks for a further £10. We would return to Woodford two days later and await notification of their arrival in England.

That evening I rang Sylvia, and her first words, as always were, "Have you managed to get me any staff?" I said I hadn't but I'd bought her six donkeys. She accused me of being drunk and slammed the phone down.

We said our goodbyes to all the friends we'd made in such a short time. We quickly forgot the abominable food, the ghastly weather, absence of fish or feather and told George we would be back next year when we had bought some new salt proof shoes. He gave us each a presentation pack of Guinness glasses, and we clubbed together and bought him a pair of binoculars. I told him if he should spot a goose through them, to telephone me immediately and we would be back. Wonderful man – wonderful beer – wonderful country.

The journey back to Dun Laoghaire was not without incident. As we neared Mulingar, I had just negotiated a series of bends when I had to brake hard to avoid hitting a very forlorn looking donkey standing in the middle of the road. I pulled on to the verge, went over, and could see its hooves were in a terrible condition, long and curled over, with maggots coming out of the crevices making it extremely difficult and painful for it to walk. There was a farmhouse nearby and I enquired from the farmer who the donkey belonged to. To cut a long story short, it was his, the feet were bad because his ground was very boggy, I asked him how much, he said £6, I gave him £4, it was female, rang George told him to tell the carrier to pick up another one, and proceeded to the docks. I tracked down "my agent" told him about the new addition, paid him his fee, caught the ferry and drove back to Woodford.

Three days later, I received a telephone call from the agent saying that all the donkeys bar one had passed the vet's inspection. The one that failed was our poor Mulingar one. He said I had two options, he could get a blacksmith to trim its hooves and try again or he could probably get 10/- for him from a knacker man. I told him to get its feet treated. He rang me the next day to say he had paid a blacksmith to trim the hooves but the vet wanted it kept under observation for a further 48 hours. In the meantime, the other donkeys would be on a boat sailing the next morning, arriving in Birkenhead the following afternoon.

Bob owned a Ford Transit type van, which he used for market and picking up Tony, the three of us set off for the docks. We encountered no problems there, we backed up to a ramp and the six donkeys were loaded in with a bit of shoving and swearing. Jack Smith had told us short of hiring a proper horsebox; the best way was to fit them tightly in a van.

In common with most vehicles at that time, the van had no form of heating, or worse still, no demisting. It was late November and the A5 took us through some lovely countryside. However, with the darkness and a heating system in the back covering the windows, roof and ourselves with condensation, any chance of seeing the beauty of Wales was out of the question.

On the outskirts of Chirk, we pulled off the main road and stopped at a pub for us to have a drink, and find some water for the donkeys. It wasn't until we got out of the van that we realized just how wet we were. We hadn't given it a thought when we left, and had no waterproofs or raincoats. The water had dripped from the roof, soaking our hair and clothes, so when we entered the pub, the landlord and locals thought we had walked there through a rainstorm. The landlord gave me a bucket of water and Bob and I went out to give the donkeys a drink. He opened the rear door carefully but not carefully enough. As soon as it was partly opened they charged, knocking both of us over. We got to our feet just in time to see them disappearing down the road with steam coming off them as though they had just climbed out of a steamer. To this day, I cannot fathom out how they managed to turn and face the door.

We returned to the pub and I asked for volunteers to help us track them down. Not receiving a lot of response, I said there would be free beer for any helpers. That was my second mistake that night; I got knocked down again in the rush to the door.

We had arrived at the pub at 8 p.m. it took us until 10 p.m. to round them up and corral them in a corner, giving them a chance to calm down, and us a chance to replenish the liquid lost running around Wales.

Having quenched our and the donkeys' thirst the next problem was how were we going to get them back in the van. At the docks, we'd had the use of a ramp and hurdles, and even then, it took time. The landlord suggested we made a ramp out of empty beer cases of varying heights. This we did and it worked, after a fashion. We all went back into the pub for further refreshment and left about midnight. Our round-up friends were happy, we were happy and my pocket was £5 lighter.

We arrived back at Woodford at around 3 a.m. and were very surprised to find a welcome home party waiting for us. The donkeys were unloaded with lots of ohs and ahs, put into two stables with clean straw and hay and left in peace after their eventful journey.

Two days later, I received a call from my agent to say the Mulingar donkey had passed the veterinary inspection and was on its way. I borrowed Bob's van and this time went on my own, having first filled the van with straw bales to keep the donkey upright. I was horrified when I saw the poor donkey's feet, I could not imagine a blacksmith would make such a mess of them. It looked as though someone had put the hooves on a block and trimmed them with a hatchet, and then painted them with tar. The poor animal seemed to be limping even more than ever. The journey back to Woodford was uneventful; being daylight helped. I resisted the temptation to stop at Chirk for liquid refreshment wanting to get my patient to a vet as soon as possible.

The local vet gave all the donkeys a thorough going over and it appeared we had a 20-year-old grey female with a two-year-old ditto, two eight-year-old brown females, a five-year-old brown Jack and the ten-year-old brown female with the bad feet. He agreed her hooves were abominable and had certainly not been treated by a blacksmith. Treatment would be possible but because of the length of time her condition had existed, her ankles were deformed and she would always hobble along. The good news was, that after treatment, she wouldn't be in any more pain. The remainder of the donkeys were given a clean bill of health though a visit from a blacksmith was needed.

I agreed terms with Frankie Southam, a local farmer to rent a paddock complete with stone barn for a bottle of Haig whisky a month. The paddock led down to the River Nene and was adjacent to the village school.

The agent sent me a bill for £9 that included blacksmith and vet's fees, plus his extra costs. I had already paid the shipping company's bill of £15 so I wrote to him stating that owing to the pain he had inflicted on the donkey I would not be paying him anything else, and if he wanted to take it any further, I would produce my vet's confirmation that the donkey had been subjected to ill treatment whilst in his care. I heard no more.

I bought saddles and bridles for the four fit female donkeys and let them out, free of charge, to garden fetes, etc. for children's rides, on the strict understanding that they would be in the control of an experienced person and not worked for more than an hour without a rest. Doris, Gladys, Mabel and Edna raised many hundreds of pounds for good causes.

Sputniks arrive in Woodford

By mid-1965, trade had increased to such an extent that we were having problems storing enough beer in the cellar. It was still being delivered in hogsheads (54 gall.) but there was only space for five on the thrall, the remainder stood on the floor. There is a knack in lifting beer barrels, which basically makes the beer work for you. You rock the barrel backwards and forwards until the momentum of the beer moving to the tap end, enables you to lift it on to its edge and with the corner of the thrall touching the centre of the barrel it is possible to lift it on to the thrall with minimum effort.

With the arrival of time and motion inspectors and union power playing a greater role in the Watney empire, it became union policy that if a dray was carrying hogsheads, three men would have to be involved in dropping them into a cellar. One man would be at the top easing it down the skids, with a rope round the barrel and two turns round a post, two men would be in the cellar to manoeuvre the barrel onto the thrall. Draymen in those days were employed for their strength and the whole idea of it taking two to thrall a barrel was ludicrous. It was one of many instances where the transformation from small brewer to large empire resulted in a loss of trust and co-operation between worker and management.

To overcome the problem with hogsheads, the brewery started installing tanks in their pubs selling a large barrelage. We were selected to be the one and only village pub to have them fitted. Their nickname was "Sputniks". To me they looked just like the divers, decompression chambers I had known in the navy. Each tank held five barrels, i.e. 288 gallons and we had six installed, the tanker delivering on Monday and again on Friday. A glass hatch on the front was secured with 10 thumbscrews. This hatch was removed for cleaning the tank, and, although the tanks were the latest technology, the cleaning routine was very primitive. The tanker driver sprayed the inside with a garden sprayer filled with beer line cleaner. This was left for a few minutes, and then flushed out with a high-pressure water jet attached to the tanker. The tank was then filled from a connection at the bottom and air escaped from a valve in the top. Low pressure CO_2 was fed into the top of the tank and an electric pump pushed the beer up to the dispense points. Cellar work was reduced to a minimum as the tank change over was carried out automatically.

I was very impressed with the system and the way it operated. However, I did find that, on occasions, the beer developed a twang after 24 hours and this meant the beer had to be pumped out and returned to the brewery for examination. The cause was traced to the tanks not being properly cleaned and residues of old beer left inside. The problem was overcome with polythene bags inserted in the tanks after cleaning. This ensured that the beer never came into contact with the inside of the tank, and the lining was changed before each filling.

Some random thoughts

It was about this time that we came up with another first in the pub trade. Our girls always looked smart but, on occasions, we had to point out that some outfits were not entirely suitable for wearing behind the bar. On one such occasion, the answer came back, "Why don't you supply us with outfits?"

I was still turning out for Rushden Thursday cricket team, and one of the members, David Willis, had a very upmarket dress shop in Rushden. I asked David if he had any ideas and he said the best way was to design an outfit and he would get them made. The design we came up with was for a pinafore dress in a French blue woollen mixture material, with a plain white blouse to be worn underneath. We had nine outfits made for the younger barmaids, and two dresses made in the same material but in a style more suited to their age for Kath and Mary. Most hotels kitted their female staff out in the obligatory white blouse and black skirt but this was the first time people had ever seen a public house with barmaids dressed in fashionable uniform outfits. The public reaction was very complimentary, well worth the considerable expenditure involved.

The 1960s were a wonderful time for party-going and generally having fun. Every Saturday evening after we closed, all the staff and their husbands stayed behind for a late drink. Most times this would last until 2–3 a.m. No one ever seemed in a hurry to go home. At frequent intervals, we organised staff parties in the dining room. Tables and chairs stacked up, the carpet rolled back, and with Rita on the piano the party commenced. Sometimes it was a fancy dress party, sometimes a tramps' ball but most times it was just a party for party's sake. The breathalyser hadn't been invented and Elvis and the Beatles were all the rage. Carnaby Street was the place to shop, tights and miniskirts were in, the Woodstock Rock Festival was two years away; Beatniks were out, flower power was in and going strong, what a wonderful time we all had! I recorded highlights of a Vicar and Tarts party on cine film for posterity; our grandchildren will never know just how short some of those mini skirts were, unless they see the film. Sylvia and I keep saying we must go back to Woodford and show it once more before we are all sitting in the Upper Circle.

Back to the water

The River Nene ran along the bottom outskirts of the village. The village parson, The Rev Louis de Casiabianco (true Englishman despite the name) was a good customer and friend, we spent many happy hours on his lawn, shooting with our .22 guns at bottles thrown upstream into the river by my young sons. One day we paused as a cabin cruiser went past and "Cassie" said he was surprised that with my sailing experience I didn't own a boat. The vicarage grounds were very picturesque and went right down to the river. He said if I had a boat, I could keep it there and he would be able to see it from the house ensuring its safety. This idea really got me thinking.

In those days, there were very few boats on the river and not many boatyards. I bought copies of a boating magazine and eventually saw one for sale at Jones boatyard, St Ives, on the River Ouse. I made enquiries and was told it was possible to get from the Ouse to the Nene via the Fens. The boat was a converted ship's lifeboat circa 1930; 30 foot long, built of pitch pine on oak frames and fitted with a Scammell 40 h.p. petrol engine. The interior was beautifully fitted out with solid mahogany panelling, w.c., a galley and four sleeping berths. The asking price was £110 and I completed the deal for £100.

I bought a navigational map of the two rivers and was somewhat dumbfounded to discover the connecting waterway between the two was listed as unfit for navigation. Enquiries confirmed that there were two options open to me: (1) I could take the boat out to sea and across The Wash or (2) I could have the boat craned out on to a low loader and taken to the Nene by road. The first possibility really appealed to me and although I had no knowledge of navigation felt this would not be a problem, after all The Wash was only a big pond!

I went to King's Lynn by car and discussed the intended voyage with some fishermen in a pub. It was soon made clear to me that without navigational experience, equipment and, even more important, knowledge of The Wash, any attempt to take the boat by water would be extremely foolhardy. With the ever shifting sandbanks in The Wash, even the most experienced skippers regularly came to grief in the short stretch between the two rivers. Having ruled out the sea trip I studied a road map and decided that if I took the boat to St Neots I would be shortening the distance, a lorry would have to travel between the two rivers. The other determining factor was I had to go to a boatyard that had a crane sufficiently large to lift me out – no travelling cranes in those days.

My crew member for the trip was Don Wilson. Apart from being a jazz pianist of some fame, Don also had a shop in Thrapston where he sold and repaired radios and TVs. He also had an old van in which he travelled round the villages, selling everything from torch batteries and candles to paraffin, mops and buckets. Nowadays you would describe him as being unconventional; in those days he was just plain eccentric

It was very rare to see Don out at night without his drinking companion, Alec Manning. Alec was a baker and another of life's characters, his bakery at Denford, a village adjacent to Thrapston, was a sight to be seen: ovens were fuelled with wood and coal and the bakery, including the preparation area, permanently covered with a thick layer of soot and cobwebs.

When we first arrived in Woodford, Alec delivered his bread at night in a horse-drawn bread van, when the horse died he relied on Don to drive him on a tour of pubs, his customers eagerly waiting for his bread. We were always their last port of call so the choice was rather limited. Alec was in his 70s and the last of an era where hygiene inspectors hadn't yet been invented. He smoked a pipe that he lit first thing in the morning and extinguished only when he went to bed. His hands were always black from stoking the fire, in winter, his nose had a permanent drip, and ash fell from his pipe into the dough.

He never wore any protective clothing, always corduroys, cardigan and peaked cap all the year round, but his bread was magnificent. On one occasion, the council tried to close him down because his bakery was structurally unsafe, but note, not because of the dirt. Such was his popularity both as a baker and character, almost every adult in the area, including all the local doctors and the Duke of Gloucester who lived at Barnwell Castle, ten miles away, all signed a petition to keep his bakery open. In the end the council gave up trying to close him down.

One evening Don asked Sylvia and barmaid Mary, if they would like to go with him and Alec to Cambridge, Don had got a bit of business to attend to there. They turned to me and said, "Is that all right with you, master?" Master was a form of speech always used by Don and Alec when addressing a male. I said that Sylvia needed a break and a day out would do her good.

They picked the ladies up in the morning and off they went, stopping at almost every roadside pub on the way. At one pub, Alec went off to the toilet and came back saying to the landlord, "Do you know your closet is locked, master?" The landlord said this was necessary because of a nearby bus stop. He went to give Alec the key but Alec told him, "You're too late, master, I had to do it in your garden, but it's all right, I did it by your rhubarb and kicked some soil over it when I finished. Should have some damn good rhubarb this year, master!"

When they got to Cambridge and Don had completed his business, they told the ladies they would go to the University Arms, a very upmarket pub, for lunch. After they had been served with drinks, Don pulled a lump of cheese from his pocket and Alec some bread from his, which Don proceeded to carve into portions with his penknife and hand to each of the ladies. He followed this up with a plastic bag filled with pickled onions, which he offered round. That was their idea of taking the ladies out to lunch!

One winter's evening, Alec told Sylvia his overcoat was getting thin and no longer keeping him warm. He asked her if I had an old overcoat I didn't need anymore. She told him I didn't wear overcoats but she had an old fur coat she no longer wanted. For the rest of that winter and the next he wore that coat every night, he looked just like Bud Flanagan. He told her he also spread it on his bed every night to keep him warm.

With Don as crewman, the boat journey from St Ives to St Neots was picturesque and uneventful. Don was gradually learning the nautical terms, e.g. port, starboard, forward, aft, bows and stern etc and, apart from his snoring keeping me awake at night, we were getting on well together.

When we reached St Neots the boatyard was ready and the lorry waiting. The haul out was completed with little fuss and the boat was soon safely secured on the low loader. Just as we were leaving the yard, the owner came running out and told us he had just received a call to say the crane at Thrapston had broken down, and we would have to go to Peterborough where the only other crane on the River Nene was based. This meant we had completely wasted our time travelling to St Neots; we had been nearer to Peterborough at St Ives, we also needed an extra day to complete the trip. Don said he couldn't spare the time and would have to catch a bus home. I told him it was common knowledge amongst sailors that ill would befall any sailor who jumped ship leaving his shipmates stranded. Whether Don fell for this story I don't know, but by the time we arrived at Peterborough he decided to complete the journey by boat. It was dark when the boat was back in the water, and too late to restart our journey. We went off to the nearest pub and spent a most convivial evening with Don playing the piano in his George Shearing style.

We set off early next morning but still not early enough for Don. He started moaning about his being late home from the very moment we got under way. At Oundle, I asked him to take the helm while I went to the heads. Don said, "Why can't you speak bloody English and ask me to drive while you have a pee?" One thing led to another and the outcome was at Wadenhoe, still six miles from Woodford, he deserted with the words, "I shall hitch-hike and don't care if I get knocked down by a bloody bus, at least I'll get a lift in an ambulance with the driver speaking the Queen's bloody English." Don truly lived up to his reputation of being a "cantankerous old bugger" as Alec frequently reminded him. I arrived at Woodford single handed, but, at least, it saved me having to remind Don to make sure one end of the rope was secured to the boat, before jumping ashore with the other.

I built a landing stage on the riverbank in a beautiful part of "Cassie's" orchard, ran a power cable from his house for lighting and battery charging and life was good. A stream ran through the churchyard to the river, which I dammed and ran a pipe to a tap that gave me cool, pure water for making tea. It was also used to add to the whisky that "Cassie", Paul Drage, headmaster of the local school, Frankie Southam my donkey landlord and Commander Carey Wilson RNV(S)R, would drink in large measures on the numerous occasions they visited me onboard *Jonquill*. We were well and truly an assorted group of friends, parson, publican, farmer, schoolmaster and magistrate.

Paul Drage was an excellent schoolteacher and scoutmaster. During the war, he had served in the army, rising to the rank of major, and though strict with his pupils, he was a very fair, respected teacher. Both my sons at Woodford, Stephen and Timothy were taught by him, and have no hesitation in saying he was their finest ever teacher. Paul was a good friend of D J Watkins Pitchford who wrote under the pseudonym of BB. I had the pleasure of meeting him when out with Paul and have since read most of his books about the countryside.

Frank Southam was a farmer and chartered auctioneer. His skill as a water diviner was in great demand. He said his success rate was 100 per cent, however, he paid a penalty for his gift; after a session, he developed very severe migraine and took to his bed for the rest of the day. A long-standing member of the Marylebone Cricket Club (MCC), he invited me to accompany him to Lords on quite a few occasions. This was my first introduction to the "home of cricket," a place I would become more familiar with in years to come. My main recollection of the first visit was seeing Wes Hall, the West Indies fast bowler, bowl unchanged throughout the day! Modern day fast bowlers – and at half his pace – have difficulty in bowling ten consecutive overs.

The Rev Louis de Casiabianco was born 100 years too late: a model for a parson straight out of a Jane Austin novel, autocratic, domineering, pompous with an ability to rub people up the wrong way. In appearance, he looked very much like Alistair Sim, the film star, especially with his glasses on the end of his nose. I liked him very much and we got on well. We spent many hours chatting together and drinking brandy (mine) in his study He was permanently short of money. He once gave me a pocket flintlock pistol in lieu of money he owed. The pistol's value increased considerably over the years, far more than the money. His wife, who was a sister at Kettering hospital, was a charming, talented lady, an expert in heraldry and an accomplished artist.

Carey Wilson was the owner of Wilson & Watson's, a shoe factory in Kettering. He lived in a most beautiful house in the village with his French wife. When we first met I asked him how long had he spent in the navy, I wasn't at all ready for his answer.

In his youth, he had spent two terms at Dartmouth Naval College where he contracted tuberculosis and was invalided out. During the war, he was appointed to a post that placed him in charge of the "upper reaches of the River Nene". Had the Germans invaded us, he would have been responsible for the defence on his part of the river. How? He never explained! When I asked, he would suck on his pipe, wink, and say, "That's an official secret, old boy!" He was given the rank of Lieutenant RNV(S)R, Royal Naval Volunteer Supplementary Reserve, but by the time I knew him had mysteriously risen to the rank of Commander.

I went to his house most weeks, and he loved to ask me about life in the Royal Navy, which countries I had visited, the people I had met. I sometimes felt that, through me, he was reliving the career he'd never had himself. His wife was a charming person, very chic as you expect from a French woman. They spent a lot of time in the South of France and she was particularly pleased I had visited Nice, Cannes, Golf Juan and Monte Carlo whilst in the navy. Each time they went abroad, they brought me back a bottle of brandy. When his gardener was ill, I mowed his lawn for him each week, with the first ride-on mower I had ever seen. His very large garden was an absolute picture, how he could ever leave it to go abroad, I never knew!

Three men in a boat

The following summer I took *Jonquil* back to Peterborough, the nearest slipway, to haul it out and tar its bottom. I became very friendly with the members of the Peterborough Yacht Club at Alwalton who owned the slipway. They gave me lots of advice and help when I had to fit a new stern; the existing one had started to rot. Their eagerness to assist me may have been partly due to the keg of beer I kept on the boat. Whilst there I noticed a lot of members busy studying charts, I asked the Commodore, Charles Critchley (Critch) where they were planning to go. He said, "Wells-next-the-Sea," but then followed it up with, "They plan the same voyage every year, but at the last minute always find an excuse not to go. No one has yet done the trip." This fired my imagination, and I too started to plan "the trip".

At the end of some of our Saturday evening sessions, Jeff, Jock Findlay, another friend, and myself would go down to the boat, cast off and cruise down to Thrapston lock where we would have a few more beers and then turn in. As soon as it was light, we would go through the lock and carry on down river to a beautiful waterside pub at Wadenhoe, arriving there at about 10 a.m. The majority of the village, including the pub, belonged to John Player the cigarette manufacturers. Only a retired JP employee could become tenant of the pub, and Ernie the landlord was such a person. We spent many pleasant Sunday mornings moored at the bottom of the pub lawn waiting, with other boat owners, for the pub to open.

On a couple of occasions we had problems en route with the engine and weed collecting on the propeller – thankfully no plastic supermarket bags then. This meant we probably looked a bit scruffy when we arrived at our destination, unlike most of the other owners who left their boats permanently at the pub and travelled by car to spend the weekend onboard. One day as we arrived we overheard someone say, "Here comes the scruffs!" Such a comment hurt our finer feelings, our boat was always immaculate due to my sons spending lots of punishment time polishing the brass portholes, hatches and boat hooks.

The following Monday I went to Plaistre & Hangars, a firm of Rag Merchants in Kettering where I had previously obtained outfits for our fancy dress parties. For a small sum, I fitted the three of us out with Royal Naval officers' uniforms, a Sub Lieutenant's for Jock, Lieutenant's for Jeff and Commander's for me!

We arrived at our usual time of 10 a.m. having purposely made our faces and hands dirty with old oil. After receiving the usual adverse comments we went below, washed and donned lily white shirts and our freshly cleaned and pressed uniforms ready to meet our critics. We planned it very carefully, waiting until the other boat owners were about to walk to the pub before we reappeared. I had borrowed a battery-operated record player from Don Wilson and, from my collection of military band music, selected the Royal Marines signature tune, "A Life on the Ocean Wave" played by the mass bands of the Royal Marines. We stepped ashore with the music playing loudly and walked to the pub with applause from pub customers and boat owners following us all the way. No one ever called us "Scruffs" again.

I talked over my planned cruise to Wells, with Jeff and Jock and they were all in favour. The boat was still at Alwalton so we took it as far as Wisbech one Sunday and returned the following week for the voyage. We had hoped to obtain a navigation chart at Wisbech but on arrival couldn't find a chandler open. We weren't worried; I had a large-scale AA road map that clearly showed The Wash and decided we could manage with that. I bought a pair of binoculars and borrowed a boy scout trekking compass from Paul Drage. We enquired about the tide times from a local fisherman and timing it, as advised, passed under Sutton bridge an hour after the tide turned.

We entered The Wash with no problems and set course for Hunstanton Pier, our first waypoint. I expected to be able to see the pier through binoculars; after all, it was only 14 miles! That was our first mistake. Our second mistake was I thought we could travel in a straight line from the River Nene entrance to Hunstanton. However, our boat was only capable of doing 5 knots and the tide was touching 8–10 knots. We wanted to travel North East but the tide was taking us North West towards Skegness. By the time we were conscious of our predicament the tide was turning and with it behind us, we very reluctantly limped back to Wisbech.

40 years later and many thousands of miles cruising accomplished, I look back and realise what absolute idiots we were. We had no proper chart or compass, no life jackets, no emergency flares, no life raft or inflatable, no anchor, no navigation lights and, most of all, no common sense. What I had, however, was a passionate ambition to be the first person to set out from Alwalton and reach Wells-next-the-sea.

After securing the boat at Wisbech, we went to the nearest pub and told a local fisherman about the setback we had suffered. He explained that even the local fishermen had problems navigating the shifting sandbanks in The Wash. A sandbank could shift its position between tides and, with their experience, they could locate the channel by the water movement. I asked if it was possible to hire a pilot for the trip. As luck would have it, he had a son home on holiday from university, who had spent his boyhood shrimping in The Wash and was an experienced navigator in those waters. He thought it more than possible he could get his son to act as pilot for a small remuneration. Without hesitation, I booked him for the following week. Peter, the pilot, had his own chart, compass, flares and enough lifejackets for all.

By now, I had a 3.8S Jaguar car, in which we travelled to Wisbech. I told Peter that once I had done the trip I was confident I would be able to navigate back to Wisbech, so in addition to his fee, I would pay his bus or train fare back. He said there was no direct bus service and it would take him a week to get back by bus, so someone had to bring him back by car. Jock didn't drive and Jeff was rather dubious about driving my Jaguar so they both agreed that as I had been to sea many times, I would have to forego the boat journey and drive my car to Wells.

It was a beautiful morning when they set out. I drove to the river entrance and watched them sail past with the boat looking splendid. While I was waiting for them, a man came along and asked if I was a bird watcher; it was Peter Scott (not yet knighted) who was visiting a nearby bird sanctuary. I told him why I was there and he said my friends were in for a rough trip! Being a retired naval officer who spent the war serving in motor torpedo boats, I guessed he knew what he was talking about, although the sea then was calm. I estimated their time of arrival off Hunstanton and set off to watch them sail past the headland.

By my original estimate, they were about an hour late passing the point. Peter Scott's forecast was correct, the sea state was quite rough off Hunstanton and they had a further 18 miles of exposed sea. When they eventually came into sight, I thought the boat seemed to be pushing out a lot of smoke, and pitching a lot. I could clearly see all three men standing in the stern. At an average speed of five knots, they should have arrived at Wells at about 4 p.m. At 5.30 p.m. I went to the Coastguard Post and asked if they had received any reports of a boat in trouble. They hadn't, but did say that sea conditions were rough and that may have delayed their arrival. The coastguard lent me a pair of binoculars and I sighted them off Wells harbour entrance at 7 p.m. There was no sign of Jeff and Jock, only Peter on the wheel. When they arrived alongside the harbour wall, I took the line from Peter and secured it to a bollard. Jeff and Jock appeared looking ghastly, white faced, glassy eyed, and I hadn't seen men look like that since leaving the Royal Navy.

As a 15 year old, I joined my first ship, HMS *Crossbow*, at Chatham Dockyard. A week later, we sailed to join up with the rest of the Home Fleet to take part in a NATO exercise. When we reached Sheerness at the mouth of the River Medway on which Chatham lies, the ship started to roll and I experienced my first attack of seasickness. The next three weeks were spent at sea off Iceland, Greenland and in the Arctic Ocean. Apart from a 12 hour stop at Trondhiem in Norway to refuel, the sea varied from rough to extremely rough, and I was sick the whole of the time. The thought that I had signed on for ten years did not in anyway help the pain. Fortunately, my next cruise was to the Mediterranean where sea conditions are much friendlier, and I overcame my proneness to the dreaded "Mal de mer".

With that experience behind me, I recognised and sympathised with Jeff and Jock. My efforts to entice them into the nearest pub were not appreciated. They just wanted to die. They told me there was no way they were going to sail the boat back to Wisbech, so I had no alternative but to leave the boat at Wells and take them back by car.

On the way back, I got the full story of events from Peter. Shortly after clearing the river entrance the engine started overheating. The boat engine was cooled by seawater being pumped round the block after passing through a filter. This had become choked with weed. In shutting down the engine to remove the debris, the boat had rolled considerably, causing Jeff and Jock to experience their first pangs of sickness. It also explained the smoke I saw at Hunstanton.

Just after passing the point, the boat was pitching violently causing the battery lead to short out and catch fire. With his crew incapacitated, Peter had to leave the wheel to extinguish the flames and in doing so, the boat had healed over sufficient for the sea to cascade over the side, flooding the bilges. Having put out the flames, Peter then had to pump the bilge after bringing the helm over. For two people, no problem, for one person extremely difficult but he managed. Such a combination of setbacks was the reason for their late arrival at Wells, and the time spent rolling around at sea carrying out repairs, was a major factor in Jeff's and Jock's acute discomfort.

Neither of them ever set foot on the boat again, not even for a gentle river cruise to Wadenhoe. They were both convinced that I was aware of the true sea state that day and purposely subjected them to a terrible experience they never wanted to repeat.

Weeks later a joke went round the village that the three of us were returning from a car trip that took us past a village fete, just as the tug-of-war had started. The team coach shouted, "Heave," and on hearing this both Jeff and Jock wound down their windows and threw up!

One good result with leaving the boat at Wells, was that Sylvia and myself plus our two sons, Stephen and Timothy, were able to have a wonderful five-day holiday on the boat, our first ever together. At low water, the harbour dried out completely, leaving golden sands and small pools that the boys fished in for crabs. Gippy, our Jack Russell terrier, loved chasing the seagulls and running with the boys. Wells-next-the-sea was an idyllic place for a holiday with young children. Stephen was ten and Timothy seven years old and, apart from camping with the Boy Scouts, had always been on holiday with their grandparents,

I got talking to the local fishermen in a pub and, as a result, Sylvia went out with them for a day's cockle and whelk fishing. The open boats provided little shelter against the elements and the lack of any cabin meant that the toilet arrangements were rather primitive, in fact just a "bucket and chucket" affair. They left at first light and returned in late afternoon so her modesty was tested on more than one occasion. The sea was quite rough but she is a good sailor and didn't let me down, in fact, she took a lot of fried bacon, egg and sausage rolls with her to give to the men, and ended up eating most of them herself. In the pub afterwards, one fisherman said she ate so much they thought her dexterity was about to be tested further. We took a large sack of cockles home with us which went down well with the customers.

Timothy takes up painting

There was another occasion when I had promised to take my sons on the boat with me, but because of Timothy's bad behaviour, I left them at home.

Following the debacle with the Vauxhall car that Riley Smith was going to give to his son on release from prison, Riley asked me if he could leave it on my car park for a few days. I said he could as long as it was not for too long as I had refused other customers' requests to do the same.

A few weeks previously I had bought a gallon tin of red oxide paint ready to prime the topsides of the boat prior to re-painting. When I returned from my trip, I was horrified to discover Timothy had somehow managed to gain entry to Riley's car and had painted the interior with the red oxide paint, covering all seats, dashboard and steering wheel. Not being able to find a brush, he had used his hands to paint the dashboard and wheel, and sat in the paint when coating the seats. Timothy was then five years old and had already acquired a reputation as the village vandal. Needless to say, Riley was not amused and asked me what I was going to do about compensating him. I reminded him that three months previously I gave permission for the car to be there for a short period, and had asked him to remove it on four occasions.

The outcome was I offered to send Tim across to Riley's house to work off the damages by doing odd jobs. Riley said he would rather not have him anywhere near his yard and accepted that it was his own fault for not removing the car earlier. We were to have many a laugh about it in the future.

When Timothy broke his arm falling off a wall at Thrapston Market, it was in plaster in a sling that he kept inside his coat or jumper. One day he was riding his bike down the hill past the pub, and collided with "Bocca" Colson who was just coming out of the hairdressers door. "Bocca", one of the village elder statesmen, suffering from failing eyesight, went to pick Timothy up but could only find one arm. He rushed back into the shop and said to Ted Templeman, the village barber, "Come quick, Ted, I've knocked a poor boy off his bike and think his arm has come off!" Poor old "Bocca", a man whose drinking prowess will be recorded in the village history, insisted to Ted he hadn't touched a drop that day.

Tim's best friend was Reg Hawes, the village milkman. He went with Reg on his round and held the horse while Reg delivered the milk. Tim's ability always to land into trouble fascinated Reg. His brother Rupert, another character, said Timothy reminded Reg of his own youth. When Reg was about, Timothy was never short of money.

When we first arrived at Woodford, we were made aware of whether we should allow Rupert Hawes into the pub. He was at 60, the youngest of the three Hawes brothers, Reg, was the eldest.

Rupert lived with his daughter and her child, whose parentage he was often blamed for. Just prior to our arrival he found his daughter dead in bed one morning; she had been murdered. Neighbours at the inquest gave evidence of hearing shouting and screams late at night when Rupert arrived home from the pub. Rupert said his daughter had a boyfriend who was in the American Air Force, and he was at the house that night. Rupert was initially arrested for the crime but released on bail. The American could not be traced and no person was ever charged with the girl's murder.

Rupert, a very articulate man, was a great one for reciting poetry and making up instant rhymes. When he drank too much, which was frequently, he would often start to cry and seem to be on the verge of announcing the identity of the murderer, and then suddenly he would laugh and say, "You thought I was going to tell you, didn't you? That's my secret and mine alone!" I banned him from the pub on numerous occasions but always relented when I received a piece of very humorous poetry from him, in which he would apologise for any of his sins.

And then there were eight

The donkeys were proving to be a big attraction in the village. Boris, the big brown Jack donkey, was a very amorous male and the five ladies in his harem kept him very busy. The paddock, in which I kept the donkeys, was next to the village school and the young mothers often congregated by the paddock gate while waiting for their offspring. They brought carrots and sugar cubes for the donkeys and at times Boris would reward them with a demonstration of his sexual technique! I sometimes wondered if the donkeys' behaviour ever caused the wives to criticise their husbands' performances! One day I received a telephone call from a very old lady who lived in a bungalow opposite the paddock. She said, "Please come quick, Mr Hackett, one of your donkeys is hitting another with a big stick!"

Jack Smith told me he thought Mabel was in foal but both Tommy Abbot and Riley Smith disagreed. I asked the vet on his next visit but he said it was very difficult to tell with donkeys. Jack, however, was so certain he bet Tommy and Riley a triple brandy. Sure enough three months later Mabel gave birth to a Jack donkey that unfortunately died at birth. We buried him in the pub garden and children from the village put flowers on his grave for months afterwards.

We were very sad at losing such a beautiful tiny donkey but the vet said Mabel had prematurely aborted her foal. A few weeks later, Jack came excitedly into the pub to tell me he had been to see the donkeys and was certain that, this time, Gladys was pregnant. Gladys was the first donkey I bought, along with her foal at the fair. Having been correct with Mabel, we were very excited at Jack's news and were determined nothing should happen to the foal this time. After four or five months had passed, Gladys wasn't getting any fatter and we came to the conclusion that this time Jack had got it wrong, though he still insisted he was correct in his diagnosis.

That November the River Nene was in flood and I thought I

had better go down and check on the donkeys. I immediately noticed Gladys wasn't with the others and started to look for her. After a few minutes I spotted her in a field on the other side of the river and I couldn't understand why she had swam there. While I was trying to work out how I was going to get her back, her foal, which had been lying in a hollow, stood up. My immense joy at seeing the foal quickly turned to alarm as Gladys started to swim back across the river towards me, I was worried in case the foal attempted to follow her. I tried to get Gladys to turn back but she kept on swimming towards my bank. Without giving it as much thought, as I should have done, I decided the only way the foal was going to get safely across was for me to go and get it.

From knowledge acquired when fishing in the river, I knew there was a spot much shallower than the rest. I think it had once been a ford hence Woodford – a ford in the wood perhaps? Anyway I kicked off my Wellington boots and part waded, part swam across the swollen river to reach the foal. Fortunately, it let me pick him up and carry him down to the river without struggling, but once we were in the water, I had great difficulty in keeping hold of the foal. The water was icy and my hands were frozen but we eventually made the other bank and reunited Gladys with her foal.

It was a most marvellous moment; at last I had a foal and had safely delivered it to dry land. The foal – a male – was very unsteady on his feet so I carried him to the pub with Gladys following me. We gave him a good rub down with towels, and put mother and foal in a stable with an electric heater for the night. The vet checked them over the next day and pronounced them both in excellent health.

I wanted to call the foal Jack in recognition of Jack Smith's correct diagnosis but Sylvia insisted in calling him William. He was an immediate celebrity in the village with a permanent queue of children at his stable; he also featured on Anglia Television and in the local press.

The chairman goes missing

As soon as I took over the licence of the Dukes Arms, I joined the local LVA, The Thrapston & District Licensed Victuallers Association. It was a much smaller association than Wellingborough, with just 48 members spread over a wide area. Although small in number the LVA had a good social side but was not large enough to hold an annual banquet.

We were fortunate in having a very good secretary in Frank Gardiner and chairman in Gerry Leach. Gerry was a real character who kept one of the most isolated pubs in the area, the Red Lion at Clopton. Both Gerry and his wife Gina had been involved in the London theatre scene, their flamboyant lifestyle making them the talk of the district. Very often Gerry would be seen behind his bar wearing a pith helmet, which together with a monocle and clipped military moustache, made him look very colonial. Gina always dressed in 1920s' style, rarely seen without an extremely long cigarette holder.

After I had been a member for a few months, I received a phone call from Gina to say that Gerry had upped and left her. I had always thought they were a devoted couple so was very surprised. I immediately went to see her and discovered Gerry had taken everything of any value, car, spirit stock, small items of furniture, all their cash and his pith helmet. He had left poor Gina in an impoverished state and she had no head for business whatever. She told me she wanted to leave the pub as soon as possible, but was concerned that the brewery would insist she gave the statutory 12 months' notice.

Gerry had left behind a battered old box file which Gina gave me permission to examine. The contents revealed they owed the brewery for rent and stock, the council for rates, electricity and water boards for services. They had a large overdraft although Gerry had recently cashed in some insurance policies.

I returned to Woodford and telephoned all the LVA members to tell them about Gerry's departure and Gina's predicament. I invited them to go to The Red Lion that evening, where I proposed to hold an auction of the remainder of Gina's stock, fixtures and fittings.

Practically all the members turned up and we had a most financially rewarding auction for Gina. Ashtrays were sold for 10/-, glasses 2/6d each, beer trays 5/- everything that could be taken away was sold, even the light bulbs. We doubled the price of drinks over the bar, and any remaining at the close, was auctioned at inflated prices. In all £150 was raised and we bought her a one-way ticket to London out of LVA funds. A good weekly wage then was £15 per week.

I took Gina to Kettering railway station the next morning and then telephoned the brewery to say I had been to the pub to see Gerry and found it locked up. Everything was in Gerry's name so there was no comeback on Gina. I heard from her on numerous occasions and luckily she had received no communication from the brewery or any of the pub creditors. For my troubles, I was elected chairman of the association at the next meeting.

Cellars are not just for beer

During our fourth year at Woodford a Mr John Hazel had replaced Colonel David Jones as managing director of Watney Mann (Midlands); he came from Head Office in London. I clearly remember the first time he came to the Dukes Arms, the first village pub in the region he had visited. We were tipped off that his favourite choice of food for lunch was lamb cutlets. I got Fred Roberts to prepare me two dozen of the very best, which we put on the lunchtime menu for the big chief's arranged visit.

He arrived with an entourage of the Tied House Regional, Area and District Managers plus Billy Marsh the head brewer, and the chief architect. While I was showing Mr Hazel round the pub, unbeknown to me Billy Marsh had gone down the cellar. He came to me very red faced and said, "Good God Tony, the bloody cellar's full of meat, I don't know what Mr Hazel is going to say to that."

Billy, a good friend of Bert Drage and Ron Loomes, had through cricket become a good friend of mine. He was an enthusiastic beagle follower and often came to the Dukes Arms with Jack Ivester Lloyd, a well-known author and artist of hunting subjects.

Some months previous, the butcher's shop next door to, and owned, by Don Wilson's father, had closed and Don told me we could have the heavy white marble slabs, and hanging rails from the shop. I had them fitted in the cellar, which, owing to the volume of food we were selling, was the only place I could store meat. Quite often, there would be two or three hindquarters of beef and never less than four gammon hams hanging there. The cellar was temperature controlled, and with the stainless steel lined walls, it made a perfect meat storage room. The day before Mr Hazel's visit, Sylvia had made a batch of sausages and three basins of brawn, and this, together with the normal meat, made quite an impressive sight.

The tour of inspection duly reached the cellar and sure enough he became very excited at the array of meat on display, but not, as Billy had feared, because of its presence in a beer cellar. His previous experience of catering pubs had all been in London where the butcher would deliver daily, this was clear proof of the amount of food we were selling and the quality of our meat. He spotted the basins and asked if it could possibly be brawn in them. I said it was and told him a customer had killed two pigs that week and had given me the heads. Much to my, and the assembled party's surprise, he demonstrated a good knowledge of meat and recognised the quality of ours. It transpired his grandfather and father had both been butchers in the East End of London, and he had grown up "above the shop".

When it came to ordering lunch he asked if he could have a brawn salad to start with followed by our home-made sausages with mashed potatoes and gravy – none of which were on the lunch menu that day. The remainder of the group had the lamb cutlets. When they finished, Mr Hazel asked Sylvia if she would sell him a basin of brawn and some sausages, which she was pleased to do. His visit was to have a bearing on our future advancement in the trade.

One other item I remember from his visit was his surprise that our public bar wasn't carpeted. Coming from London he had never seen a bar without a carpet before. While they were all having lunch I rang Alec Horrell, a farmer from across the green, and asked him and his son, to come across to the pub with the dirtiest wellies they could manage. When Mr Hazel saw the mess they made, he fully understood why village pub bars weren't carpeted.

We were receiving a lot of requests from the brewery to instruct other publicans and their wives in pub catering. Initially we felt flattered and pleased to pass on our acquired knowledge. However, after we had trained five or six couples, we objected to the brewery using us as unpaid instructors; some of the couples' pubs were near ours, putting them in direct competition to ourselves. The brewery offered either to pay us for each couple trained or for Sylvia to run classes for licensees at Northampton Technical College for which she would be paid a very good hourly rate. After giving it thought, we decided that what with the increased market catering which was a very good money earner, running the Dukes Arms and bringing up the children, she had all that she could manage without taking on more responsibilities. Anyway, it would have meant our taking on extra staff to replace her, and we were already employing all the available women in the village.

We move on

In spite of our success, and the wonderful atmosphere at the Dukes Arms, we were beginning to look for further challenges. We were still in our early 30s, tremendously ambitious, and our accountant Mr Guy, warned us about staying in one place for too long and getting into a rut.

Alfred John Guy came into our lives after we had been in business at the Dukes Arms for about a year. With all the strain of moving in, alterations, etc. I had never got round to obtaining the services of an accountant. After a while I received a demand from the Inland Revenue for £15 income tax that I thought was very fair and sent off a cheque. Many months later, I received a demand for £25 tax, which, this time, I thought, was getting a bit excessive. I was talking to our LVA secretary, Frank Gardiner, and I asked him if he had an accountant. That's how I came to meet Mr Guy.

He had been a partner with Thornton Baker, travelling the whole of the country carrying out audits, but pressure of work resulted in him having a heart attack at the age of 52. This made him decide there was more to life than being a high flyer in a large company. He bought an old gamekeeper's cottage in a tiny hamlet near Thrapston and started doing the accounts for small local businesses. He enjoyed meeting his clients socially and being involved in their private lives.

From the very first day we met, he became a very good friend, counsellor and adviser. Many years later when Mr Guy retired, his practice was taken over by Michael Wildman who was a Woodford boy. Michael was to be our accountant until our retirement and, like Mr Guy, we were to value his advice and friendship.

It was due to Mr Guy's prompting that I contacted Bert Drage at the brewery, and asked if he had any suitable larger pubs for us. He had nothing at the time, but said he would keep us in mind if something appropriate came up.

In the meantime, we travelled to Broad Haven in Pembrokeshire to look at a hotel that was for sale. It was a lovely place, in a beautiful spot and had tremendous potential. The function room held 150 people for a sit-down dinner and opposite the main door, across a narrow road, was a magnificent Victorian conservatory overhanging the beach. As with all good things, there was a snag.

The owner of the hotel was a local developer who had many business ventures. In the lounge bar was an enormous garish electric organ, the owner's pride and joy. Even though I would be buying the freehold, a clause in the sale stated that the organ must remain at the hotel and the present owner would be allowed to play it at weekends! If that wasn't bad enough, we made enquiries and it appeared he was a dreadful player. Another of his business interests was an amusement machine dealership, and a further sale clause was that the new owners must install his machines – jukebox and fruit machines – for a period of ten years. I sent Mr Guy down to try and get him to either lift the clauses or failing that, find out how much it would cost to write them out of the sale agreement but the seller wouldn't budge. It was a pity because it was a lovely place. Other places we looked at were The Red Lion Hotel at Ashburton in Devon, another nice place but very dilapidated, and hotels at Diss, Skipton, Banbury and Peterborough. All had a downside, one way or another.

In late February 1968, Bert Drage came to see us and said he had a hotel in Towcester that could be just the place for us. He gave us the basic details and it sounded good, but it didn't have a function room, and this was an avenue where we wanted to expand. The functions held at The Dukes Arms were very profitable but we were restricted by the size of the room; consequently we had to turn down bigger dinners. Bert told us not to write it off without viewing, as Mr Hazel was very keen that we should take it over and turn it back into a successful business.

From publicans to hoteliers

The Brave Old Oak Hotel was well situated in the centre of Towcester's market square that breasted the A5: Watling Street. An impressive building that had once been three separate businesses, a bank, later a bakers, an ale monger and a saddlers. The oldest parts dated back to 1627 and were two of the few premises in the town that survived the Great Fire in 1676, which destroyed 85 buildings. It was said to be Prince Rupert's headquarters during the siege of Northampton in 1643 when the Royalist Army camped in the town for five months.

Different theories were put forward for its name, one was that it was named after HMS *Royal Oak* that fought so bravely at Trafalgar, built from timber grown in the nearby royal forests of Whittlebury and Silverstone. Another was that it got its name from an old oak tree in Whittlebury Forest that had been struck numerous times by lightning.

The M1 motorway had opened the previous year taking most of the through traffic away from the town. The doom-mongers had stated it would be the end of Towcester but in the opinion of most people, it was the making of the town. They said the day before the M1 opened it took five minutes to cross the main street; the next day it was possible to walk down the middle without meeting a car.

The existing tenants of the Brave Old Oak had previously run a hotel in Dartmouth. I don't know what brought them to Towcester, but they told the brewery they owned the Dartmouth hotel and were in the process of selling it, once sold they would transfer the assets from there to the Oak. This situation had existed for almost a year in which time local trades people were owed considerable sums of money, and eventually so was the brewery. It transpired the hotel in Dartmouth was rented from the local council and the only assets they owned were the fittings and stock.

A succession of managers were sent up from Dartmouth to run the Oak; they more or less helped themselves to food and drink without payment, further adding to the tenant's financial difficulties The deteriorating state of affairs led to them being declared bankrupt, and this was the position when we went to view.

The tenant's son and some of his hippy friends from Dartmouth were running the place. We went one evening, without an appointment, as we didn't intend to disclose our interest in the place. We wanted to gain an insight into the type of business it offered before viewing officially. The place was in semi-darkness lit only by candles in bottles. Three scruffy hippy types were behind the bar standing over an electric fire which appeared to be the only form of heating in the room. The shelves were bare apart from a couple of optics containing half-empty spirit bottles. The only beer they had was in bottles, and not too much of that. A youth with long ginger hair served us and then said, "I suppose you've come to have a look at the place?" Though taken by surprise by his remark, I thought I might as well tell him this was so as we intended returning officially the next day. He turned out to be the tenant's son and I asked him how he knew we were possible viewers; he replied that as customers were thin on the ground, he assumed anyone he didn't know must be prospective tenants.

There was little point in trying to view that evening, the electricity had been cut off and we would have needed torches to get around. I made an appointment to view at 11 a.m. the next day.

In daylight, we could see more clearly the immense character of the hotel. The air of neglect didn't detract from its charm and we immediately fell in love with the place. After inspecting the ground floor, we asked to see the 16 bedrooms and were told, "This wouldn't be possible as residents are still in the rooms" – at midday? I said we hadn't travelled this far to have to come back again. The telephone had been disconnected so I went outside and found a kiosk to ring the brewery and tell them the problem; they sent a man out immediately.

He told Nigel, the tenant's son, we must be allowed to see the whole premises and he accompanied us upstairs. The first room we came to looked and smelt like a doss house. The bedlinen was filthy and the floor was littered with dirty plates. This was the pattern for the rest of the rooms, except that in two of them, youths were still in bed.

We had seen enough to interest us and before we left Towcester, visited the town's other hotel, The Saracen's Head of *Pickwick Papers* fame, and four pubs in the main street. We agreed that the competition was nothing to worry about.

Six wonderful years come to an end

The years we spent at The Dukes Arms were some of the happiest of our lives. We had arrived at a run-down village pub six years previously in 1962, an impoverished young couple with lots of ideas but very little money. Now we were considering taking over a town hotel. None of our success would have been possible without our dedicated and conscientious staff:

David Knighton, who for the first two years never received any wages; the debt we owed him could never be repaid in money. He was a barman, chef, cellar man, toilet cleaner, child minder in fact anything we needed doing he willingly did.

He had problems passing a driving test so we bought him a moped to get to work. In the winter, he always wore a deerstalker hat, and late one evening after arriving home, he telephoned asking if he had left it behind at the pub. He said he thought he was wearing it when he left but it wasn't there when he reached home. He stuck a notice on the village notice board offering a £1 reward for anyone finding it. Two years later, a small boy came into the pub holding a piece of soggy rag that was just recognisable as David's hat. He said he had found it in a ditch a mile outside the village and asked if the reward was still being offered, I gave him the £1 rewarding his initiative.

David went to Wellingborough School and was a contemporary of Sir David Frost – the TV star. On leaving, he joined Wellingborough Iron Company as a trainee metallurgist. When the company closed down they wanted him to transfer to Corby but not being able to drive, meant him moving from home. He obtained a job with another firm in Wellingborough until, after his tenth attempt, he finally passed his driving test, an achievement that opened up new opportunities for him and he joined Watney Mann as a Free Trade representative. His limitless energy and likeable personality made him a very good rep and it was no surprise when after a few years he obtained a better position with Carlsberg Brewery.

During all this time he played a key role in the development of Irthlingborough Diamonds Football Club and, after his untimely death at the ridiculous early age of 49, a room at their new ground was named after him. He was godfather to Timothy and Michael, a good friend to Stephen: a man much loved by all who knew him.

Betty Peck wasn't the first barmaid who worked at the Duke, but without in any way detracting from the others, she was the best. Betty was a tiny bundle of energy, with a wonderful smile. She had a laugh that sounded like a machine gun and an accent that defied anyone but a trained linguist in tracing its origin. Her sudden shrieks could reduce the hardest man to a trembling jelly. Living just doors away, she was always the first to be called upon in a crisis and never once did she let us down. Together with her husband Gordon they were very good friends and, like David, we owe them a great debt of gratitude, not least for her help filling in gaps for this glimpse of our time spent at Woodford.

Kath Forscutt was a grey-haired version of everyone's idea of a perfect granny, so full of life she always had time to listen sympathetically to any body's problems. She had amazing stamina that kept her going when others flagged. Her husband Len, whom she adored, helped with getting glasses in, bottling up and washing up during peak periods. They were a very well matched couple and we loved them both dearly. Len died in 1971 aged 71 and Kath in 1977 aged 74.

Iris Clipston, tall and elegant, apart from working at the Duke helped Sylvia at the Market Restaurant, her husband Peter was our darts captain and he helped behind the bar.

Doreen Allan with a complexion like Dresden porcelain had a lisp that always reminded me of Violet Elizabeth in *Just William*. She was a waitress at lunchtime and in the evenings, and held the record for the fastest descent from the dining room, and the breaker of the most crockery. A lovely natured girl who, like Betty, could be relied on to keep us informed of all village "news".

Mary Pendered was our first barmaid: always immaculate and "Aunt" to our boys. She ran the PX at the local American air base and often brought us the most delicious giant pizzas. Mary was an excellent cook too.

Then there was Margaret Cockings. How she found time to work for us with having such a large family was always a mystery. She too had a lovely personality, another very hard worker.

Joyce Paine was an athletic girl who had represented Northamptonshire at 100 yards in the same National Schools Sports Championships when I represented Leicestershire at high and long jump.

The cast was star-studded: Bridget Green, an accomplished baker and confectioner, won National awards for her wedding cake decorating and her bread baking. Bridget came back into our lives at Blakesley when she worked as a representative for a frozen food company.

Jeff and Rita Stamford were a husband and wife team: Rita, a girl with many attributes not the least of which was a profile that would have made a superb figurehead for any sailing ship. A hugely talented girl, her piano playing and singing made a big attraction at weekends. No one has ever sung "Yesterday" as well. Jeff was a good friend, easy-going, I could talk him in to doing anything – except going on my boat again – a good barman always immaculately turned out. Sadly the last we heard of them, they had separated.

Jock Findlay too had a powerful singing voice much appreciated by the customers. A good friend, sadly never quite the same person health-wise after his boating experience. I never knew whether the cruise really did affect him that much. Jock also helped behind the bar.

There were others: the Houghton brothers, David and John, always willing to help – and Stan York, our first barman during the "Disco" era. Others who worked for us included Jean Fletton, Gladys Clipston, Mrs Smart, Mrs Marriott, Barbara Dunphy and Joan Abbott.

Although it is 36 years since we left the Dukes Arms, we still remember a lot of our customers with great fondness. Some, although their faces are imprinted on our minds, many names escape us, but with help from Betty and Gordon Peck I will list those we remember. Sadly, a lot have died.

Gordon & Betty Peck, Mary Pendered, Len & Kath Forscutt, Peter & Iris Clipston, Teresa Clipston, Doreen Allan, Clive Allan, John Allan, Graham Allan, Tommy Abbot, Tony & Melba Gent, Riley Smith, Margaret & Don Cockings, Jeff & Rita Stamford, Arthur, Molly and Andrew Brown, Herbie Green, Bridget Green, Fred & Trevor Roberts, Dennis Price, Stan & Olive York, Frank Clipston, Eddie Groom, George Groom, David Houghton, John Houghton, Albert & Beryl Headland, Alvina Headland, Michael, John & Jenny Pendered, Harold Skelly, Tom Blowfield, Melba Blowfield, Jack Parker, Alf Bosworth, Terry Bosworth, Sam Skelly, Cliff Elmore, Wayne Waters, Roger Baker, Gerald Baker, Daphne Waters, Jock Findlay, Jack Smith, Reg Hawes, Rupert Hawes, Hector Hawes, Paul Drage, Frank Southam, Bob Britton, Alec Horrell, John Horrell, Richard Burnham, Barry & Joyce Payne, Stan Gamble, Bunny Warren, Terry Warren, Richard Drage, Alec Coyle, Bud & Joan Abbott, Charlie Robinson, Ted Templeman, Brian Graley, Bennie Smart, Dick Gunn, Daisy French, Charlie French, George Wilson, Bill & Jean Fletton. Des & Jean Blackwell, Malcolm Langley, John Dunmore, Mick Dunmore, Colin Munton, Sid Templeman, Freddie Crouch, Frankie & Mr Marriott, Ken Marriott, Len & Cis Warren, Stan Bates, Tim Davis, John Hawes, Derek Hawes, Charlie Mabbut, Michael Wildman, Michael Bosworth, Ivan Brown, Richard Turner, Steve Cullam, Eileen Cullam, David Turner, Ernie Rice and all those other names will, no doubt, come to mind once this has gone into print.

Almost certainly, I have missed someone from the roll call of customers and friends who, in some small but essential way, helped make our business the success it was.

We went back to Woodford last year, with our eldest son Stephen and his wife Mary. It was our first visit for many years and coincided with the annual Church Flower Festival. Before visiting the Dukes Arms, we went to the church and after seeing the flowers, had a tour of the graveyard. It was a very sad, moving experience seeing the graves of so many old friends, folk whom I had hoped to meet later that day in the "Duke".

Jock Findlay had died in the 1980s, Peter Clipston very young, Riley Smith that year aged 83, and Jack Smith aged 70, not long after we left.

They say he had gone down hill very quickly after our departure. He couldn't afford to run his car so it had to go. His finances allowed him to drink only half-pints of ordinary beer and smoke ordinary cigarettes. His quality clothes had reached the end of their life, although he still doffed his trilby to a lady. A big blow to his dignity was when he could no longer afford to have his own room at Aggie Cumley's.

We were very sad we hadn't learnt sooner about his reduced circumstances, it would have been a pleasure for us to have assisted him in some way. He was a fool to himself and had many critics, but even so he symbolised an era when being a gentleman didn't just entail going through a toilet door bearing the correct title.

Paul Drage, Frankie Southam, Alec Horrell, Cassie and his wife, Reg, Hector and Rupert Hawes and most members of the RAOB lodge were in the graveyard. So many customers had died whom we expected would still be alive. Bob Britton had moved away, as had Betty and Gordon, although when they heard we were back in the village, they came to have a drink with us. Tony Gent was in a home but very few others had left the village.

The Brave Old Oak Hotel

We paid further visits to the Brave Old Oak and the more we saw the more we liked it. I knew the brewery were very keen for us to take it over as soon as possible which put us in a strong bargaining position. I suggested that we take the Brave Old Oak but keep the Dukes Arms for a year. At the end of this period, we would decide which place to keep. First of all the brewery weren't very keen; they still had long waiting lists of people who wanted tenancies, and for one person to have two was unheard of. Eventually with pressure from Mr Hazel, they gave in and we achieved another trade first in having two pubs at the same time. Although there were a few cases of dual tenancies in London, we were the first in the Midlands.

We had to tie up loose ends at Woodford quickly. The donkeys were taken to Thrapston market where, having told the auctioneer we would not let them be sold to dealers, all found very good homes. Gladys and her foal went to a disabled children's home near Oundle, the vet who had been treating her bought Agatha with the bad feet, and farmers bought the others for their children and grandchildren. They would be so much happier than they were in Ireland, and would never have to work again. I never worked out exactly how much they cost me i.e. original purchase, shipping costs, vet and blacksmith bills, but one thing was certain, bringing staff from Ireland would have been much cheaper than donkeys.

The village had a very good boy scout troop run by Paul Drage. I told the senior scouts that if they looked after my boat they could use it for organised trips. Six months after we left, I received a phone call from PC Ron Dowdy to say my boat had been set adrift and was overhanging a weir. I returned to the village and Frankie Southam organised a tractor to pull if off, but unfortunately its back was broken. Riley Smith offered me £25 for it as scrap. In view of what happened to his car, I gave it to him with much sadness at such a beautiful boat suffering the ignominy of ending up in his scrapyard.

Betty and Gordon had shown an interest in having a pub, and we thought if they ran the Dukes Arms for us, they would stand a good chance of taking it over if we decided to give it up. Leaving them in charge, we moved to Towcester.

Pub changeovers rarely go according to plan, and this was no exception. On the day the transfer should have taken place, the outgoing tenants failed to show up at court. I was granted a temporary licence for a week when it was hoped they would put in an appearance. The actual pub changeover went ahead with Nigel representing his parents.

Before they were bankrupt, the brewery had taken possession of the entire outgoing tenant's fixtures and fittings, furniture and stock. They were entitled to do so under the tenancy agreement. This meant I was buying everything from the brewery who used their own valuer. I had Peter Stiles working for me, as he had done at Woodford. Stock should not have been a problem as they had virtually ceased trading. However, in the kitchen were eight dozen small tins of Lusty's Bird Nest Soup, eight dozen of their Real Turtle Soup and four dozen Sharks Fin Soup. Neither of the valuers had the slightest idea of their value, nor had Nigel or for that matter, from where they came. Apart from a few part-empty jars of spices, the kitchen was devoid of any other stock.

One or two items of furniture were of good quality, the remainder rubbish. I argued that as we would have to refurnish the premises completely I didn't see why we should be forced to buy the brewery's tatty furniture, bedding, linen, carpets and soft furnishings. Peter Stiles agreed but the brewery wouldn't relax the normal procedure between the two parties on a changeover. I told them we would return to Woodford if they insisted on my purchasing the inventory and, after a phone call to Bert Drage, they relented. Because they were anxious not to create a precedent, I was told that if I agreed to pay a token amount, an acceptable scheme would be worked out. With this assurance, I handed over a cheque for £200 and we were the tenants of The Brave Old Oak Hotel.

The scheme the brewery came up with fitted our plans perfectly. Although we chose the items, they paid for the complete refurbishment of the hotel and rented it to us on generous terms. The total cost of furnishings for the bars, restaurant, residents' lounge, lobby, stairs and landings plus the complete refurbishment of the 12 letting bedrooms and five staff rooms came to £9,000 for which I paid £200 a year rent. The £200 I paid at the changeover was counted as the first year's rent. The rent for the premises was £250 a year and, within six months, the brewery redecorated the whole premises, inside and out. The kitchen was refurbished and a new reception area was built, a new boiler installed and new suites were fitted in the four bathrooms.

All the letting bedrooms were furnished with Stag Minstrel furniture – then very up market – and the best quality carpets and curtaining. The stairs and landings were carpeted in a bright cherry red Wilton which when combined with the wall and ceiling beams and white walls, gave a light airy appearance.

Not having to spend out on refurbishing, we were able to go to town on light fittings, pictures, including some very good oil paintings for the lobby, stairs and landings, and all new kitchen equipment. We had GPO telephones installed in the bedrooms and an exchange fitted in reception. Very few three star hotels had telephones in their bedrooms. Hotels generally were not installing televisions in bedrooms at that time, but we fitted them later. The windows were very old leaded glass, lovely to look at, but not very good at keeping out noise. To reduce the sound of traffic we had secondary double-glazing installed that had the added advantage of being invisible from outside.

While these furnishing descriptions may sound commonplace today, in 1968 most of it was considered absolute luxury. Our main competition, The Saracens Head, still had linoleum and iron bedsteads in their bedrooms four years later. Was it any wonder that our celebrity guest list was so impressive?

About the only improvement the previous tenants made to the premises, was to buy all the panelling from the Old Customs House in Dartmouth prior to its demolition. This panelling lined the walls of the bar and lounge in the hotel: very impressive, each panel containing a handpainted coat of arms and name in gold lettering. The earliest crest had the name Bastard, dated 1040. The panelling blended in with the character of the building and was a great topic of conversation with foreign tourists, especially Americans. I must confess I told them the coats of arms belonged to past owners of the hotel, whereas in reality, I understood them to be past Mayors and Burgher masters of Dartmouth. I could never understand why the Elders ever let them leave the town.

A very large fireplace and panelled surround from the same source dominated the restaurant, and we had our own crest painted in a panel above it. The room held 12 tables each with four covers, and with the charcoal-coloured carpet we fitted, the red tablecloths and red lampshades created a very inviting sight for anyone passing the windows.

The public bar contained a magnificent inglenook fireplace and the lounge bar a walk-round chimneybreast in the centre of the room, with a fireplace either side. The bowed beamed ceilings in the two bars varied in height from 7' at their highest down to 5' 10" at their head banging lowest.

At the far end of the public bar was a cold buffet counter with refrigerated display unit, quite innovative for the period. At the other end was an entrance door leading to the street, and a further door that led down to the cellar. The cellar was in three sections, each with vaulted ceilings. One section was caged and formed a large wine store with racking for 500 bottles, another was used as a bottle store and the main part was the beer cellar stretching the whole width of the building

An opening with glazed panels either side linked the two bars. We installed fitted red leather upholstered seating in the lounge bar, and chose a very good quality Tudor patterned carpet for the floor. The public bar had a flag stoned floor and we plumped for high backed dark oak refectory seating which together with oak circular tables and the inglenook fireplace, gave it a circa-1700 tavern appearance. Most of the bar furnishings were antiques, bought from local dealers.

Leading off the main entrance lobby was the ladies and gents toilets. The ladies was very well fitted out with three cubicles and a long vanity unit containing four basins along one wall.

The residents' lounge was in the newer part of the hotel, which also housed the restaurant, reception desk, foyer and main staircase. It had a high ornate ceiling and large French windows that looked out onto a small paved area. A large walk-in safe in the foyer was a legacy of the days when that building was a bank.

The main kitchen was fitted with two double oven cookers, two large plate and food hot cupboards, two four-pot bains-marie, two salamander grills, a griddle and a double fryer. A large pantry led off the main kitchen. The preparation room contained a large walk-in refrigerator, chest freezer and potato peeler; the scullery was fitted with double stainless steel sinks.

The elegant stairs in the foyer, led to the first floor which contained three double bedrooms, one with a four-poster, four twin bedded rooms, one en suite, and four single rooms. Also on this floor were our personal en suite room, main office and large airing cupboard and linen store. A flight of steps adjacent to our room led to two attic rooms, Stephen and Timothy slept in one and the other was their play room – until I took it over for a very large Scalextric track.

At the end of the long landing, a further staircase led onto another landing, off which was a large family room containing a double and two single beds, and a further landing leading to one twin and two single staff rooms.

The yard at the rear of the premises had originally contained six stables but these had long been demolished to form parking spaces for 14 residents' cars. The boiler house and fuel store were attached to the building and a bottle store next to that. Our big bonus was the market square provided ample parking immediately in front of the hotel.

We bring new life to an old hotel

The outgoing tenants turned up at the adjourned licence transfer and now the Brave Old Oak was truly ours. The Chairman of the Bench, Commander Lawson RN (rtd) welcomed us to Towcester and said he hoped we would return The Brave Old Oak to its former glory.

Our biggest problems for successfully running the hotel were staff and supplies. We inherited two members of staff neither of whom had been paid for a month. The previous tenants had very kindly told them that the new owners would pay them.

Elio de Gregorio was a 24-year-old 15-stone Italian who had originally worked at the Castle Hotel in Dartmouth as a commis chef. How he came to be in Towcester was a mystery. His English was very limited as were his cooking skills. He lived on the premises and for the last few weeks had existed on tinned salmon and sharks fin soup. He had a lovely smile but initially was very sad faced, which we discovered was brought about by his fear we were not going to employ him. We heard of an Italian girl living in the town, married to an Englishman. Every time we wanted a detailed discussion with Elio, we brought in Marie to act as interpreter. For the first few weeks, this was not a big problem as we were not yet ready to serve food. Later on, his limited English became a matter of convenience for him.

Barbara Spanton had been employed as a chambermaid. A Norfolk girl, she was hard-working and conscientious. Like Elio, she too was worried about her future employment. She had worked at the Oak for five years under three previous tenants and was able to give us a good run down on their pros and cons. That was the extent of the staff but we didn't mind at all, we much preferred to engage people we knew we could work with, training them to our standards. We were most fortunate in having David Knighton to help us at weekends although his increased involvement with Irthlingborough Diamonds FC somewhat restricted his hours.

The main reason we were not serving food was due to problems with suppliers. A telephone enquiry invariably resulted in us being told, "When you pay what you owe, you may place an order." This applied to the milkman, baker, coal merchant, heating oil supplier, laundry, newsagent and, worst of all, wholesale grocer. In those days, there were no Cash & Carrys, just two main suppliers of catering food in the county. The firm we dealt with at Woodford came from Kettering and didn't deliver to our side of the county. I had to get the brewery to write to firms and state that we had no connection with the previous tenants. But all this took time. However, the decorating and refurbishment were going ahead and it gave us an opportunity to know our customers and learn about the town.

Towcester, whose Roman name was "Lactodorum", was the main shopping area for many surrounding villages. Most items could be purchased in the town, from a new hunting outfit and pair of hand made rugby boots, to medical supplies and electrical goods. There were three banks, a main post office and a firm of solicitors, a cinema built in 1939 by the first Lord Hesketh, a birthday present for his wife, a racecourse belonging to the same family and three schools, grammar, secondary and primary.

Being astride the Watling Street, the town had been well supplied with hotels and public houses. However The Talbot and White Horse Hotels had closed together with The Criterion, The Goats Head, The Dolphin, The White Hart, The Pomfret Tap, The Crown, Nelsons Arms, Albion, Wheat Sheaf, The Bell, The Star, The Sun,

Horse & Jockey and the Horse and Groom, public houses. This still left the Saracens Head and Brave Old Oak Hotels, and The Bull, The Plough, Sun Inn, Pomfret Arms, Peacock, White Horse and Folly pubs. There was also a Conservative Club in the town, but no Working Men's Club, an indication of the affluence in the area. At one time, the town had two breweries that were both bought by Phipps Brewery of Northampton. Dominating the market square is the town hall built in 1865 and nearby the Chantry House, built in 1452, the town's oldest building.

Towcester is probably best known for its racecourse that held its first race in 1876. The Empress of Austria who was staying at Easton Neston Hall as the guest of the then owner, Sir Thomas Fermor-Hesketh, first had the idea of holding a race meeting in the park. She was a fine rider, who rode side-saddle, and was sewn into her outfit each time she rode. It was once claimed that when the Grand National's future was in doubt at Aintree, Towcester was a possible alternative venue. Before winning the Grand National in 1908, a local horse, Rubio pulled a wagon owned by the Saracen's Head Hotel.

The main employer was the electronics company, Plessey, which had two premises in the town, and their main research laboratory in a neighbouring village. The South Northamptonshire District Council, employing 150, also had their offices in Towcester. These two concerns, together with the nearby Silverstone Racing Circuit and Towcester Racecourse were to provide the basis for our residential trade and a large part of drink and food sales.

I joined the local Chamber of Trade and LVA. The LVA had 52 members, a well organised and supported association. The area was bounded by Oxford, Banbury, Daventry, Northampton and Buckingham Licensing Districts, Although small compared with their neighbours, Towcester often set the pattern for extensions etc that was followed by the other branches. They had a good secretary in Tom Underwood, a landlord of many years' experience, and a sound chairman in Arthur Powley from Cosgrove Lodge Hotel where they held their social functions.

On the same day I applied for my licence the new licensee of The Bull, Ivor Denny, applied for his. Together with his wife Joan, we were to become very good friends. John Smith the landlord of the Saracens Head also became a good friend, but after he turned teetotal, our "outings" together were reduced. Other licensees Gordon Cowley, Jack Adams and Rex Groombridge also became firm friends.

Alterations and redecoration nearing completion, we started looking for staff. We were fortunate that my mother had recently retired from her public house, and was living with us then. Between the three of us and David Knighton, who stayed with us at weekends, we coped very well with staffing the bars. The layout at the Oak made it possible to serve with less staff than at the Dukes Arms. The L shaped bar counter meant you could serve both rooms from a central position, whereas the Duke had three separate counters.

Our first requirements were for kitchen and waiting staff. We decided to keep Elio for the time being so the initial food was purposely kept simple. One day Elio had a visit from a friend of Marie's, an Italian lady named Mrs Bandini; her English was not as good as Marie's but far better than Elio's. Sylvia asked her if she knew anyone who wanted a kitchen job and, as luck would have it, Mrs Bandini did. She was an Italian version of Kath Forscutt, the wrong side of 60 but a tremendous worker who never ever let us down, and had the added advantage that she could act as a go-between with Elio.

Sylvia was getting up at 5.30 a.m. preparing the residents' breakfasts, and before that, calling them with a tray of tea. Initially she was also the breakfast waitress, and when we had a full house she was having difficulty coping. Barbara was starting at 6.30 a.m. cleaning the bars before moving upstairs to act as chambermaid. She too was feeling the strain so Mrs Bandini was able to help Sylvia cook the breakfasts before assisting Barbara upstairs.

You may wonder what I was doing all this time, and you wouldn't be the first. I was night porter and very often stayed up late serving residents, sometimes till early morning. On more than a few occasions, I was still be serving drinks when Sylvia came down to do the morning teas. During Towcester race meetings, it was quite common for residents to ask if they could have a refund for not using their beds! Racing teams testing at Silverstone, in the days when motor racing was an enjoyable pastime, often stayed up late, as would the drivers. I once stayed drinking with Piers Courage until 2 a.m. the night before he drove in the British Grand Prix. Those were the days.

Our next staff acquisition was another gem. Betty Walters had recently moved to the area from Poole. Her husband was a well-paid scientist at Plessey and she had no need to work, but she was bored staying at home. Betty had gained her experience as a waitress working at the Royal Bath Hotel in Bournemouth as a young girl. We had started employing older schoolgirls as part-time waitresses and Betty proved an excellent tutor, instructing them in the duties of a silver service waitress. There must be many women still working as waitresses in the Towcester area who first learnt their skills from Betty. Her ability enabled Sylvia to concentrate on the kitchen side of the business and Elio in particular.

He was a very willing worker and was keen to learn more about his trade. One problem we had was overcoming the bad habits he had acquired along the way, mainly to do with hygiene. He had been taught to spit into fat or oil to determine its temperature. I know this is a common practice throughout the trade but Elio would delight in bringing it from great depths. We had to eat his prepared food and found it very offputting.

Sylvia got very irate with him and, on occasions, hit him with kitchen cloths. When admonished his face resembled a Labrador dog that had been shouted at. Mr Bandini's regular expression was, "No, no, Elio, Madame she no like it, smack you heavy." He was an impulsive picker of food, continuously eating while working, if he was stripping the meat off a cooked chicken, half would go in his mouth. His worst habit, and one which I threatened him with dismissal over, was his habit of going to the fridge and grabbing handfuls of prawns, then cramming them into his mouth. Apart from the hygiene aspect, the cost was getting out of hand.

Lady Hesketh, the mother of the present Lord, had a very good Italian chef in Mario. He had been head chef at the Talk of the Town nightclub in London, and, due to health problems, brought on by the work pressure, left to take up a less stressful position, albeit temporary. Together with George the butler, they were regular customers and I told him of our problems with Elio. Mario was in his late 30s and Elio hero-worshipped him, so anything that Mario spoke to him about was instantly noted. I told Mario that unless Elio improved, both in ability and cleanliness, we would have no alternative but to dismiss him. Although the conversation between them was in Italian, the effect on Elio left us in no doubts. He burst into tears and rushed upstairs to his room with Mario and Mr Bandini following close behind him. All it needed was the presence of Gina Lolobrigida, and we would have had a proper Italian farce.

Whatever was said it had the desired effect. They returned to the kitchen and, on Mario's prompting, Elio said, "Me no spit in pot, Mrs, me no eat food, Mrs, me good chef like Mario!" Mario explained that he told him we were disgusted with his dirty habits and good chefs never eat while working. He went on to say that he was prepared to give Elio tuition and, if he learnt quickly, would we continue to employ him? It was about that time Elio discovered the delights of drinking cider, so I went and got him a pint then we all shook hands and from that day Elio was a new man.

One day a young chap arrived at reception and asked if he could see Mr Hackett. Mother came to me and said a parson wanted to see me. He wore a white turtle necked sweater that mother had mistaken for a parson's collar. This apart, I could well understand her thinking he was from the church, which in some respects he was. He was 6' 4" tall, thin as a rake, wore horn rimmed spectacles and had a mop of unruly curly hair. He spoke with a soft educated accent and said he had come for the barman's job advertised at the local Labour Exchange.

I would like to name his parents; sufficient to say they were titled and not immediately local. Tony had indeed spent a year training for the ministry, but, being discovered in a situation that was then illegal, it resulted in expulsion from his theological college. He was perfectly frank with us and said he would fully understand if we didn't give him the job.

He travelled six miles on his bicycle to work each day whatever the weather, and never once was he late. He was an excellent conversationalist who could speak on a variety of subjects, was excessively polite to the customers and in all respects the perfect barman. He told us that Canon Curtis, the local vicar, knew his parents and the circumstances behind his change of career, but Curtis never let on that he knew him.

Douglas Curtis was one of our most regular customers; he would pop in at various times of the day for a half-pint of bitter, and again early most evenings. It was unfortunate for him that a programme called *All Gas and Gaiters*, an ecclesiastical TV comedy starring amongst others, Derek Nimmo, was very popular at the time. Douglas spoke similarly to that rather comical sing song voice used by Derrick Nimmo It made him appear snobbish, but he was a good friend and one of our earliest supporters.

When we first arrived at Towcester, we were quickly made aware of a certain supercilious clan who lost no time in telling us that if we looked after them, they would look after us. We later learned that they had played a major role in the downfall of the previous tenants, and, in fact, the tenants before that. Their loud voices and exaggerated accents kept a lot of people away from the Oak. At full strength, they numbered twelve though from the noise they made, often sounded more like twice that number. Their main form of communication involved using the word "darling" as frequently as possible. All in all, they were a pain in the backside and I was determined to get rid of them as soon as possible.

Customers and characters

Alan was the manager of Philadelphus Jeyes, the local chemists, and a very mild mannered gentleman. He needed to be, living with Kate. When we first arrived at the Oak, she had bright red hair that changed colour at regular intervals, and was an alcoholic, a chain smoker and perhaps a smoker of something else. Not a lot was known about her background, other than she once lived at Lambourne where she bred racehorses. She often spoke about "the servants". Now all that was past history – and she was left with Alan, her personal slave.

It was a traumatic moment when Alan lost his job due, it was said, to discrepancies in his drugs register. They had to vacate the flat above the chemists, and moved to a house in the town. Kate died a few years later and Alan married the owner of an electrical repair shop in the town.

Other morning customers who were eager for me to ban the "darlings" included Mr Morris, a retired bank manager, his son John, a sports reporter on the local rag, later to become the Secretary of the British Boxing Board of Control for many years. Another customer was Commander Lawrence Rich, RN (rtd) a true gentleman and war hero, together with his charming wife.

Mr B, the manager of one of our local banks, was always our earliest customer for the first of his many aperitifs. Throughout the course of a morning, he paid us frequent visits drinking the best part of a bottle of dry Martini. Most days he took a bottle of gin away with him. He lived above the bank in a flat that he shared with numerous caged birds.

After we had been at the Oak for nine months, I noticed a commotion at the bank early one morning, and a ladder being placed against an upstairs window. Mr B had failed to open the door to let the staff in and it proved impossible to raise him. We next saw an ambulance arrive and Mr B was brought out on a stretcher and placed in the back. Some time later Mr B's mother, who lived in a nearby village, came across and told me her son had been found in an alcoholic coma and was taken to hospital. She asked if I would go across and clear out some empty bottles.

I took a couple of boxes to put them in and followed her up the stairs. The sight that greeted me was unbelievable. One room was full of built-in cages that contained birds of many species, budgerigars, canaries, love birds, cockatiels and finches. Many lay dead and decomposing in the bottom of the cage and sprouting birdseed covered the room floor. In his bedroom were numerous tin beer trays piled high with cigarette ends and enough empty gin and martini bottles to fill ten cases.

His mother asked if I knew anyone who would take the birds away. My colleague, Ivor Denny who had an aviary in his pub garden, came and collected them, 26 in total. He estimated that the remains of a further 15 littered the bottom of the cage. We never saw Mr B again though his mother told us he spent a week in hospital, followed by a long period in a clinic. He was a very nice man and we were very sorry for him. His mother said the drink problem had been with him for a number of years and had been exacerbated by pressure from the bank head office, all of which led to him having a mental breakdown.

Jeremy and Sharni Grey had a spice factory based in an old mill in the village of Slapton, just outside the town. They were a lovely couple and Sharni, Indian by birth, was noted for the food she served at barbecues held at their beautiful house. Most of the food had an exquisite spicy flavour, and to get an invitation to their barbecues was a sign you had arrived on the local social scene. Sadly, Jeremy died at a very young age a few years later.

Albert Kightley was a retired gas fitter: his face had more creases than a dried prune. Originally from London, if you met him in Cornwall his craggy face and complexion would suggest he had spent a lifetime at sea. His wife had died shortly before we arrived at the Oak, and he decided he was going to see the world before he too died. In the next few years, he enjoyed many cruises and, just before his sudden death, he was eagerly planning his next one. A lovely chirpy little chap, he was greatly missed by the "morning crowd".

Mr Winn was a gentlemen's outfitter and bespoke tailor. His tiny corner shop opposite the Oak was a complete fashion statement. You could buy the latest fashionable Daks suit or a pair of 1930s' suspenders. At noon every day he would shuffle across the road for his tot, ignoring all oncoming traffic and shouts from his wife reminding him not to stay too long. He was a very dapper little man who looked and walked like a veteran Charlie Chaplin. His daily ration was three scotches with half-pint beer chasers. His return journey took half as long as the outward one. The eventual closure of his shop left a big hole in the town's facilities.

The Reverend Fred Smith, vicar of Silverstone, was a Scotsman who loved good company, and the odd drop even more so. Fred was a real character; he rarely wore his dog collar which helped when he was involved in his many arguments with strangers. A chain smoker and raconteur, his tales encouraged listeners to insist he had "just one more nip". How he managed to drive home was a mystery.

Jason Roberson, a true gentleman and proprietor of H E Roberson & Son Ltd, Ironmongers. Jason started working for his father in the 1930s and retired in 1979 in a shop that simply oozed old-fashioned standards. On all the occasions I visited the shop to buy items; I never once stumped Jason or his willing staff with my request. It may have taken time and it often did, but they always found what I wanted. The last time I bought a single six-inch nail was at Jason's. He was the chairman of the Chamber of Trade and a very active Scoutmaster. Jason was not a regular drinker but was often enticed in by fellow tradesmen.

In those days, all the shops in the town closed for lunch, and more Chamber of Trade business was conducted at lunchtime in the Brave Old Oak than at their monthly meetings. Apart from the above people, lunchtime sessions often included all or some of the following: -

Derek Hughes, jeweller and watch repairer, Derek Leeding, bespoke shoe shop owner, Jack Everson, postmaster and ex-professional footballer, David Henshaw, estate agent, John Newman, grocer, Ken Orme, bank manager, James Arnold, solicitor, Mrs Downing, haute couturière, Dave the bookie, Ken Sketchley, grocer, George Skey, grocer, Michael Green, antique dealer, Bill Williams, coal merchant, Diane Rush, haberdashery, Bill Gordon, café owner, Norman Teer, plumbing supplies, Bob Freeborough, baker and milkman, Wilf & Don Derby, garage proprietors, Mick Dunkley, taxi owner, Bernard Cross, shoe shop, David Hunt, manager of Wiggins coal merchants, Talbot Morgan, seedsman and nurseryman, David Groome, garage owner, Ian McCullough, manager of the local mill, Tom Matthews, blacksmith, Bob and Maureen Bruce, good friends and even better customers. Like-wise Jim Baker a great conversationalist – when sober – George and Cyril Buckland, amongst other things, collectors of antique cars and fire engines, Dick Higham, Ian Hetherington, a Guinness representative who lived in the town. He rarely conducted any business after 12 noon. Ian's brother was Sir Peter Hetherington who at the time was Director of Public Prosecutions, John Goodwin, solicitor, who later left to set up the Crown Prosecution Service at Liverpool, and many local farmers.

Any list of lunchtime customers would not be complete without the name of Harry Williams. Along with Jason, Harry was Mr Towcester, a walking history of the town. One of my most enlightening experiences at Towcester was when Harry took me up the church tower to help him with his regular task of winding the clock. The view from the tower enabled me to see parts of the town I never knew existed. He wound the clock until 1982 when it was electrified, Harry was then 80. Although a member of the local coal merchant's family, Harry was the secretary at an engineering firm on the outskirts of the town, who made milling equipment. He cycled to the pub each lunchtime for his glass of Guinness. Even when he suffered a stroke, he still came for his Guinness which he drank through a straw.

I shall always be grateful to Harry for introducing me to Mr George Law, a shoemaker in the town. I felt very honoured to shake the hand of the man who made running shoes worn by famous athletes. His many clients included Chris Chataway, Chris Brasher, Gordon Pirie, Harold Whitlock, Lord Burghley and the most famous of all, Roger Bannister. Roger was wearing a pair of George's shoes when he ran the first four-minute mile in 1954. George was still making shoes up to his death in 1969 at the age of 89.

Harry had the most beautiful handwriting and it was always a pleasure for Sylvia to receive her birthday card from him. Each year it contained a different verse of his own making, written with a quill pen in exquisite script. He died in 1994 aged 92.

As it turned out, I didn't have to ban the "obnoxious crowd". Not long after we arrived, they split up, due I think, to matrimonial shenanigans among them. It was always difficult to work out just who was married to whom!

All is not gold that glitters

With the completion of the re-decoration and refurbishing, trade started to increase in all departments. We took on another waitress, Jean, and three more barmaids, Sue, Pat and Mary. Elio was improving under Mario's tuition and we were able to expand the choice of food on the menu.

We opened up the buffet bar at lunchtimes; this was one of our best moves. The food served at the Plessey staff canteen left a lot to be desired, and we started getting many of their office staff in for food. It was very hectic as they only had 45 minutes in which to be served with food and drink before returning to work. We were averaging 75 to 100 snacks each day, and Sylvia employed Mr Guy's daughter, Ursula, to live in and help out at the buffet bar.

Elio also needed more help in the kitchen and we obtained it from a most unlikely source. In the village of Tiffield on the outskirts of the town, was a boys' approved school. A lot of the boys came from broken homes, but all had been in trouble with the law for one reason or another. Although run by our local authority, most of the inmates came from other areas, their own authorities paid their fees.

The boys were trained in catering, horticulture and building trades, and had extremely well equipped, modern facilities. The instructor to pupil ratio was far in excess of a normal school, consequently the boys received a very good training. I had recently been elected a member of The Hotel & Catering Institute, the leading trade standards organisation. The head asked me if I would like to serve as an assessor at the examinations taken by the boys on completion of their training. This brought me into contact with the instructors, and through them, I learnt that the boys were encouraged to obtain temporary local employment, prior to their release.

Usually this was daytime work until 6 p.m. as they were "locked up" at night. I said I was prepared to employ two boys but needed them until 9.30 p.m. when we ceased serving food. The head agreed providing Sylvia or myself drove them back to the school on completion of their shift. For the next year this arrangement worked perfectly, and we had numerous boys, aged between 15 and 17, working as Elio's assistants. We did have one blip, however, that threatened to end our partnership with the school. So that the older boys could work later at weekends, the head gave special dispensation for them to stay overnight.

I was working down the cellar on a Saturday morning, when I noticed a flash of something shiny between the empty beer cases. Closer inspection revealed it was the gold cap on a bottle of Teachers whisky. It had obviously been hidden there to be retrieved later, but the problem was by whom. Elio, Ursula, and two Tiffield boys were living in that weekend, also we had John the kitchen porter and Mr Bandini in the kitchen, Betty and Jean as waitresses and Tony with Sue in the bar. All were under suspicion.

We had a very large police station in the town and most of the

CID personnel were very good customers. I asked one of them, Tony Skerratt, what I should do and he went away and came back with a bottle of powder. He dusted the bottle with the powder, and explained that when someone touched it, after a short period, the moisture on their hands would turn the powder into a bright green dye.

The next morning the whisky bottle had gone and the banister was covered in green dye. Numerous handprints led to the Tiffield boys' room. One of the boy's hands was bright green. We had found our thief. In his bag was the whisky bottle together with numerous letters. He said the bottle was taken when Elio sent him to the wine cellar on the Saturday morning. He had hidden the bottle where I found it, and retrieved it that evening while we were all having a late drink. Letters in his bag from his mother, living in Coventry, revealed why he took it. In one, she said she was pleased he was still working at the hotel. She was looking forward to his next leave, and if he had an opportunity, would he get her *another* bottle of "comfort for her nerves".

He admitted to taking a bottle previously and the head disciplined him by adding a further three months to his sentence. It was a very upsetting experience. We liked the lad, as did the staff, but he had put them all under suspicion and betrayed our trust. The head told us it was due to pressure from his mother that initially caused him to steal, and result in his sentence. She didn't deserve to have a son like William who was basically a nice lad.

Under normal circumstances, his misdemeanour should have resulted in all boys being withdrawn from outside work. However, in view of the circumstances and my not pressing police charges, our arrangement continued. The worst part of the whole episode was the damage done to the walls by that dye. The redecoration cost ten times the whisky!

The arrangement with Tiffield School finally ended a year later. It was Grand Prix weekend, things were very hectic, and one of the boys had to return to the school that night. He could see that Sylvia and I were extremely busy and said that if he could borrow our eldest son's bicycle, he would get himself back to the school. I telephoned the head and he gave his permission. We never saw the boy or our son's bicycle again! The head was reprimanded for letting the boy return to the school unaccompanied, and it brought to an abrupt end what had been a very satisfactory arrangement for both parties.

Silverstone, the home of Grand Prix racing

Our very first Grand Prix at the Brave Old Oak was the 1969 and 14th event to be held at Silverstone Circuit, four miles away. We had been warned about how busy we would be, but nothing could have prepared us for what took place. GP week started on the Sunday before the event the following Saturday. Old hotel records showed that in the past, Mike Hawthorn, Pedro Gonzalez, Reg Parnell, Roy Salvadori, Peter Collins, Graham Hill and Innis Ireland had all stayed.

Accommodation was booked from one year to the next but because of the problems experienced the previous year, most of our residents were new to the hotel. However, reports regarding the quality of our rooms soon spread around the motor racing circus and we had our share of celebrities. We had Jo Bonnier driving for the Lotus team and Piers Courage driving for the Brabham team both staying with us. Those were the days when seeing Grand Prix drivers walking round the town was a common sight. All drivers stayed in the area, there was no flying backwards and forwards to London and the Continent. However, it was not long before a combination of traffic chaos and the emergence of helicopter travel meant all would soon change.

The town was overrun with racing supporters from all over the world, and we found ourselves having people sleeping overnight on the floor in both bars. New Zealanders, Denny Hulme, Bruce McLaren and Chris Amon were driving in the GP, and had a large following of their compatriots. For some reason we seemed to be the HQ and watering hole for all the antipodeans in England, that week. We sold as much lager as we normally sold in a year. I had three brewery deliveries to meet the demand. We experienced many other major racing car and motorcycle events during our term at the Oak, but nothing ever reached the trading heights of that year.

For the record, Jackie Stewart won the race, Piers Courage was 5th and Jo Bonnier retired. Piers Courage booked rooms for the 1970 *Daily Express* International, (there was no GP at Silverstone that year), where he finished 3rd to Jackie Stewart. In addition, he booked for the 1971 Grand Prix. Very sadly, he was killed during the 1970 Dutch Grand Prix. He was a great guy and lived life to the full.

We cut our ties with the Duke

Trade continued to increase all the while, although beer sales never reached the phenomenal barrelage achieved at The Dukes Arms. Even so, at the end of our first year we had averaged six barrels a week. Spirit sales compared with Woodford were ten fold and wine sales in the restaurant were showing a steady increase.

It was now obvious that we would be staying at Towcester, and I informed the brewery that we would give up The Dukes Arms as soon as they wished. Our time at the Oak had been so hectic that we had neglected Woodford shamefully. Looking back, we felt very guilty that the pub that had given us so much and put us on the road to success, had to take second place to our new venture. With hindsight, it would have been far better for our old customers, if we had made a clean break from The Duke when we first went to Towcester. Having said our goodbyes once before made it an anticlimax the second time. I think most friends and customers knew we wouldn't be back in residence. Many of them had been to Towcester and realised the extra opportunities The Brave Old Oak offered would win the day.

Gordon and Betty didn't want to take it on as a tenancy. Gordon had carried on with his job during the year, and with bringing up two young girls, it was really too much for them. I went back for the transfer of the licence, and, standing in the courtroom brought back so many memories of the day I stood there with Ernie Goodman. Colonel Stopford-Sackville thanked me for the way we had run The Dukes Arms and Carey Wilson had a tremor in his voice when he wished me well for the future. He died within the next year. I did not think a lot to the new tenants. They were too flash.

Joe Burgess, Esq

I first met Joe Burgess when I was at The Dukes Arms. He, like Jack Smith, had also been a leather representative. With Charles Clore massacring the shoe trade, Joe, like many of his colleagues, became redundant. At the age of 57, not a lot of new avenues of employment were open. He obtained a job selling accessories to ladies and gents hairdressers, and it was whilst calling on Ted Templeman at Woodford, that I was introduced to him.

Joe was an authority on cricket, soccer (mostly the Corinthian Casuals) and church music. He was a friend to many, including Sir Neville Cardus and John Arlott. He had developed his love of church music as a young man, from his friendship with Sir Edward Elgar. He once told me his idea of heaven, was watching Tom Graveney bat on Worcester Cricket Ground whilst listening to Elgar's *Enigma Variations*. Players from all counties knew Joe, at cricket grounds throughout the land.

Joe first introduced me to the Corinthian Casuals Football Club (CC) when I went with him to a dinner in London. It was there that I met, among others, Sir John Waldron, Commissioner of the Metropolitan Police, a 6' 6" ex-centre half, Denis and Leslie Compton, Jimmy Hill, Doug Insole, Richard Hutton, Bob Willis, Graham Roope, Hugh Doggart, Trevor Bailey, Ken Barrington and Mickey Stewart all past and present CC players and Jim Swanton, Brian Johnston and John Arlott, the cricket commentators.

I joined the Casuals that night and was proud to wear their

chocolate & pink striped tie. Corinthian Casuals, an amalgamation of The Corinthians and The Casuals Football Clubs, were first formed in 1874 and is the only football club whose coat of arms is registered at the Royal College of Heralds. In 1887, they went on tour to South America, which is why so many football clubs on that continent are named after them.

I took Joe to numerous CC games in London and on one occasion was introduced to W C T (Tadge) Webster, an old CC player, who was to be the President of the Marylebone Cricket Club (MCC) the following year. He agreed to propose me for membership of the MCC, Doug Insole, who later became the Secretary, seconded my application and five years later in 1976 I became a member of the most prestigious cricket club in the world.

Joe and I together attended every test match at Lords Cricket Ground for many years. More recently, I accompany my three sons to the Saturday's play of each Test match. Whereas Joe and I spent the lunch interval walking round the ground, meeting and talking to the many celebrities known to Joe, my sons treat me to a lunch in the Warner Stand. Good as it is, it cannot compare with the pleasure I had meeting the brothers Alec and Eric Bedser, G O "Gubby" Allen, Dennis Compton, Leslie Ames, Len Hutton, Bill Bowes, Willie Watson, Cyril Washbrook, Freddie Brown, Garry Sobers and Jack Ikin. I particularly remember Joe introducing me to the great Learie Constantine – later Lord – who captained the West Indies before the war.

Nine months after relinquishing the tenancy of The Dukes Arms, we engaged the best member of staff we ever employed.

Steven Walsh, an Irishman was then about 26 years old. He had attended Blackrock College in Dublin, and was a most competent barman, waiter and chef. He had worked alongside the new tenants of The Dukes Arms at a hotel in London. When they left to take the Duke, Stephen went with them to help run it. Things didn't work out, and after nine months, the new tenants were bankrupt and Steven was out of a job. Betty Peck suggested that he approach us regarding a position, and with his experience and training, we had no hesitation in taking him on. His lovely wife, Nora, came with him so we gained a kitchen help as well.

All three staff rooms at the hotel were occupied, and, not wishing to lose Stephen, we bought a six-bedroomed house in the town for £3,500 and turned it into staff accommodation. We immediately put him in charge of the restaurant and he stood in as chef when Elio had his day off. He was a star, popular with all the staff, and, even more important, with the customers. Nora was a lovely girl and a very good worker, but unfortunately, for us, but not for them, she became pregnant after a few weeks so we were shortly to lose her services

It was also about this time that Sylvia decided we should increase our family. Stephen was now 13 and Timothy 10 so there was going to be quite a gap between them. Although she was working just as hard as ever, by having more full-time staff than previously, Sylvia would be able to take things easier than was possible at The Crows Nest. At least that was the plan!

Michael was born in June and Sylvia worked until the day before he was born, starting again the day she came out of hospital. Mr Sellars would have been very pleased with her!

Trade was increasing in all departments, and we were finding it more and more difficult to employ local girls. Plessey offered work to women on a shift basis, e.g. they could work a minimum of four hours a day whenever they wanted. Some worked odd nights when their husbands came home. In 1969, it was impossible for hotels to employ foreign staff. The ridiculous regulation, at that time, allowed them to be employed by hospitals, care homes and as domestics in private houses, but not hotels. One way round the regulations was to employ au pair girls.

Germans invade us

We had a German resident, Mr Schell, staying at the hotel while installing equipment at the Plessey Research Centre. Sylvia was talking to him about our staff problems, and he said he knew a family in Germany who were very keen for their daughters to come to England to improve their English. I wrote to them and received a reply from Bearte their daughter.

Mr Schell had an amusing incident during his stay. On his first morning, he came down early for breakfast and Ursula (Mr Guy's daughter) was on duty in the dining room. Talking to him that evening, Sylvia asked him if everything was to his satisfaction at the hotel. He said he was rather curious about the breakfast served that morning. When Ursula asked, "What would you like?" he said, "Ham & eggs." Ursula went away and came back much later with a plate containing some almonds and figs! In his broken English, Ursula had mistaken his request for "harm und iggs" for almonds and figs.

Almonds were no problem for her, trout & almonds were on the menu, but she panicked over the figs. Mrs Bandini who was working in the kitchen, went home and came back with a jar of green figs in syrup, which she had left over from Christmas. Sylvia asked Mr Schell what he thought of his dish? He smiled and said, "I thought it was to eat while waiting for the proper breakfast." When asked for her version, Ursula said, "I thought it strange, but decided it must be a German's breakfast." Poor girl, she never lived it down.

Bearte was 20 years old. Her father was a professor at Freiburg University and she was the middle one of his three daughters. Her English was very good and her lovely smile made her very popular with our younger male customers. Although officially she was an au pair girl, once a permit had been obtained the authorities never checked on them. She was experienced in all departments, having worked at hotels in Germany during her student days.

We were so pleased with her performance that after a few months we asked if any of her sisters wanted a job. She said her youngest sister wanted one during her school holidays, which lasted from June to September. Sylvia was due to have her baby in June, so we thought it would be perfect for her sister to be a genuine au pair and help look after Michael. Before her sister arrived, Bearte asked if we could also find a job for her sister's friend, Rosa. The room in the staff house contained three single beds so we thought why not.

Victoria, Bearte's sister was 17 years old and 6' 1" tall! Like her sister, the first thing she did after settling in, was to shave her arm pits and chop inches off the bottom of her skirts. A tall raven-haired 17-year-old beauty in a mini skirt was too much for Elio and Steven. Every time they heard her walking along the landing, in her size ten suede desert boots, they would rush to get cleaning materials from a cupboard at the bottom of the stairs. My mother was frightened to death that Victoria might drop Michael. With her height, he certainly wouldn't bounce if she did. Her friend Rosa was another nice girl, 18 years old and the daughter of a solicitor. She too had worked in a hotel before and was very proficient.

So there we were, it seemed as though our staff problems were solved for the time being. We had Elio, Stephen, Nora and the three girls living in, plus Sue, Barbara, and Mary full-time, with Betty, Mrs Bandini, John and the Tiffield boys, part-time.

One evening when Mario and George were in the bar, they asked me about our staff situation, and I said we were fortunate to have the German girls for the summer and so we were OK. George said, "That's a pity because Lady Hesketh has a Spanish under butler, Pepe, who is surplus to her requirements." His older brother was head butler to a family who lived at a large Hall in a village near Stony Stratford, and, if he couldn't obtain another position, he would have to return to Spain. Looking to the future when the girls returned to Germany, we agreed to take him on.

The name Pepe really suited him. He could have been Irish Steven's brother. They were both about 5' 5" tall, dark haired with swarthy complexions. Steven once told me he came from a small town on the west coast of Ireland, where, after the break-up of the Spanish Armada fleet, one of their galleons was wrecked on rocks by his town. The Spaniards raped all the local women and, as a result, ever since then, all males in his village have been small, dark and swarthy. Steven was a great storyteller but I believed his tale to be true.

There was a lot of rivalry between Steven and Pepe. Steven was much more qualified than Pepe and his immediate superior, but because Pepe had worked for Lady Hesketh, he thought he was more "regal"! If he could put one over Steven he was in his element, Steven thought he was a creep!

When on early duties, he would bring a plate of his freshly made biscuits with our morning tea. He said he always made them for Lady H and she said he was the best biscuit maker on her staff. It didn't stop her from letting him go though! Steven liked his drop of Guinness and Pepe loved nothing more than to tell Sylvia that Steven was "drunked". For all their rivalry, Elio, Steven and Pepe worked as a good team, and we happily overlooked any shortcomings.

Varied guests

The week before Michael was born, Worcestershire were playing Northants at the County ground. The team were staying at the Grand Hotel in Northampton, a hotel that had seen better days. Joe Burgess telephoned me at about 9 p.m. to ask if I could do him a favour. The Worcestershire team had returned to the hotel and was told they were too late for any food. He asked if we could supply them with something. I told him to bring them over and that was the first time we met Tom Graveney and Basil D'Olivira. The team arrived and we cooked them all 1½lb T Bone steaks. After a day fielding they were very hungry and all cleaned their plates.

This was the start of a very good relationship with the Worcestershire team, and, as a result, they called in most times they passed through the county. They were a very good side, with Don Kenyon as their captain, and, apart from Tom and Basil, had Norman Gifford, Ron Headley, Van Holder and Glen Turner in the side. Bill Alley, the old Australian player, was one of the umpires for the game, and he came with them. He was one of cricket's great characters and at 1 a.m., when they were leaving, he asked me if I had any food they could take back with them for breakfast.

I went to the fridge and took out a 20lb-cooked turkey, which I wrapped up for them and sent them on their way, a little worse for drink. Next morning, Don Kenyon opened the batting and was out for a duck. Tom told me afterwards that Don was still drunk when he walked to the wicket. A few weeks later, I received a thank-you letter from the team, a signed team photograph, a club plaque and county tie. After the 1975 England v Australia test match, Bill Alley sent me a signed photograph showing him umpiring with the first ever streaker leaping the wicket at Lords. He wrote on the back, "This was the best carcase I have seen, since your turkey!"

It was about this time that after a very hectic drinking session, England and Northamptonshire cricketer Colin Milburn went upstairs to bed early. After his friends unsuccessfully tried to wake him up, I placed two cartridges in my shotgun, and discharged both barrels into the ceiling, directly under his bed. Colin came back down immediately, and I was left with a large hole in my ceiling.

Colin was a regular customer – a claim we shared with many other pubs – and it was a sad loss to English cricket when he lost an eye following a road accident. Even sadder was his early death.

Running a hotel on a main road like the Watling Street meant we had guests from all walks of life, Lords, MPs, and film stars, mechanics and miners, and some quite strange people. A double room in pre-decimal 1971 was £3.10s 0d and single £1 17s 6d. per night. (£3. 50 and £1.75) The average price for a 3-course table d'hôte dinner was 17/6d, and a la carte £1. Bar snacks varied from 5/– to 7/6d (25p and 38p).

Stowe School was four miles away and many parents stayed at the hotel when attending events there. We were always surprised at the extent to which some of them would go to spend as little money as possible. It was quite common for them to smuggle fish & chips into their rooms, rather than pay for a meal in the restaurant. Some asked if they would have to pay extra for their offspring to share a room with them. Most of the boys were aged 12 upwards.

A Stowe parent, who stayed at the hotel on numerous occasions, each time asking for our cheapest single room. She was always very well dressed, and wore lots of jewellery and make up. On her last visit, she asked if we had any objection to her son sharing the room. We told her that all the put-you-ups were in use in other parents' rooms, but we did have a vacant single room he could have. She told us not to worry as she would make other arrangements. When Barbara called her with her morning tea, she was very surprised to see a man sharing her single bed! It turned out to be her 17-year-old son! In some respects, we felt very sorry for her and wondered if it was at all to due to reduced financial circumstances.

We felt equally sorry for a lot of the other parents. In spite of the high fees they were paying for their sons' education, some of the boys had atrocious manners. They were rude to staff and very demanding. Most of them couldn't start a sentence without saying "I say". We had to prohibit five families from staying again, all because of the unruly behaviour of their sons. I often wonder if Richard Branson – an old Stoic – ever stayed at the Oak while we were there.

A man, well known in the financial world, stayed with his wife at the end of each school term. She was, to put it mildly, a stuck up bitch! None of the staff liked serving her. In the restaurant she would complain loudly if Steven didn't personally serve her. The wine was never to her liking, and in the bar she would try and embarrass staff by ordering obscure cocktails.

They wanted breakfast in their room, and it always had to be fresh kippers. Sylvia arranged a delivery from a firm in the Isle of Man when we knew they were coming. One particular weekend, she stayed at the hotel on her own. In the morning, she came to reception, looking extremely embarrassed, and told mother she'd had an accident. Apparently, she had fallen asleep and somehow tipped the plate with the kippers into the bed, and then laid on them. The oil from the fish had penetrated the mattress and ruined it. We sent them a bill for the cost of a new mattress which was eventually paid. They never stayed with us again.

As a contrast, Lady Docker – of the gold Rolls Royce fame – stayed with us on four occasions. She was always extremely polite towards the staff, easy to please, and very generous with tips.

We once received a booking from Arkansas, America, specifically requesting our double-bedded room with a four-poster bed. When the couple arrived, they were both young, very similar in looks, and extremely large people. Steven showed them to their room and came back to tell mother that they were brother and sister. Apparently he noticed the labels on their luggage stated Mr and Miss X. At about midnight, we heard a loud crash and the man came downstairs shortly afterwards to say the bed had broken. I did a temporary repair by putting a beer case in place of the shattered leg. Next morning when they paid their bill, the man apologised for the damage to the bed, and left £2 to pay for it. Mother naively asked him how the bed broke, to which the man replied, "Blame my sister!" He offered no other explanation.

On another occasion, a lady from Cheltenham booked the same room. When she arrived she was accompanied by another lady, both in their mid 40s. The next morning, Barbara proudly displayed a pair of man's underpants she found in their bed!

In our first year, we didn't have a master key for the bedrooms. We had spare keys for each individual room but guests were always taking these away with them.

Leatherby & Christopher, a large London company, were responsible for the bars and catering at Towcester racecourse. They brought a coach load of staff from London, and employed about 30 temporary local staff. I became very good friends with the manager who was in charge of the event. Dave was a South

Londoner who had worked for the company at Wembley Stadium, Wimbledon, Ascot and Henley. He was a lovely cheerful fellow, at 36 the same age as I was. We often went on a tour of local pubs the night before the meeting, on our return, we never went to bed before 1 a.m.

Dave booked in as usual for a race meeting in November but, due to a previous engagement, I would not be there to entertain him.

I had been elected the East Midlands representative to the British Hotel and Restaurant Association. Our monthly meetings were held at the associations HQ in Upper Brook Street, London. The meeting took place in the afternoon and was always followed by a splendid dinner, often at the Café Royal.

I travelled down that morning with Leslie Barton, proprietor of the Angel Hotel in Market Harborough. Leslie was the North Midlands representative, he drove to Towcester, and I drove to London. We usually returned at about 10 p.m. but on this occasion thick fog had delayed us, and we didn't arrive back at Towcester until well past midnight. Pepe and Steven were still up but Sylvia had gone to bed. Because of the fog, Leslie stayed the night, and after a nightcap together, we both retired. Next morning Sylvia said Dave had been very agitated and kept asking if I'd returned. He went to his room at 11 p.m. asking Sylvia to call him if I returned before midnight.

Nurden & Peacock's Cash & Carry had opened a branch in Northampton and Dave's company had an account with them. It was quite common for him to go there for supplies before going to the course. When he didn't come down for his breakfast, Sylvia thought that because he had gone to bed earlier than usual, he had decided to go to Cash & Carry first. At 10 a.m. he hadn't returned so I tried his room. Finding the door still locked I assumed he had probably left money in the room and had taken the key with him. This was common practice for Dave. At 11 a.m. his assistant came down from the racecourse wanting to see him. He needed the cash floats and the staff was waiting for supplies. I tried his room again and then phoned for Tony Skerrat to come down from the Police Station.

Tony gained access with a credit card and Dave was lying on the floor. Empty tablet bottles were strewn on the bed, and it was obvious he had taken an overdose. Dave was still alive but unconscious and we called an ambulance. He never recovered consciousness and died on the way to hospital.

Sylvia and I both attended the inquest. His wife, whom we had never met before, gave evidence saying they had no financial worries and enjoyed a very happy marriage. She was a lovely person, just how I expected Dave's wife to be. His employers said there were no problems from their side, and his death was a big loss to the company. Two of his colleagues who had driven up from London with him, said he was laughing and joking quite normally during the journey. The coroner returned an open verdict, saying there was no clear evidence that Dave intended to kill himself.

To this day, both Sylvia and I contemplate what might have happened had I returned earlier from London. She didn't tell the Coroner that Dave was agitated that night, but we both wonder what caused his agitation. Could I have helped with any problem he had? He was a charming person and was missed by all who knew him. The whole sad business retains an air of mystery.

Because of our experience with Dave's room, we had all new locks fitted with master keys. Again, we wondered: if we had reached Dave sooner, could we have saved him?

The Forsyte Saga was the most popular series on television during that period. The parents of Margaret Tyzack, who played the part of Winifred Dartie, lived at Plumb Park on the outskirts of Towcester. Her younger sister was getting married locally, and that weekend we had a hotel full of celebrities. Kenneth More, Nyree Dawn Porter and Eric Porter from the cast and June Whitfield and Kenneth Williams were but a few of those attending.

Well after midnight, they started to play party games. One game involved the men leaving the bar, and then six ladies lifted their dresses, bared their bottoms and knelt on the seats facing the wall. Another lady proceeded to draw a face on each bottom with considerable skill. The men were then let back into the bar, and had to guess whose face was on which bottom.

Pepe walked through the bar while all this was happening and almost suffered a heart attack. He soon recovered and rushed to tell Elio and Steven of his good fortune. Some weeks later, he tried to involve the German girls in a similar game! Most of the wedding guests looked very much the worse for wear at breakfast, but all said they had enjoyed their stay and would return.

People from all over the world came to Plessey at Towcester, mainly to the Alan Clark Research Centre at Caswell.

During the war, the government set up an electronics research establishment at a place known as Caswells Farm on the outskirts of the town. I understood the reason for selecting this site was to avoid detection by enemy aircraft. From the air, it still had the appearance of normal farm buildings. Most of the scientists put down roots in the area, and, after the war, the establishment was taken over by the Plessey Company.

The two factories in the town made microprocessors and other components for the electronics industry; satellite companies were set up in different parts of the world. It was in conjunction with this overseas business, that we had six Romanians, five men and a woman, stay at the hotel for a month. We were told the woman was a political official, sent so that the men didn't stray from the party line. The five men slept in the family room – one double two single beds, and a put-you-up – and the woman had a double en suite to herself.

Plessey paid all their accounts, and no restrictions were placed on what they could order in the restaurant. We were told they would have to pay for any drinks from the bar, but after dinner, they all retired to the family room. By then, we had installed televisions in the bedrooms. They kept very much to themselves and never had any contact with the other residents or customers.

One morning Barbara told Sylvia that their room had a strange smell that she couldn't place. Sylvia went to investigate and discovered that in a chest of drawers were large salami type sausages. The oil or fat from the sausage had leeched into the drawers and this was causing the smell. Through the Plessey interpreter, Sylvia explained to them that this was not permitted and in future all food would have to be kept in a refrigerator in the kitchen. She then left them to discuss the problem with the interpreter. He returned to say that the Romanians did not like English food and if they were not allowed to have food in their room, they would return to their own country. It was clear we had the makings of a diplomatic incident on our hands. What made it particularly hard to believe was the fact that they ordered large steaks at dinner every evening and Steven said there was never anything left on their plates.

Plessey, as a company, were our best customers and most of the local management and their wives regularly used the hotel. We didn't want to do anything to cause them embarrassment, but we felt we had to be firm. The smell was beginning to waft along the landings, becoming very unpleasant.

The impasse was finally resolved by Plessey buying a fridge which was installed in their room. It was curious that after the fridge arrived, apart from the sausage it was always full of Romanian wine and brandy. Where it came from was a mystery. But we were soon to find out.

After the incident, they seemed to thaw out and we got to know them much better. On the rare occasions when the woman was absent, they could be quite jovial. They were still staying with us at Christmas, though they spent Christmas Eve, Christmas Day and Boxing Day at their embassy in London.

In 1971, licensed premises were not granted an extension of hours for the New Year. It was not considered a "special enough occasion" to warrant one. We closed as normal that particular year and organised a buffet supper for residents and staff. What I remember most about that New Year was at midnight, Sylvia, mother and I were the only English people present.

We had the six Romanians, three American and two Australian residents, three German girls, Steven and Nora from Ireland, Pepe from Spain, Elio, Mrs Bandini and husband from Italy and John the kitchen porter from Scotland. Quite the United Nations!

The Romanians sang national folk songs, Elio, and Steven, who both had good voices, chipped in with their own renditions. To toast the New Year, the Romanians produced some bottles of their brandy – it was rank, and I told Elio to ask them as best he could, "Where did you get it?" It seemed it was delivered weekly to Plessey, together with the sausage, from their embassy in London.

They returned to their country the following week, but before they left, they went to London and returned loaded with Marks & Spencer carrier bags, at least ten each. In a very nice gesture, they presented Sylvia and me with a lovely cut glass vase.

Unwanted changes

Early in the New Year, Elio announced that his wife was coming to England from Italy! This caused quite a stir because no one knew he was married. What made it even more remarkable was he had never met his wife! Mario explained that Elio came from a village high in the mountainous area of Northern Italy, and, in that region, it was possible to have a marriage by proxy if both families agreed. Elio was a good-looking lad who always had an eye for the ladies. Sylvia took him to Northampton station to meet the train bringing his new wife.

Palmina was short, plump and not at all attractive. Sylvia said she thought Elio was going to burst into tears when he first set eyes on her. When they arrived at the hotel, Elio went straight to his room and left her standing at reception. It was very embarrassing for all concerned. Fortunately, Mrs Bandini had waited for Palmina's arrival and was able to talk to her until Sylvia was able to get Elio to come downstairs. It was obvious he had been crying which made Palmina even more depressed.

Sylvia gave her a job in the kitchen but it never really worked out; Elio would rarely talk to her. He changed from being a cheerful character to a morose, sulking type. He started drinking a lot and one day Palmina came down for work sporting a black eye. Pepe thought the whole episode was a hilarious joke and his antics did nothing to improve the relationship.

It therefore came as a complete shock when one day Elio told Sylvia that Palmina was pregnant! She had only been in the country a couple of months and, in fact, the baby was born nine months and two weeks after she arrived. We all hoped that the baby would improve their relationship with each other, but if anything, it worsened. Elio was very proud of his son but was drinking more and more. Eventually Elio decided to return to Italy, having worked for us for six years. We were very sorry to see him go. His skill as a chef had improved out of all recognition, and Elio, Steven and Pepe had worked well as a team.

Steven took over as chef while we advertised for a replacement for Elio. Over a six-month period, we had five chefs. Three came from agencies to whom we had to pay commission equal to one week's salary. All were useless. Two were complete alcoholics; one lasted just a day. It was disaster all-round. In the end, much to our relief, Steven took over the position as chef. He didn't really want to do it permanently, but he was a good chef and we increased his salary accordingly. Pepe, who had become a very competent waiter, was put in charge of the restaurant and we were back on an even keel once more.

I meet his Lordship

When we had been at the Brave Old Oak for a few weeks, I was serving behind the bar one morning when I heard a screech of brakes and saw a car stop halfway across the pavement by our main entrance. A few minutes later a youth came in and asked for a half of bitter. When he returned to his seat, he sat with his feet on a stool. I went over and told him to remove his feet off the stool, which he grudgingly did. A few minutes later I noticed his feet were back on the stool, so this time I told him to drink up and leave. That was the first time I met Lord Alexander Hesketh. Fortunately this animosity was not to last and we were to become good friends.

Easton Neston House, then the home of Lady Hesketh and her three sons, is situated at the rear of the Brave Old Oak. In the stables of the house, Alexander formed a team that started building racing cars which were to become the talk of the racing world. The climax was winning the important 1974 International Trophy meeting at Silverstone followed by the Dutch Grand Prix in 1975.

The Brave Old Oak was the unofficial HQ of the Hesketh Racing Team. At any one time you were likely to find the team Patron Lord Hesketh, the designer Harvey Postlewaite, team manager "Bubbles" Horsley, driver James Hunt, and all the mechanics, design and office staff standing at the bar. All the other customers were influenced by the team's progress and celebrated their success.

When the team won in Holland, Alex telephoned me and said, "We shall be back at Towcester in the early hours of the morning, will you stay open for us?" There was no need to ask. When he walked in carrying the trophy, the bar was full of supporters who erupted with applause. The celebrations lasted for days.

The Hesketh Racing team were probably the last Formula 1 team to treat racing as an enjoyable pastime. This was, in no small way, due to the exuberance of James Hunt. In his all too short life, he lived it to the full and broke all my barmaids' hearts.

It was unfortunate that the ever-increasing cost of maintaining a Formula 1 racing team was beyond even the funds of his Lordship, and the following year the racing team folded. They carried on for a while building cars for other teams and then changed over to building motorcycles. It was a very sad day for the town and in particular, The Brave Old Oak. Hesketh Racing had brought fame to the town and a breath of fresh air to the hotel.

Motor Racing Stables was the forerunner of the Jim Russell

Racing School, which still operates from Silverstone Circuit. Its purpose was to teach aspiring young drivers the intricacies of motor racing. The training initially took place in TVR sports cars and then went on to single-seater Formula Fords. The MRS main school was based at Brands Hatch, and the instructors came to Silverstone most weekends during the winter. They always stayed at the Oak, as did their pupils.

The boss was Marc Anthony, a real smoothie, with Instructors, Gerry Corbett, Jock Dalziell, Peter Baxingdale, Bernard Unett, Tony Dron and Martin Blackie. Martin became a very good friend and went on to achieve success in the Club Sports Car championships. His selection of sponsor however, was a rather unfortunate choice. The company sponsoring him was called Peter Humble Ltd and the logo on Martin's car said "HUMBLE BLACKIE". I somehow doubt whether it would be allowed in today's pc world! Bernard Unett in his 1300 Hillman Avenger was to make the 1300 Class in the British Saloon Car Championship, his own in the 1970s. Thanks to the lads, both Sylvia and I had the pleasure of driving one of their single-seater Fords round Silverstone Grand Prix circuit.

Nottingham Sports Car Club was the main organiser of club racing at Silverstone. Their Secretary and organiser, Betty Shaw, was the dominant force behind the club. I don't think she would be offended if I said Betty was a "larger" than life character. Before Formula 1 teams established workshops at Silverstone and used the circuit daily for testing, apart from the Grand Prix, club racing was the circuit's main source of income. If, and when, the history of Silverstone Circuit is written, Betty must feature prominently.

Other clubs to make the hotel their Silverstone HQ were The MG Owners Club, Aston Martin OC, Bentley OC, Lagonda OC, 750 MC, Vintage Sports Car Club and The Jenson OC.

I took my two eldest sons, Stephen and Timothy, to the circuit on many occasions. Grandstand seats and Paddock Transfers for the three of us cost a total of £10. One grandstand seat today costs more than £100. The boys walked all round the paddock, asking drivers for their autographs, and having a close look at the racing cars. It was a small boy's paradise.

I was a member of the Silverstone Club. This was a licensed club where you could go for a drink and something to eat during meetings. When racing was taking place on the club circuit (a shortened course), it was possible to watch it from the clubhouse windows. Membership of the club was £4 a year and on weekly club nights, members could drive their road cars round the circuit for three laps at a time. All good fun.

The British Racing Drivers Club owned the circuit and its President, The Hon Gerald Lascelles, the Track Manager, Jimmy Brown and Secretary, Anthony Salmon were regular visitors to the hotel. Other motor racing celebrities and aficionados who frequently stayed at the Brave Old Oak included Colin Chapman, Graham Hill, Jack Brabham, Barry Sheene, Roger Clark, Gunnar Nilsson, Raymond Baxter, Lord Montague, Viscount Downe with his magnificent Aston Martin gracing our car park, and staff of the Grand Prix Mobile Medical Unit who always stayed with us.

Non racing celebrities who stayed at the Oak included TV host Hughie Green, war hero Douglas Bader, comedians Les Dawson and Bob Monkhouse, politicians Lord George Brown, Airey Neave, who was blown up by an IRA bomb, and Enoch Powell. Writer Graham Greene, actress's Pat Phoenix from *Coronation Street*, Noelle Gordon from *Crossroads*, and Joyce Grenfell. Actors Richard Harris, Richard Todd, Peter Finch and Wilfred Hyde-White. Round the world sailor Sir Alec Rose, racehorse trainer Fred Winter and my namesake, General Sir John Hackett.

Motorcycle Grand Prix were not held at Silverstone until 1977. Prior to that, numerous International meetings attracting top riders took place at the circuit each year. All these events were well attended, with spectators coming from all over the world. Generally they were a well behaved crowd, but, one year, matters got rather out of hand.

On this particular occasion, the town was taken over by some 300 Hells Angels. The A5 was sealed off at each end and they then spent the evening doing "wheelies" through the town. Quite a number, male and female, were stark naked which went down well with Elio, Pepe and our female staff. When the police finally broke through the barriers, all hell was let loose. Eventually the police withdrew and left them to it. At an enquiry afterwards, the police said they feared for the safety of their officers.

The following year, steps were taken to contain the hooligans on the circuit. A marquee was provided for their use, and a rock group was laid on to entertain them. Quite early in the evening the marquee was set on fire, and when the fire brigade arrived, tent poles were thrown through the windscreen of the tender, badly injuring a fireman. They then descended on the village of Silverstone and caused havoc. It was a shame that out of the thousands that attended, a tiny minority should give motorcycle racing such a bad image.

Our one foray into the sponsorship side of motor sport was with Graham McRae, a New Zealand Formula 5000 driver. F5000 was considered by many to be more exciting than F1 and attracted many top drivers to its ranks. Graham raced a Leda-Chevrolet and in 1972 won the Rothmans European F5 Championship meeting. He operated very much on a shoestring, acting as his own mechanic and towing his racing car on a trailer behind a Chevrolet Camaro. I had Brave Old Oak Hotel stickers printed, and in return for free accommodation, he carried the hotel name on his car at six International Races! Talk about cheap sponsorship. The best publicity came when Graham spun at Copse Corner during the *Daily Express* International meeting, and there filling the television screen was our logo.

A sad occasion

Graham was partly involved in a very sad incident whilst staying at the hotel.

Sylvia had always wanted a Morris Minor traveller and one of our customers had a splendid example for sale. I bought it and as well as Sylvia, we let the staff use it. Working for us at the time was Christine, a live-in barmaid who came from East Anglia. She gave us the impression she had lived a sheltered life and was now making up for lost time. At every opportunity, she went night clubbing in Northampton. The German girls had returned home at the end of the previous summer, and for this year, we had taken on two Scottish students.

We had rented a house in Sandbanks, near Bournemouth for a holiday, and were leaving after closing time on this particular Friday evening. Christine asked Sylvia if she and the two girls could use the estate to go to Northampton, providing they could get a driver. She asked Graham if he would drive them but he was racing the next day and wanted an early night. One of the Scottish girls had a provisional licence and Christine came back to say they had found someone to go with them who had a licence.

It was raining heavily when they left and after midnight, Sylvia got the children out of bed for us to leave as well. As we were moving off, a local policeman, Barry Gunn, waved us down and told us there had been a serious accident involving our staff, on the outskirts of the town. I went with him and saw the bodies of two men lying on the verge and our girls on stretchers being placed in an ambulance. Sylvia's car was such a mass of twisted metal; it was a wonder that anyone survived.

It transpired that after leaving the hotel, they picked up two local men who Christine had arranged to go with them to Northampton. George was a very stout man and his friend, who was home on leave from the Army, was also well built. The two Scottish girls were in the front seats; they were both very small girls. The two men were in the rear seats and Christine, who was a big girl, sat in the boot. All this weight at the back made the car very unstable.

At the inquest, the police stated the car had reached the brow of a hill and oncoming vehicles had possibly dazzled the driver. On braking, a combination of the wet road and the weight in the back caused the front tyres to lose grip and the car went into the path of oncoming traffic. Four cars collided with the estate after the original accident. The two men shot forward and were ruptured internally on making contact with the front seats; they died instantly. Anne, the girl who was driving, suffered a broken jaw, collarbone, arm and ribs. Sandra in the passenger seat had a broken arm, leg, ribs, and nose, badly cut face and severe bruising. They both recovered after a long spell in hospital but never returned to work at the hotel. Christine, who must take the blame for what happened, had the least injuries.

The police examiner gave evidence that in his opinion, a contributory factor was uneven tyre pressures and worn steering bushes. The car had covered 26,000 miles and had been regularly serviced. The local paper reporting on the inquest carried the headline, *Faulty car causes death crash*. I arranged with the RAC to have the car inspected by their top man, and his report completely contradicted that given by the police "expert". I was told by one of my police contacts, a senior officer, that this was the first examination ever carried out by their man. I made an appointment to see the chief constable and, armed with my report, extracted an apology from him which was printed by the local paper, again, on the front page.

It was a very sad and unnecessary incident. George had served in the Royal Navy for seven years and was married with two small children. He was a very popular man. The chaplain from his last ship officiated at his funeral.

When the German girls returned home, Beartie's eldest sister, Angelica, joined our staff. She was so different in looks from the others. Tall and blonde, truly Germanic in every way, but, like her sisters, a lovely girl. She worked for us for two years and then married a local boy. Her father was a very lucky man to have three such charming daughters.

By the start of 1972, the business was booming. The lunchtime trade was exceptionally good with staff from Plessey, the enlarged South Northants District Council office staff and racing teams swelling the takings. We were averaging well over 100 bar snacks each day and often had a long queue at the buffet bar. We were operating at 90 per cent room capacity, both weekday and weekends. I had installed a telephone exchange in reception and phones in all bedrooms – only found in four star hotels in those days. This gave mother a greater role as receptionist and telephone operator, although I cannot really say she ever truly mastered the intricacies of the exchange operation. A pint of beer cost 12p and a tot of whisky 15p. The barrelage had almost trebled since our first year and the restaurant trade was on a permanent upward curve.

Here are some typical prices shown on the restaurant a la carte menu for 1972, all prices of main courses includes vegetables:

Prawn Cocktail	27p
Soup of the Day	10p
3 Egg Ham Omelette	65p
12oz Dover Sole	90p
2 Rainbow Trout	80p
12oz Sirloin Steak	£1
Duckling à l'Orange	95p
Coq-au-Vin	80p
8 oz Fillet Steak	90p
Steak Mixed Grill	90p
Prawn Curry	75p
½ Roast Chicken Salad	85p
Choice of sweets	15p

A Bottle of Chablis £1.90, Beaujolais £1.60, Chateauneuf du Pape £2.10

Favourite dishes at the buffet bar included Shepherds Pie, Braised Faggots and Steak and Kidney Pie, all priced at 40p.

Decimalization had taken place with very few problems, in spite of all the propaganda from the anti-decimal brigade. The only argument of theirs that proved correct was prices did increase alarmingly. Whereas an old penny increase on a pint of beer was greeted with threats by customers to stop drinking, a new penny increase was very quickly accepted. We, along with most retailers, were guilty when converting, of rounding up to the higher sum. The takings had reached £162,000 p.a. (net of VAT). Our rent had gone up in stages to £600 and was due to increase to £1400 at the next review. This was by far the most profitable period of all our years in the licensed trade. Rents and wages were low and prices and profits kept creeping up.

More banquets and balls

After I had been a member of my local LVA for a couple of years, I was appointed social secretary, a role that entailed organising the Annual Dinner (or Banquet as it was still known). Towcester LVA Dinners had previously been lacklustre occasions for members and wives only. They had been held at the previous chairman's hotel and, because of its size, were restricted to about 80 people. With assistance from my good friend, Ivor Denny, we decided to go big, and booked the Cornhill Hotel on the outskirts of Towcester. Nearly 120 people sat down to a splendid meal and the evening was a resounding success. Unfortunately, shortly afterwards, the hotel was sold to an organisation called The Jesus People and turned into a commune. This promptly put an end to the Cornhill as a venue.

The next year, 1972, we decided to go for bust and booked the function room at the recently opened Saxon Inn in Northampton. The room held 400 for a sit-down dinner, and despite the sceptics who said we wouldn't half fill it; we sold all the tickets with ease. The cost of the five course banquet was £4. 50. For dancing, we had the Douglas Day orchestra, a 10-piece band. The highlight of the evening was a mannequin parade put on by Vanity Fare, a Towcester boutique that Sylvia modelled for on occasions. She modelled at the dinner and persuaded Tony Penny and Miles Clark to join her. It was a showstopper.

The most memorable banquet was in 1975 when after inviting Lord Hesketh to be our Guest of Honour, I persuaded him to let us have his Formula 1 car on display in the banqueting room foyer, the car that won the Dutch Grand Prix. It was brought to the hotel in the team's transporter, and then to every one's dismay, there wasn't a door in the hotel large enough for it to go through! Not to be beaten, I rang Alex and he sent extra mechanics who proceeded to dismantle the car, take the parts into the foyer, and then reassemble it. It looked magnificent. By begging from brewers, spirit companies and other trade suppliers we amassed 80 prizes for a raffle that raised over £2,000 during the evening for trade and local charities.

Ivor and I continued to organise the banquets for a number of years until his untimely death in 1983 at the ridiculous age of 50. Before his death, we were both concerned at the drop in dress standards of both licensees and their guests. Although the dress for men had always been dinner jackets or lounge suits, most men wore a DJ. From 1979, we noticed some men started wearing blazers and inappropriate "loud" evening jackets, bought, no doubt, for their holiday on the Costa del Sol.

Another disturbing trend that started to creep in was when "trendy" publicans carried their takings around on their bodies. A lot of the men wore more jewellery than their wives. The noise couples made whilst dancing was deafening, and the noise of their gold necklaces and bracelets clanking against each other often drowning out the sound of the band. Moreover, that was only the men. As the standard of dress deteriorated, so did the behaviour. At times, it was often difficult to hear what the guest speaker was saying due to the amount of noise. We both found this disrespectful and knew that it spoilt the evening for many members and guests.

Unfortunately, this was the start of a gradual deterioration in the standards expected from licensees in general, a trend clearly illustrated at the Brewster Sessions.

Once a year all licensees were expected to attend the local Magistrates Court to have their licences renewed, an opportunity for the Justices and landlords to meet each other. I was brought up in the trade and showed respect to the bench by dressing as smartly as possible; I had never seen a scruffy magistrate.

Over the years, the obligation to attend court had lessened with the Association's solicitor representing members. Long before this however, licensees were attending court in jeans and T-shirts which I personally found very discourteous. It was often difficult to tell which were the licensees applying for various extensions, and which were criminals waiting to be tried: a view also shared by many senior police officers I knew.

I acquire a record

Talking of criminals, reminds me how I became one.

When Michael was about three years old, he came into the lounge one afternoon with blood running from a cut to his head. He said that some youths were throwing stones at Gippy, our Jack Russell dog; one had hit him and another had broken a window. I could hear the youths shouting when I stood at the rear entrance of the hotel, so I crept unseen along a wall, then rushed at them. They scattered in all directions except one youth who was holding a moped. When he saw me approach, he hesitated at first then dropped the moped and ran. I chased after him and grabbed him by the shoulder of his denim jacket. I told him what would happen to him if I ever caught him throwing stones at my dog again, and then let him go.

The next day I was visited by two police officers, neither from our local station. They told me they had received a complaint that I had assaulted a local youth and took a statement from me. I was told unofficially I would hear nothing more about it. I was therefore very surprised some weeks later; to receive a summons accusing me of causing Actual Bodily Harm – ABH, and in addition, damaging the youth's moped. I consulted my solicitor who said it was a formality and the case would be thrown out.

I attended court on the given day, and was rather surprised to see all six of the youths, very smart in their school uniforms, also in attendance. I was handed photographs that showed grazes on the youth's neck together with another photograph that showed the moped with a broken rear light. At the time of the incident, the youth was wearing a very coarse denim bomber jacket, and it was more than likely that when I grabbed him, the rough denim grazed his neck. He was a fleshy boy, the sort who bruises easily. In evidence he said I tried to strangle him and kicked his moped breaking the light, all of which was absolute rubbish; the light was broken, if at all, when he threw the moped down.

The five other boys confirmed his evidence and I was found guilty and given a year's conditional discharge. In the hotel that lunchtime, both the Clerk of the Court, and the prosecution solicitor Anne Pemberton, told me the case should never have been brought to court. Once it had, they both blamed my solicitor for not challenging the youth's evidence sufficiently.

Many years later, the father of one of the boys admitted to me that his son told him he lied that day, and said the "injured" boy made the marks on his neck himself. The father said he had considered informing the police of his son's dishonesty, but had worried about action being taken against his son. I told him he would have to be ruled by his conscience. I heard no more.

The Southfield's Gun, Gutsing and Gambling Club

In 1970 together with a group of my friends, we formed The Southfield's Gun Gutsing and Gambling Club. The original shoot members were Ivor Denny, Fred Dixon and Rex Groombridge, fellow licensees, David Powell, Rob Cockerill, Peter Penn, Eric Dickens and Norman Reeve all local farmers, Bob Freeborough, our local milkman, Richard Selby a professional gambler, Jim Wallis a plant hire manager, Ian Hetherington, a Guinness representative and, when on leave, Dick Martin, a Merchant Navy officer.

Rob, Ivor, Fred, Bob, Jim, Norman, and myself were all either Vice Presidents or members of the Northampton Rugby Club ("The

Saints"). We travelled together to all England rugby matches in this country and abroad. David (Piggy) Powell made 370 appearances for "The Saints" and captained the side for five seasons. He was a member of the British Lions on their tour of New Zealand in 1966, and went on to gain 14 England caps.

Our first clay pigeon shoot was held at David's farm, and afterwards we drank in an old barn by the light of candles. It was at this first shoot that we adopted the name TSGGGC and decided we deserved more salubrious surroundings to drink in afterwards.

Rob had such facilities to offer at his farm at Blakesley, a village near Towcester, We turned two stables into a shooting lodge, complete with cooker, easy chairs and most important, heating and lighting. Dick Selby was in his early 20s and a compulsive gambler. On a visit to a casino in Brighton, he broke the bank, and in lieu of winnings was given the roulette table and chips which we installed in the shoot HQ. Later on we were joined by Richard Amos who owned The Crossroads Motel at Weedon and builders Tony Penny, Roy Andrews, Brian Stanley, Doug Groome, farmer Lloyd Evans and believe it or not, another Tony Hackett, an artificial inseminator of cattle! (Hope that's the correct title, Tony.) I was christened Charles Anthony and Tony No 2 was christened Anthony Charles. Even Dick Selby couldn't work out the odds of us meeting and becoming friends. Others were Steve Nunn, a very talented silversmith who made the crown that the Prince of Wales wore for his Investiture. Steve trapped for us and for many years, he and Mick Gulliman, another trapper, drove us to internationals in Rob's ten-seater Land Rover Safari.

We were well known at Twickenham for having the largest flagstaff in the car park. Rob made it out of tubing and when erected stood some 30 feet above the ground. We drove to the game with a keg of beer mounted on the front of the vehicle and piped along the roof to a dispenser at the rear. This made our group very popular with the Northants contingent, though we often had to repel boarders. I think we were one of the first groups to take a barbecue

1 Sylvia, Timothy and Stephen with donkeys at Woodford, 1965. Brewery versus ublicans annual Golf Day 1972. l to r: Brian Newton, Bert Drage, Ivor Denny, Tony Hackett.

7 Sylvia and Tony on the water.
8 At Buckingham Palace Garden Party 2000.

9 Our Cornish cottage – first snow for 21 years.

to Twickenham and serve hot food, though it wasn't long before other groups copied us.

Sometimes we drove into central London after the game and visited a friend of mine who kept the Swiss Tavern in Soho. Other after game watering holes were the Stag and Hounds Pinkney's Green and The Bull at Bisham. We have enjoyed many scrumptious dinners at the latter. Later we all chipped in and bought a full size 20 seat luxury coach, fitted out with a galley, bar, tables and toilets.

On a few occasions, I drove David Powell's father, Willie, to international matches. One I remember most was to Cardiff in 1969 for Wales v England.

Prior to the game, we drank in the exclusive Town and Country Club, which, before they built the new stand, overlooked Cardiff Arms Park. Willie's brother-in-law was a member. Willie was a Welshman and before becoming a farmer had served in the Glamorgan Police Force. He once told me the story about when they were sent to Cornwall to subdue striking Cornish miners. He said they inflicted such extreme punishment on the miners that Cornish clubs never played rugby against Welsh teams for many years afterwards.

Whilst in the Town and Country Club we were surrounded by club members and reporters who wanted to speak to the father of an England team member. The drinks were being provided fast and furious until one person said to Willie, "How does it feel being a Welshman having a son playing for England?" Tact was never one of Willie's strong points, so it was typical of him when he replied, "I would have strangled him at birth rather than let him play for Wales!" Willie was one of a very rare species, namely, a Welshman who disliked the Welsh! Because of Willie's lack of tact, we quickly went from being the most sought after people in the room, to the most despised. Needless to say, the supply of free drinks ceased immediately.

With 15 minutes to go before the kick-off, I told Willie we must get to our seats in the stand. Willie had a gammy knee and walked with a stick so he decided to stop and watch the game from the club. In those days, the club lounge was a favourite place for elderly members to watch the game.

I went outside and, seeing a senior police officer, gave him Willie's ticket with the instructions to give it to any young boy who hadn't got a ticket. I was therefore somewhat taken aback when after five minutes a middle-aged man occupied Willie's empty seat. If that wasn't bad enough, he spent the next few minutes berating the England players in a strong Welsh accent.

The seats were in a group allocated to players' wives and guests. His favourite target was John Pullin the English hooker whose wife occupied the seat next to mine. After listening to his tirade for a few minutes, I threatened to throw him out of the stand if he didn't stop his abuse. This had the desired effect, and he was silent until half time when he left, presumably to go to the toilet. I followed him and once clear of the aisle told him that if he returned to his seat, I would report that Willie's ticket had been stolen and have him arrested. He never returned.

For the record, England were thrashed by 30 points to 9.

We stayed at a lovely hotel in Cowbridge, a small town on the outskirts of Cardiff. In the hotel bar that Saturday evening, Willie, Rob Cockerill, Dick Martin and I outdrank an illustrious company who included, writer broadcaster Winford Vaughan-Thomas, Welsh Rugby International and Glamorgan cricketer Wilf Wooller, and Peter West the BBC commentator. Willie and I retired to bed at 3 a.m. with sore throats from singing and arguing, but happy that we had at least beaten the Welsh at something that weekend.

As an indication of how the game has changed, players were expected to make their own way to internationals, arriving at the team hotel on the Thursday night. They stayed the two nights before the game at the Royal Hotel next to the ground. The players walked from the hotel to the ground a couple of hours before the kick off. A dinner was laid on after the game and the next morning they made their own way home.

That year I gave a lift back to Towcester to David, England

selector and ex-International, Ron Jacobs and a young Fran Cotton, then an England reserve. Fran was a student at Loughborough University and had an appetite like a horse. He, together with David, Ron and Ian Wright, also a reserve, enjoyed a slap-up meal at the Brave Old Oak before making their way home.

I count myself very lucky in having such a wonderful bunch of friends. For over 10 years, we did everything together, much to the concern of our wives. Many tried to join our group but few succeeded, and it was sad that our numbers were reduced by the early deaths of a few.

I start to lose my friends

Ivor was the first to die at the far too early age of 50 and I lost a good friend. Apart from running The Bull at Towcester with his wife Joan, he also owned a newsagents and printing business. After a very busy Christmas period, he complained of chest pains and after spending a few days in an intensive care unit passed away. He was a Governor of the Licensed Victuallers National Homes, an organisation that provided bungalows at Denham and Rugby for retired publicans and their wives. Ivor and I attended all trade conferences together, and for years played golf on a different course each week but I rarely played after his death. Joan has remained a very good friend to Sylvia and myself.

Roy Andrews also suffered a fatal heart attack while working in Saudi Arabia and was next to die, followed by Peter Penn who died after a long illness which he bore very courageously.

In 1993, Rob was knocked down and killed by a car when walking back to his hotel at Le Mans. He lived life to the full and, like all my friends who have died, the packed churches at their funerals reflected their popularity. I still miss Rob to this day; he was one quarter of a very inimitable quartet, Rob, David Powell, Jim Wallis and myself. It was ironic that Rob should be killed walking along a road. He owned an E type Jaguar car that he drove like a maniac, but with much skill. He once drove me to Murrayfield in icy road conditions for an international, and I never stopped shaking all weekend. £400 was collected at Rob's funeral for new gates at the village cemetery, the timber coming from oak trees in his woods.

In 1996, Bob Freeborough heard that Sylvia and I were back in Northants and came to Blakesley to see us. After he left, he had a heart attack and died shortly afterwards. He was an accomplished rally driver, part of the British Leyland Mini Cooper Rally team. He completed in the Monte Carlo event for a number of years, and the first London Mexico World Cup Rally.

Fred Dixon died in 2002, having suffered a number of strokes. A Royal Tank Corps National Serviceman, his father, a Regimental Sergeant Major in the Household Cavalry, was the last cavalry instructor at Weedon Barracks. He taught both King George VI and the Duke of Windsor to ride.

Fred and Val kept the King's Head at Farthingstone for a number of years. They were originally tenants of Watneys but when they sold the freehold to Frank Brierley, a local cut-price superstore owner, the name changed to The Pirates Den. For a number of years it was the meeting place on a Monday night for Rob, Jim, David and myself. Many times it was daylight before we left.

Rex Groombridge died in 2003 aged 72. A most genial person with a laugh that could be heard the length of Towcester race course. Rex was born at The Red Lion, Foster's Booth, a pub he took over from his father and ran for 40 years with his wife Pauline. When decimalisation took place we all had to buy new cash registers, but not Rex; he didn't trust them and up to his retirement still kept his takings in a drawer under the counter. If any customer had drinks on credit, Rex would chalk their names and amount owed on beams behind the bar. It was possible to lean over the counter and see who owed how much; as a result, customers never owed him money for long.

Ian Hetherington moved away from the area and died shortly afterwards. His father was personal physician to the Duke of Argyll. Ian never believed in working after his lunchtime drink. He would leave ashtrays and other Guinness items with me, to give out to any publican who complained about not having received a visit from him.

As I am recalling friends who died at an early age, mention must be made of Jimmy Hunter. While we were still at Woodford, Jimmy, an old rugby playing friend from Malta days tracked me down and for a number of years; we made an annual pilgrimage to Twickenham for the England v Ireland game.

Jimmy was a short service dental officer (three years service then a good gratuity). After he left the service he built up a very large practice in Burton-on-Trent and his charming wife, Biddy, was a consultant surgeon at the local hospital. They both came from Northern Ireland and spoke with a lovely, gentle, lilting accent. Jimmy played for Queen's University and was reserve for Ireland before joining the Navy. He captained the Navy in Malta and the Combined Services when he returned to Portsmouth.

When Jimmy arrived for the rugby weekends, he was always accompanied by John Richards and Ken Gleason. John was a Welshman with a marvellous singing voice and a matching sense of humour. He was an executive with Woolworth's. Ken was head brewer for Bass Brewery at Burton. On the many occasions when I paid return visits to Jimmy and Biddy, we always ended up at the Bass sample room.

For Burton Rugby Club's Centenary, David Powell organised a team for me to take there to play them. The cost to me was £20. Today it costs that amount to get a player's autograph! Ten Internationals took the field that Sunday, including Jan Webster, Martin Horton, Keith Fielding and Sam Doble for Burton. Sam was to die tragically in 1977 at the ridiculous age of 33.

When he was in his early 50s, Jimmy, who was a fitness fanatic, was working in his garden with Biddy. He shouted to her that he had a pain and died of a heart attack almost immediately.

David Powell married Sara Monk, a county tennis champion, in the early 1970s. They booked every room at the hotel for their guests. These included six British Lions and ten Internationals in total. With our very low ceilings, it was hilarious watching 6ft 6" men trying to stand upright at the bar. Peter Stagg, a Scottish International, was the tallest at 6ft 11" This was the first time I met John Currie the England second row forward.

Harold Wilson saves our bacon

Having items stolen from the hotel was one of the accepted risks of the trade, usually involving coat hangers, towels, ashtrays and other "consumables".

The local rugby club organised an annual Tug-of-War across the River Tove, and teams, mostly from rugby clubs, came from a wide area. The event increased in popularity each year and was a very profitable evening for us. We usually suffered from having bags of flour thrown at our windows and other acts of "spirited fun", nothing too serious.

This particular year, we were informed that the rugby club had received a record entry, including teams from four Oxford colleges. I had promised to take Joe Burgess to Lords that day, but before I left, I removed all the coats of arm shields from the panelling and anything else that I thought could be taken away.

I arrived back from London at 9.45 p.m. and as we entered the town, was greeted with a scene of devastation. All the buildings were white with flour, and broken glass littered the street. When we arrived at the hotel, I was horrified to see Steven and Pepe squeegeeing beer out of the front doors onto the pavement. Three windows were broken, the RAC and AA hotel signs had gone and the roof looked as though we had suffered a heavy snowfall.

Inside was chaos. Flour bags had been thrown through the broken windows, and had burst against the back fittings, covering all the bottles and glasses with flour. The carpets and seating were covered in a grey grunge, a mixture of flour and beer. Worst of all, six light fittings had been wrenched off the walls and two very nice carriage lamps, either side the main door, had disappeared.

Every pub in the town had suffered damage of sorts; The Saracens Head had probably come off worst of all.

I learnt that the vandalism reached its peak at about 9 p.m. and the police then advised all licensed premises to close their premises. Sylvia took action straightaway, which probably reduced further damage. In all we had about 500 glasses broken or stolen.

The next day we got all the licensees together for a meeting, and it was decided to inform the rugby club that should they hold an event the following year, we would all close our premises. They agreed not to hold the event again, and I will give the club credit; through various "channels", my carriage lamps were returned! It was a great shame it turned out this way; the idea to hold the event was a good one, and it had raised a lot of money for charities.

One morning Sylvia's attention was drawn to the number of butter dishes missing from the restaurant. These blue Denby ware pots cost about £1 each. She told the staff to replace them for the next day's breakfast and to keep their eyes open.

Among the residents, at that time, was a couple with a boy aged about 12. They had booked in for a week and this happened on their second day. The following day two-condiment sets were missing, these were also Denby ware. I went to the couple's room to check whether the lost items were in their possession. They had lots of large luggage, all double locked making it impossible to examine, and there was no sign of any of the items in the room.

At that time, an investigation was underway regarding a possible illegal land deal at Wakefield in Yorkshire, involving, if my memory serves me right, Lady Marcia Faulkender's brother. As Marcia Williams, she was Prime Minister Harold Wilson's private secretary and lived at Blisworth a village three miles from Towcester.

Staying at the hotel while investigating the case was Detective Chief Superintendent Alan Jones and Detective Sergeant Ron Peters, both from Scotland Yard. They had been carrying out enquiries in the area for the last ten days, and I became very friendly with them. When they came into the bar at night, I mentioned about the missing items, and where my suspicions lay. Alan said they would look into it the next morning.

The couple and boy left the hotel at around 9.30 a.m. whereupon Alan and Ron went upstairs to check their room. Ron came down after a few minutes and asked Sylvia and myself to go upstairs. The cases had been opened and inside were our missing items, plus some of our cutlery, towels and a small picture taken from the landing. The strangest item of all was a pack of bacon, which could only be obtained from Nurden & Peacock cash and carry. None of the additional items had been missed. Also in the cases were many other effects obviously taken from a variety of hotels. We were particularly interested in a solid silver dish engraved with the crest of the Duke of Bedford, obviously stolen from Woburn Abbey. Everything was put back in the cases and they were relocked. How Alan and Ron opened them, I never knew.

I thought Ron would tackle them that evening but he surprised me by saying, "It's best done in the morning." He went on to explain that fraudsters, such as this couple, often left after paying their bill with a dud cheque or without paying at all. They say, "We are waiting for the bank to open and will return to settle our bill." That would be the last we would see of them. He made it seem such a common occurrence, that I wondered why it hadn't happened to us before. Perhaps we had just been lucky – or selective with our guests.

When the couple came down for breakfast, Alan and Ron were waiting for them. Alan showed them his warrant card and said, "I am Chief Superintendent Jones from Scotland Yard and this is my colleague Detective Sergeant Peters, we are here to investigate the theft of items from Woburn Abbey and other places." The woman screamed and the man collapsed. The woman then grabbed hold of the boy and shaking him screamed, "This is all your fault, you little sod!" It was easy to imagine the effect it had on them. There they were, being apprehended by a senior police officer from Scotland Yard, in a small Northants market town hotel.

Alan and Ron took them all into the residents' lounge and reappeared later to say they were admitting everything – including stealing bacon from our kitchen – but hadn't enough money to pay their bill. However, they had a number of National Saving Certificates in their possession which could be used to reimburse us. We all trooped into my bank, and by some means, sufficient certificates were credited to our account to cover their bill. It all seemed very complicated but, thanks to Alan and Ron, the proceedings were satisfactorily concluded.

Once he was satisfied we had been paid, Ron telephoned the local police and the three were arrested. They were charged with umpteen cases of theft and deception, and, surprisingly, released on bail. They failed to show for their trial and we never heard anything of them again.

Alan and Ron stayed with us for another month carrying out their investigations into the Wakefield affair. Much was written in the press at the time, about the possibility of a criminal offence having been committed, but nothing ever came from it. I remember Alan's telephone bill was astronomical.

Enforced staff changes

Pepe and his brother, Jose, had arranged to return to Spain for a holiday, the first time Pepe had returned to Spain for three years. So he was eagerly looking forward to his holiday. He had been to Northampton on the last three paydays, buying gifts for his mother and relations. Pepe went to bed early the night before his flight, though he was so excited; we doubted if he would get very much sleep.

At about 11 p.m. we received a telephone call from the housekeeper at the home of his brother's employer where Jose was the butler. She said that a bee had stung Jose and he wasn't at all well. Jose's wife thought Pepe should go to see him urgently.

I got Pepe out of bed and drove him the eight miles to where his brother was. As we pulled up on the drive, the housekeeper rushed out and told Pepe how sorry she was, Jose had just died! Pepe let out the most dreadful scream, rushed into the house and up the stairs. I went into the kitchen with the housekeeper and she told me what happened.

In the early evening, Jose had been in the garden picking flowers, and had been stung in the mouth by a bee. His tongue started to swell but initially they were not too worried. They phoned the doctor and he told them to give him plenty of ice cubes to suck. A couple of hours later, Jose was experiencing a lot of pain and had difficulty in swallowing. They called the doctor again and he told them to give him aspirin. But the aspirin did not improve his condition and they again telephoned the doctor. The doctor arrived just as he died.

Pepe hadn't returned downstairs after an hour, although we could still hear him and Jose's wife crying. The housekeeper said she would make a bed up for him, so I said I would drive home and return the next day.

When I arrived the next day, his employer was there. He had been on holiday in France and flew back as soon as he received the news. He was a very influential person.

He said he was paying for Jose's body to be flown back to Spain accompanied by his widow and Pepe. I asked him, "When will the inquest be held?" and was very surprised when he said there would not be one. I asked him if he was happy with the action, or lack of action, taken by the doctor and he said, "The poor fellow wasn't to know the seriousness of Jose's condition."

I pressed the point but he said there was no point in upsetting Jose's wife and Pepe. He dismissed my accusation of incompetence and, rightly or wrongly, I concluded there was to be a cover up. He seemed to imply that because Jose was Spanish, his life counted for rather less. I refused his offer of a drink for two reasons: it was far too early and I disliked the man intensely.

I asked to see Pepe but was told he was still sedated, I never saw him again. I shall never forget that dreadful night and Pepe's reaction to the news of his brother's death. Pepe worshipped him and was always showing people photographs of "my brudder". I sent Steven with Pepe's belongings and the many gifts he had bought for his family. Steven said he saw him but Pepe was still too upset to talk.

Everyone missed Pepe; he was always so cheerful, so eager to please. We all sent letters of condolence to him in Spain but never received any replies. I think the shock had affected him deeply. To this day, I still cannot understand why an inquest wasn't held.

Pepe's departure left a gap in our staff, and it was at this stage that we employed the "terrible twins". Janet and Christine were local girls, both married with young families. Janet worked behind the bar and Christine in the restaurant. Both were extremely good workers, when they weren't gossiping. Their favourite position was standing at reception gossiping with my mother, but they were such likeable girls, you felt you couldn't admonish them. Janet was to work for us for many years.

In 1970 we felt that the ever-increasing amount of paperwork, i.e., wages, PAYE tax and insurance, invoices, hotel reservations, general correspondence, etc. warranted us employing a part-time secretary. Through one of our customers, Bob Turpin – no relation to *the* Turpins, but a good amateur boxer all the same – we employed his girlfriend Pam. She was a very efficient secretary who worked for the local solicitors, and after her work there, assisted Sylvia with our paperwork two nights each week. This arrangement worked very satisfactorily until, shortly after her marriage to Bob, she ceased working when their baby was on the way. By this time we were employing ten full-time staff and as many as twelve part-time. The wages bill was approaching £350 per week, with the onset of VAT, even more time was spent in the office, and that was how we employed Mrs Taylor.

Edith Taylor was in her early 40s. At first, I thought she was a rather reserved person, but, in a short time, we got to know her better and both she, and husband John, became very good friends. The extra workload meant we needed to employ her four mornings a week. Initially we turned a room at the staff house into an office, but when Steven's wife Nora had her baby, they needed more room so we rented an office in the town. Edith was to work for us for the next 25 years and she played a very important role in what was fast becoming a form-filling society. She was a very conscientious person and we owe her a great deal for the efficient way she dealt with all our accounts and secretarial duties.

It was about this time that the trade newspaper *The Morning Advertiser* (the oldest newspaper in the world) ran a competition for the best looking barmaids in the country. I had no hesitation in forwarding a photograph of our ten girls; they won the Midlands group and were runners-up in the final.

While on the subject of awards, I should mention that our flower displays at the front of the hotel were the pride of the town. We won the Chamber of Trade floral competition so many times, they asked us not to enter any more so as to give other premises a better chance.

We won 1st Prize in the Watney (Midlands) floral competition and our prize was for Sylvia and me to visit Watneys Mortlake Brewery, accommodation at the Dorchester Hotel and dinner at Quaglino's Restaurant. When I drive past the pub now, I feel I want to go in and ask, "What has happened to the flowers?" The frontage lent itself to floral displays.

Up for the Cup

Each year, the Rugby League Cup Final was played at Wembley Stadium. In our second year at the hotel, we received a booking for eight rooms for the Friday and Saturday nights of that weekend. We were very nervous as to what we had let ourselves in for, and as it turned out, justifiably so.

They started arriving at midday on the Friday. Jack Lewis the organiser, Taffy, Alan, two Joes, Jess, Les and Bob. They started drinking the moment they arrived and it continued unabated the whole weekend, apart from brief sojourns to sleep and eat. They paid into a fund throughout the year to finance their weekend.

The intention was that any money left over would be distributed to the staff, there was never any left, but they always looked after the staff very well.

They all came from Swinton in Lancashire. Jack had a newsagent tobacconist's shop, which was used by the workers from three nearby factories. In his own words, it was a goldmine. His new car each year carried the number MED1F. Jess was a builder, Alan an undertaker, Les, Taffy and two Joes, miners, and Bob was a plumber. They never went to bed before 2 a.m. on the Friday night but always looked fresh when they left at 10 a.m. the next day to travel to Wembley. 6 p.m. would see them back again wanting more refreshment before dinner. After that it was solid drinking until the first ones drifted off at about 3 a.m. In the early days, both Joes, Taffy and Les often stayed drinking all night. Many arguments took place between them and my regulars regarding the pros and cons of the two rugby codes.

Altogether, they stayed with us at Towcester and Blakesley for 24 years. During that time, some passed away but they were always replaced by fresh faces. Of the originals, Jack, Taffy and Alan were still going strong when we left the trade.

Dark clouds looming for the licensed trade

In early 1972 Grand Metropolitan Hotels, under Mr Maxwell Joseph started making overtures to the Watney Mann shareholders with a view to taking over the company. To defend themselves, Watneys started reviewing the rents they charged their tenants; some proposed increases were as high as 500 per cent. My proposed new rent was upped from £1,400 to a new figure of £3,500! The terms of a tenant's agreement stipulated that the brewery had to give a year's notice to increase his rent. At the same time, rumours started to circulate in the trade that Watney Mann were planning to turn their best tenanted pubs and hotels into managed houses. Under management, they would receive all the trading profit from a house, rather than just a rent. Having been a manager and experienced the manner in which they operated their managed houses, I was extremely concerned. The majority of the company's tenants shared my concern.

A meeting of Watney Mann tenants was held at the Salon Ballroom in Northampton. 500 licensees attended from the Watney Midland's region, which encompassed the counties of Northants, Leics, Warwick, Beds, Oxon, Hunts, Bucks and Lincs. The tenants were greatly concerned about the management issue, rents and other changes being made by the company. To fight them on these issues, it was decided to form a Watney Mann (Midlands) Tenants Association. Brian Newton from The Bell Inn, Coventry was elected chairman, Jack Clifton from The Golden Horse Northampton, was elected secretary and I became the vice chairman.

I had never met Brian before but this was to be the start of a great friendship between us. Brian and his lovely wife Thora, had a big busy pub in Bell Green, a suburb of Coventry. It was in a rather run-down area but very close to a large residential college and Brian's pub was the only watering hole nearby. In the very large garden there was a full-size, four-lane ten-pin bowling alley. He sold so much beer that he employed a full-time cellar man. During opening hours, he stayed in the cellar, just to change over barrels and kegs. At its peak, The Bell was selling 28 barrels a week. I knew Jack Clifton very well; he was secretary of the Northamptonshire Licensed Trade Association and had a very busy house, The Golden Horse in Northampton.

One of the proposals that came out of the meeting was tenants should increase the price of a pint of Red Barrel beer from an average of 13p to £1. Watneys were in the middle of a £2.5m advertising campaign promoting the beer, and it was felt this action would force them to re-think their policy.

Similar meetings were held in London, covering the London and South East area of the Watney empire, and in Manchester covering the North West. Later on further associations were formed in East Anglia and the South West. A national executive was created consisting of the chairman and vice chairman of each region. Gerald Richardson was elected as national chairman; he had two large tenancies in London. Most importantly, the press and publicity officer was Jack Murphy, who had a pub at Hayling Island.

Jack, an Australian, had worked for many years as a reporter for various national newspapers; his experience was to prove invaluable. The chairman for the London area was Eddie O'Connor, a larger-than-life Irishman, with The Monkey Puzzle pub in Sussex Gardens, just off the Edgware Road. His vice chairman was David Bance who had the New Inn on Ham Common. In the North the chairman was the irrepressible Ronnie Crook who ran a large pub at Heaton Norris near Manchester. Ronnie's beaming face appeared on posters advertising Wilson's Bitter throughout the North.

We had numerous meetings with the directors of Watney Mann, and these led to them confirming their intention to change the most profitable of their tenanted estate from tenants to managers. From this moment, the fight was on.

In the latter half of the year, Grand Metropolitan Hotels (GMH) won the battle, and Watneys were taken over. They had fought a long and often bitter battle to retain their independence but to no avail. It was the beginning of the demise of family breweries that had existed for hundreds of years. Gradually the influence of accountants was being felt throughout the whole trade, none more so than at Watneys. Many large public houses on corner sites in London and other large towns and cities, were sold off for development. Other large pubs were turned into "Birds' Nests", a type of very noisy disco bar.

For the next year Brian and I, sometimes together, sometimes separately, attended LVA meetings throughout the region, whipping up support for the cause. In no time, we had over a thousand members. In view of the amount of correspondence involved, my accountant, Mr Guy, became our paid secretary and treasurer. On many occasions, he was to have a steadying influence on our more outlandish publicity schemes.

WMTA fights back

Brian went abroad on holiday in early 1973 and shortly afterwards Jack Murphy rang to say he wanted regions to organise publicity stunts to bring to the public's attention the plight of Watneys tenants. He said he planned for the Midlands to lead first, to be followed by the other regions.

I arranged for Ivor Denny to print 1,000 posters with the words *"Keep Watney Tenants, Tenants"* on bright yellow paper. This was a play on the posters Watneys had asked us to display during the Watney/GMH battle, which said *"Keep Watneys, Watneys"*. My scheme was to plaster Watneys brewery in Northampton with these posters. I had experimented with various strengths of wallpaper adhesives, until I reached the required strength.

I organised a team consisting of Bob Freeborough with two of his milk floats, Jim Wallis in charge of providing ladders, Rob Cockerill who made us long handled paste brushes, and with those three, plus Ivor, Steven the chef, Rex Groombridge and myself, we descended on the brewery at two o'clock in the morning. I had arranged for local newspapers and two television companies to meet us at the brewery and they were already set up when we arrived.

We parked opposite the brewery offices, lifted the sides of the milk floats, which contained the ladders, paste and brushes, and while Jim, Rob and Bob erected the ladders, the rest of us started pasting. The offices were four storeys high and we started at the top with Rob and Steven on the ladders, Jim and myself passing the pasted posters to them. The others carried on pasting, running across the street with the prepared posters.

After we had placed 100 at the highest point, we lowered the ladders for the next row. Just as Steven was going back up the ladder, he slipped and let out a loud oath. Unbeknown to us, there was a security guard on duty that night because of the IRA's bombing campaign in this country. The guard heard Steven shout in his Irish accent and thought we were planting bombs! A few minutes later police cars encircled us.

A police inspector, asked who was in charge, and I stepped forward. I explained to him what we were doing and why, saying that if Watneys had their way, the town would be full of "Birds' Nests". One had opened in the town a few weeks earlier, and had been a constant source of trouble for the police, with fights and drunkenness. I pointed out that I was responsible for the TV companies and press presence, and would hardly have done this if we were terrorists! He asked me if we had finished and I said we needed another 15 minutes to make a good job of it. He told us he would be back in 10 minutes and didn't want to see us there on his return. In total, we put up 500 posters on the building and walls surrounding the brewery.

I knew that the Chairman of Watney Mann (Midlands), Michael Gow, arrived for work each morning at 8.45 a.m. and I had arranged for the TV companies to be present to record his reaction to our night's work. I arrived at 8.30 a.m. and the sun shone directly on the office frontage, making the posters stand out superbly. Mr Gow arrived and, when asked for his reaction, refused to comment.

Later that morning, I received a telephone call from his secretary, asking me if I would go to the brewery to see him. I rang Jack Murphy and told him what we had done that night, and that I had been summoned to the brewery.

I was ushered into Mr Gow's office where Bert Drage and Dillon Welshman, the Tenanted Trade Director were present. Gow started by reading me the riot act, and then said, "My first reaction was to ask the police to prosecute you." He went on to say, "However, after consulting with Head Office, if you will give an undertaking not to repeat this disgraceful escapade, the company will take no further action." I told Gow, "I have many plans for a variety of further protests, so there is no need for me to repeat the previous night's action."

At this point, Gow turned purple and started making threats, when his secretary came in to say, "The *Daily Mirror* are on the telephone and want to speak to Mr Hackett." Immediately his attitude changed and he told her, "Tell them Mr Hackett is otherwise engaged." He turned to me and said, "Unofficially, I do not agree with the management policy, but I cannot be seen to condone your actions." I said I fully understood his position; we shook hands and I left.

Bert Drage told me afterwards that, prior to my arrival at the brewery, Mr Gow had been in touch with their legal department to see if I had given them grounds to discontinue my tenancy. I never knew the advice he received, but, I was still with the company a year later and he had departed!

I telephoned Jack to let him know how I got on and he said, "Did the *Daily Mirror* trick work?" I might have guessed it was his ruse! He went on to say that he had been asked for a statement from the *Mirror, Mail, Express, Telegraph* and *Financial Times* regarding our night's work. They later contacted me and I explained why I felt we had to take such action.

Our local evening paper's front page was filled with photographs of Steven, Jim Wallis and myself. Inside were two further pages of photographs and text. That evening, scenes of us putting up the posters and interviews were shown on BBC, Anglia and Midlands ITV. A week later, I featured in a five-minute interview on national television for the BBC *Man Alive* programme which had a large viewing audience.

Brian telephoned me on his return from his holiday and asked if anything new had happened!

Flushed with success, my next protest demonstration was to have involved an elephant. I contacted Riley Smith and he assured me he could provide me with an elephant at no cost. I was going to have a coffin made with the letters "RIP Watneys Tenants" painted on it, fixed to the elephants back, and then to parade it round the one way ring road in front of the brewery! Mr Guy talked me into delaying this tactic until a planned mass lobby of Members of Parliament had taken place. This happened a few weeks later, supported by 600 tenants. Prior to the lobby, a mass meeting was held in the Central Hall, Westminster.

While all this was going on, the property next door to the hotel came onto the market, for £29,000. It was a large shop, used for bicycle sales and repairs, and had twelve rooms above it. It would have been easy to knock an opening through connecting the hotel landing with that of the shop. This would give us at least an extra nine badly needed bedrooms, plus three more bathrooms.

Thinking we would buy it, I formed a limited company, Towcester Sports & Games Ltd, to sell sports goods from the shop. Sylvia and I were to have 90 per cent of the shares. I had asked David Knighton if he would run it and had made David Powell, Roger Arneil the Scottish Rugby International and England cricketer, Colin Milburn directors. Once it was up and going I intended asking Tom Graveney if he would also become a director.

Roger was working for the Wool Council and had many contacts for supplying clothing to major teams and schools. The idea was we would obtain contracts supplying schools with clothing and equipment by offering the services of our directors as sports advisers and coaches. They would be paid a percentage of any sales they achieved. There wasn't a sports shop in the town and only one in the whole of Northampton. To think that in those days, the main items bought by parents were football and rugby shorts, tennis and cricket clothing and odd items of equipment. Compare that to the sports goods purchased today by bullied and intimidated parents, for their ever-demanding offspring: trainers, tracksuits, replica football strips, tennis racquets and cricket bats, ski clothing and equipment, the list is endless.

I thought, at the time, I was on to a winner, and when one considers the enormous market that now exists in sports equipment, it makes me wonder about our future had we gone ahead with this project.

I approached the brewery with my scheme to incorporate the upstairs of the shop into the hotel. At the same time, I told the brewery I would be interested in purchasing the freehold of the Brave Old Oak should this be possible. I was told they would give me an answer after they had consulted their legal department. Later events were to rule out all these possibilities.

Our meetings with Watneys continued at regular intervals and, in 1973, they announced that they had reduced the number of houses they were taking for management from an original 500 to 280. The fight then started to get adequate compensation for the displaced tenants. At this stage, all we knew was that the 280 selected pubs would be the most profitable houses from Watneys 3,500 pub estate.

After many hours of negotiation, Watneys agreed to compensate displaced tenants with a sum equal to one and a half year's net profit, or thee years' rent, whichever was the greater. The brewery would have the choice of selecting which year was to be used, for calculating purposes, from any of the tenants' past three years' trading accounts, and the half year from their last year.

After a long battle with the Inland Revenue, it was agreed that this would be treated as an ex-gratia payment, thereby making it free from Income Tax liability. Credit has to be given to Watneys for employing the finest tax experts available in obtaining this ruling. Additional sweeteners included no increase in a displaced tenant's rent during the year of notice and the brewery to pay all valuation fees and removal expenses.

One result of the generous terms negotiated was that many tenants were hoping their house would be one of the selected 280. When the list was finally published, The Brave Old Oak was one of only eight from the Midlands Region. For some obscure reason, Brian's pub was not one of them.

A further benefit was that all displaced tenants would have first choice of any vacant Watney tenancy in any part of the country, for a period of 12 months. We received a weekly list and Sylvia and I must have looked at a dozen or more but none were suitable. We did try to persuade David Knighton to run the The Countryman at Staverton near Daventry for us but without success. David would have made an excellent publican but he had his sights set on working for Carlsberg Brewery.

The brewery had just brought out a 20-year turnover lease agreement. This enabled a tenant to take on a business for 20 years with a rent based on a percentage of turnover. The rent would be reviewed every three years and if trade had not reached a stipulated figure, a penalty sum would be applied. The tenant would be responsible for all repairs and replacements, excluding the main structure and roof. If the tenant wanted to sell the lease, a sum of money would be arrived at to cover dilapidations. Tenants would be known as "Inntrepreneurs".

The brewery offered us The Queen Victoria Hotel at Rushden, a large Victorian ex-railway hotel on a turnover lease. This was the first one offered in the Midlands, and a brewery accountant came from London to explain the workings of the lease to us. The hotel had 24 bedrooms and a large function room but was in a very dilapidated condition.

The initial rent would have been 6 per cent of turnover. We went and viewed it but it was not for us. It would have been difficult for any place to come up to the standard of the Brave Old Oak. At one stage, the brewery said they would permit us to have up to three pubs of our choice.

Many people were disappointed that their houses hadn't been selected for management and a certain few suggested that the WMTA executive had only been interested in "feathering their own nests". It is true that of the 12 executive members, 10 lost their pubs to management. What has to be remembered is that only people with successful businesses could have spared the time and expense needed to do the job properly. Apart from Mr Guy, no one else ever claimed expenses, Brian and I spent at least 30 nights staying in different hotels in the capital. In addition, we spent five nights in Manchester, four in Norwich and three each in Trowbridge and Brighton. Goodness knows how much we spent on travelling, telephone, postage and paying extra staff to cover for us.

I had enjoyed my campaigning with Brian, he was an extraordinary person who did not enjoy good health, suffering from angina and diabetes. If that wasn't enough he was also asthmatic. This, in no way, curtailed his activities, both he and Thora worked extremely hard at their busy pub. They were accomplished ballroom dancers and Brian and I enjoyed many rounds of golf together.

He once told me about the time they were undergoing live-in training at a large pub in London in the early 1950s. At Christmas, they sat down for dinner with the manager's family and other resident staff. The manager's family had turkey with all the trimmings and the staff had roast pork. The manager said his staff food allowance didn't stretch to giving them all turkey!

The time had arrived for Sylvia and me to decide in which direction we wanted to proceed. We were still young and both enjoyed the hotel trade enough to warrant buying a larger hotel. Finance would have been no problem, but neither of our two elder sons showed any interest in the trade. Stephen had helped in the dining room on occasions, but not very willingly. We envied couples who ran hotels with assistance from their children.

We had been very fortunate in obtaining satisfactory staff at the Oak, but it was always a problem getting the right ones. With just a public house, at least customers will, if necessary, wait to be served. With a restaurant, customers want to eat at their chosen time. They may engage babysitters and it is no concern of theirs that the chef has turned up drunk on the busiest night of the week, or that the headwaiter had sliced his finger off!

Our career takes another turn

While we were still weighing up the pros and cons of our future direction, a free house came onto the market in a neighbouring village. At that time, there were very few free houses, only about 5 per cent of the pubs in the country.

The late Mrs Bolton, a member of the Gilbey Gin family, had owned The Red Lion at Blakesley. Her husband was a "Mr Big" in shipping insurance and a prominent member of the Baltic

Exchange in London. Mrs Bolton had died the previous year and the pub was being sold on behalf of her executors by Jackson Stops & Staff, a company that originated in Towcester. Mrs Bolton had lived in the house next door to the pub, and so it should not interfere with her tranquillity, had installed her retired chauffeur as the landlord.

Joe and Annie Coghill, the landlord and landlady, were an elderly Scottish couple who were eager to return to the Orkneys. Mrs Bolton let them have the pub for a nominal rent and, apart from a few old codgers, the trade was minimal. The busier pub in the village, The Greyhound, a Watney pub, had closed some six months previously, part of Watneys policy to realize the value of their rural pubs by selling them off delicensed, a policy they came to regret years later.

The asking price for the Red Lion was £30,000 and I rang Jackson Stops and offered £29,000. Max Lee, their man handling the sale, phoned me shortly afterwards to say they had received an offer equal to the asking price and did I want to up my bid. I told him we would go to £31,000 but that was our final bid. A week later he called at the hotel to say our offer had been accepted.

We were very familiar with the village of Blakesley and its inhabitants. When the Greyhound pub closed, a lot of their customers started using the Brave Old Oak. It was a very picturesque village with most of the properties, including the pub, built from the lovely rich brown local stone. Apart from the pub, the village had a primary school, post office, village stores, butcher and a garage that also sold petrol. The neighbouring village of Woodend was joined to Blakesley; it had a baker but no pub.

The village lay in a triangle formed by the A5, A43 and A361 situated midway between Northampton, Banbury and Daventry. Oxford was 22 miles and Silverstone circuit 4 miles away. The combined population of the two parishes was 630. It was a very prosperous village with property commanding prices well above the average for the area. Quite a few villagers worked at the Plessey

Research Centre, some at Northampton and one or two travelled as far as London.

The Red Lion, a three storey building, was situated on the main road in the village. On entering the front door, the two bar rooms were to the left of a passageway that led to the yard at the rear. On the right was a small off-sales shop which would be Mother's department and, behind that, the private lounge, kitchen and stairs. On the first floor were five bedrooms, a bathroom and toilet. The top floor contained two further bedrooms and two attic rooms. A large clubroom on the first floor had been blanked off for Mrs Bolton's use. A new doorway and stairs had been built to give them access from their property. They used this room for Grafton Hunt parties, and it also served as a playroom for their children. The lawn at the rear of the property had also been sealed off and incorporated into their garden. A two-storey garage and five stables surrounded a small courtyard.

At a conference a few years previously, I met a couple who were tenants of a public house in Maidenhead. David and Val's pub was a very large catering house on a new estate. At the 1975 conference, Val was on her own and she told me that she and David were splitting up. She said she had fallen in love with a customer and if I ever wanted a couple to manage a pub, they would be willing to do it. I contacted her regarding the Red Lion and, after consulting her boyfriend, they agreed to run it for me for a year. Her boyfriend Patrick was a Southern Irishman, he and his brothers were self-employed plasterers in the Maidenhead area. Pat was a very likeable fellow, but I never thought he was suitable for Valerie. David had spoilt her terribly, and she never knew what it was to be short of money. She was about to find out!

Bartholomew Arms

We still had almost a year left at Towcester before our move to Blakesley, and we were determined to make it as memorable as possible. Right up until the actual day we departed we were still increasing the trade. We were averaging twelve barrels of beer per week, substantial quantities of wines and spirits and 150 bar snacks a day. A change in the law enabled us to open at 5 p.m. and we often had a full house within minutes of opening. A lot of customers started calling in for a drink before they went home from work. Our takings were averaging £4,500 a week which, considering beer was around 18p a pint, a set lunch £1, a bottle of Nuits St Georges £2.60 and a double en-suite room £7, wasn't bad going.

We discovered that behind the scenes the tenanted department were trying their hardest to get the Brave Old Oak Hotel removed from the list of transfers, and some of the customers organised a petition to present to the brewery in an attempt to keep us there. Whilst feeling flattered by everyone's efforts, we had resigned ourselves to leaving and had started to look forward to the new challenge.

Things weren't working out too well with Pat and Val at Blakesley and I had to spend a lot of time there sorting out problems. I thought that Val's daughter Julie – her only child – who had been terribly spoilt by both her and David, was the main cause of a lot of their problems. She had attended a private school in Maidenhead but at Blakesley went to the local primary school. At the age of 10, she was years ahead of the local children in both knowledge of the world and sexual matters. After school, she wore make-up, jewellery, stockings and high-heeled shoes. Pat had no control over her and this, combined with Val's laid-back attitude was a recipe for disaster. Events were to take a disastrous twist a few years later. To make matters worse, Pat was a confirmed gambler and drank quite heavily, bad habits for someone running a pub.

When the time came for us to leave the Brave Old Oak we laid on numerous farewell parties, the most memorable one was for all the brewery employees we had been involved with during the 16 years we had been with the company, both as managers and tenants. Many tears were shed, some with relief on the brewery side! At one party, Peter Davis, the Chairman of the Council, said it was being arranged that we should be appointed Freemen of the town but we never heard any more about it. Peter was the only Labour councillor we ever voted for – he did a lot of good work for the town.

One of our saddest moments was saying goodbye to all the staff. Barbara Spanton was the only one that had been with us from the start, but all of them were like family. Steven wanted to go with us to Blakesley but the volume of trade did not warrant employing him for some time, and, anyway, he was far too talented for what was then just a small village pub. We were however very pleased that Janet Bull went with us to work as a barmaid, and once again we were able to call on the services of David Knighton.

On the actual day we left the Brave Old Oak Sylvia was very tearful; we had been very happy there and although just moving four miles away, it felt as though we were severing all connections with the area. We had taken over a run-down business, badly in need of TLC, and turned it into the best small town hotel in the region.

Nigel Horne in his book, *Taverns of England,* wrote, "That comfortable old bon viveur, Dr Johnson, is reputed to have said: 'There is nothing which had been contrived by man, by which so much happiness is produced as a good tavern or inn.' Surely, The Brave Old Oak Hotel at Towcester would have pleased him."

A Spaniard with an English wife took over as the first managers, and in the next seven years, a total of six managers came and went. The reputation of the once famous hotel went from bad to worse, so much so, that it eventually closed. After two years, during which time it was boarded up, it was sold to Bank's Brewery and became a youngsters' theme pub: The end of an era for Towcester.

Val and Pat left Blakesley and became stewards of a Working Men's Club in Northampton. They had many moves and, eventually, after Pat had been caught with his hand in the till, he left Valerie and went to live with her daughter! Poor Val stayed in the Northampton area and died of a heart attack some 10 years after leaving Blakesley; she was in her early 50s. Pat was employed as a barman in numerous pubs in the area and eventually died of cancer of the tongue in his early 50s. I never knew what happened to the daughter, nor did I care.

Trade at Blakesley was very good for a village pub, but a good week equalled only two days' beer trade at Woodford. Initially we stocked Watneys beers because they were the most popular in the area. Having spent a most enjoyable evening in the company of Mike Hurdle, Managing Director of Marstons Brewery during a visit to Burton-on-Trent Rugby Club with Jimmy Hunter, I also stocked Marstons Pedigree Ale, which, over the years, was to prove our most popular beer. After a year, we were selling a total of five barrels of beer a week and considerably more spirits than we ever sold at Woodford. Beer in 1976 was 21p a pint and we were averaging £1,200 takings a week, boosted somewhat by having five letting rooms.

Once we settled in, I started to think about alterations. A back room, which had been used as a skittle room, had a most magnificent inglenook fireplace covering the whole width of one end. The only problem was at some time a breezeblock wall had been built at the back and had been painted with apple green gloss! There was a young talented bricklayer in the village and I got him to demolish the breeze blocks and replace them with local stone.

In one of the out buildings was an old baker's oven from the days when the pub had also been the local bakery. Phil Cowgill, the builder, removed the oven and built it into the inglenook fireplace. He did a splendid job and it looked as though it had always been there. With new carpet and furniture, these alterations gave us a very comfortable lounge bar. We were doing quite a few functions in the large upstairs room in which I had built a bar counter with back fitting, installed electric panel radiators and bought new tables and chairs.

I arranged for an old friend, Bob Carvell, an architect with Watneys, to draw up plans to completely re-arrange the ground floor area, which entailed turning our private lounge into a public bar. New toilets were to be built to the rear of the premises and the kitchen area extended. Two new bathrooms would be built above the new toilet block and the area above the garages converted into a three-bedroom flat complete with lounge, kitchen and bathroom for us. The plans were submitted to the local council and, after a few minor alterations, approved.

However, an extended dispute with a developer who I thought I was a partner with, delayed the start and it was some years before we could consider carrying out alterations.

We make our mark on village life

One of the first alterations we made was changing the name from the Red Lion to the Bartholomew Arms. There were five Red Lions in surrounding villages and I always thought it a rather insipid name for a pub, "Arms" seemed a much grander title. We considered various names, e.g. Mountbatten Arms (I only knew of one other), the Grafton Arms, after the local hunt, but not being very pro hunting, I didn't want it to become the HQ of the "unspeakable".

The Bartholomew family had once owned most of the village

and were very well thought of. The last squire, Charles W. Bartholomew, who died in 1919 was a very generous benefactor to the village. He lived at Blakesley Hall, which was built in 1100 as a hospice by the Knights of St John of Jerusalem. In 1903, he laid down a 15-inch gauge railway in its grounds. The track ran between the Hall and village station on the Northampton to Stratford-on-Avon railway line. Two American-built steam locomotives pulled a train with family guests in open carriages, and wagons of coal for the hall boilers. During WW2, the Army used the hall and in 1957, sadly, it was demolished.

With one or two exceptions, the change of name was much appreciated by the village elder brethren. I had the sign repainted with the coat-of-arms of the Bartholomew family and the pub was soon known as "The Bart".

Our first regular customers from the village in the early days included: the brothers Doug and Peter Blake, Tony Salmons, Bill, John, Les, Derek and Gordon Bodily, Brian Paine, Albert Kelcher, Reg Reynolds, Bob Patterson, John Ford, Stanley Pickworth, John Bourne, Tony Penny, Miles Clark, George Powell, Mick Gulliman, Gerald & Muriel Townsend, Brian & Phil Cowgill, Mickey Brown, Dick Bird, Gerald Chidwick, Don Boon, Keith Wheeler, Bill Darby, Roy Cunningham, Ted Kirkham, Cyril King, John Weekley, Colin King and Graham Jones. Farmers Rob Cockerill, John Sheppard, Eric Broomfield, Barry Osborne, Frank Osborne, Roy Wilson, Joe and Linda Jefferson. Village tradesmen Peter Tanswell, garage owner, Doug Brown, baker and shopkeeper, John Ivens, builder and David White butcher. Many of their wives were also customers.

The village had an excellent parson in Bishop Alan Rogers; he had previously been the Bishop of Mauritius and originally bought a house in the village for his retirement. When he finally retired and moved to Blakesley, the Bishop of Peterborough asked him if he would help out in the area which he agreed to do. He was a very good lunchtime customer. As soon as we were organised and commenced serving bar snacks, a lot of our Plessey and Towcester

RDC customers from the Brave Old Oak started using the pub at lunchtime.

Our first real involvement in village life came with the Queen's Jubilee celebrations in June 1977. While there were quite a few events organised for children, to my surprise very little had been organised in the way of entertainment for adults. The streets were strung with banners made from Union Jack fertilizer bags, and in the evening, a barbecue was held in local farmer John Sheppard's barn. Very little else was planned.

Blakesley once had had a thriving cricket team, but, due to personality clashes, had not fielded a team for a number of years. Some weeks previously, following a challenge from Roy Cunningham, I mowed a wicket on the cricket square and we had a most enjoyable game between two teams drawn from the pub customers. As a result, with help and encouragement from Doug and Peter Blake, Miles Clark and John Bourne, I organised a fun cricket match as part of the village celebrations.

Held on Jubilee Day, it consisted of two teams each of 25 men and women, representing the top and bottom halves of the village. The women dressed in St Trinians outfits and the men as country yokels. I donated a barrel of beer and numerous flagons of cider. Before going into bat, each player had to drink a half-pint of beer or cider and repeat it when given out. If a batsman hit a four or a six, he had to leave the field and drink another half. If a bowler bowled someone out or a fielder took a catch, they too would have to leave the field and do likewise. If a fielder dropped a catch, he would have to drink a pint. Most people taking part finished the match in a very merry condition and all voted it a resounding success.

During the match, hilarious as it was, I was aware that we had some very good cricketers in the village. As a result, I arranged a couple of friendly matches against neighbouring pubs and the seeds were sown for next season's Bartholomew Arms Cricket Club.

I started to work on the playing field early in 1978. The local council had a contract to mow the field once a month. This had been satisfactory for normal everyday use but unsuitable for a cricket arena. At my request, the playing field committee bought a set of gang mowers and I bought a small tractor with which to tow them. The actual wicket area (the square) had deteriorated considerably through lack of maintenance, and I had to spend many hours getting rid of the weeds and moss.

I affiliated the club to the Northants Cricket Association and, as a result, was invited to attend a five-day goundsman's course at Motspur Park in Surrey. The lectures were given by groundsmen from Lords and Oval Cricket Grounds, Wembley Stadium and Wimbledon Lawn Tennis Club. It was a most interesting and informative week and I learnt a tremendous amount about the care and preparation of grass surfaces.

As the playing field soil was very sandy I sent a sample to Motspur Park for analysis and they recommended the incorporation of five tons of Nottingham marl into the wicket area. This marl was a combination of brick dust and clay ground to a fine red powder. We had no club funds so I paid for it, which, with delivery, cost about £100. I also hired a mechanical aerator, which took out plugs of soil to be refilled with the marl. The effect of this treatment was to provide a solid wicket surface, hardwearing and true.

We were very fortunate that one our players, my friend Jim Wallis, was manager of a plant hire business in Northampton. He provided me with a mechanical roller which saved hours of preparation. A further member of the team was another friend, David Powell. He let us have a knapsack sprayer and chemicals to kill the nettles surrounding the outfield, and trimmed the boundary hedges for us. Gradually the playing field took shape and we started raising funds to purchase kit.

Under the supervision of Brian and Phil Cowgill, we laid a concrete practice wicket and, when funds allowed, purchased netting and matting. Bob Allen, our American player who lived in the village, obtained caps for all the players from his base PX, with the initials BA on them. We also had sweater badges made with the Bartholomew coat of arms on them and a club tie with the same motif.

I contacted local teams and in no time, we had a very good fixture list, playing 20 games a season – all home matches. One particular attractive fixture was an all-day game against Ben Collins's XI. Ben, an ex-captain of Northampton FC, the proprietor of a sports shop in Northampton and his team consisted of ex-Northampton FC players and local personalities. We started playing at 10.45 a.m. and adjourned to the pub for lunch at 12.30, restarting at 2 p.m.

Our early teams were picked from Tony Salmons, Brian Payne, Gordon Bodily, Derek Bodily, David Powell, Jim Wallis, Tony Penny, Brian Stanley, Roy Andrews, Dick Finch, Doug Blake, Peter Blake, Steven Bodily, John Bourne, Bill Brown, Roy Cunningham, Miles Clark, yours truly and Bob, the American. Later on Norman, a coloured American airman, became our secret weapon. Fielding in the dark shadows on the boundary, he would emerge into the bright light, to the surprise of opposing batsmen, and take some splendid catches.

We had mixed fortunes during the first few seasons but, over the years, as village youths became proficient enough, we usually won more matches than we lost. Up and coming young village players who were to play for the team, included the James brothers, Willie & John, both good batsmen, David, Jamie and Paul Cunningham, Peter Bodily, Roger Bird, a very good all-rounder and county youth player, Simon Weekly, also a county youth player, became our No 1 strike bowler, Simon Bourne, Peter Diamond, David Smith, Raymond Paine as dour a player as he was in character (he later became headmaster of a school at Bedford), Peter Sheppard and Richard Heritage. David Cunningham joined the Royal Navy and the last I heard he was a Lieut Commander; all credit to him he was a very nice lad.

Other players who played an important role in later years included Brian Smith an excellent all rounder who I had played with at Rushden, Frank Hunter, a very stylish batsman, Jim Wastell, small in statue but with a heart as big as an ox's, David Bailey, Dave Halliday and Alan Whiffel who left us to captain Towcester Town. Gerald Chidwick, Ivor Denny, John Currie England Rugby player, and Mike Dilley an ex-Northamptonshire County speed merchant, all made appearances.

I brought Mike into the side as our secret weapon against Ben Collins's XI. In the four years we had played Ben's team, they usually gave us a drubbing. I thought they were beginning to rub it in a bit too much so, through Brian Smith, I made contact with Mike who had played for Irthlingborough Town XI before he joined the county side. In his prime, he was an extremely fast bowler with perfect physique for the part, but the years had taken its toll reducing him to medium pace. Even so, he was faster than any bowler we usually faced and as his bowling speed decreased, his batting improved. On the day, Mike took five wickets for 16 runs and scored 46 helping us to a resounding victory. In an unexpected show of bad sportsmanship, Ben's team never played us again.

John (Muscles) Currie was a big friend of David Powell. At 6' 4", he made 25 appearances for England 1956-62 alongside his second row partner David Marques. Their partnership for England was spoken of in hushed terms; two living legends. They were tremendous jumpers in the lineout unaided by the lift-up technique now legal in modern rugby. It was once said that Marques jumped so high in a match against Ireland that his marker despaired of ever getting the ball. He became so frustrated that at one lineout he decided the only way to counter Marques as he went up was, as it were, to grab a handful of genitalia. As he landed and passed the ball to his scrumhalf, Marques turned to the Irishman and enquired: "Are you trying to prove something?"

John was a talented, fluent batsman and an asset to the team on the all too few times he turned out for us.

I averaged 30 hours a week working on the playing field, mowing the outfield, preparing wickets and cleaning the pavilion. Although the majority of villagers were full of praise for my efforts, there was opposition from some quarters. Over the years the village cricket and football clubs had been run and dominated by the larger village families. Some of their elders did not take too kindly to an "outsider" muscling in on their territory and were quite vocal in their opposition.

Most people knew that it was because of the infighting that occurred within these families that the teams had ceased to exist. Certain members of the playing field committee accused me of using the village facilities for my own financial advantage and wanted the team to be called Blakesley CC. I put this proposal to the team and they voted unanimously for it to remain "The Barts".

As for the accusation that I was using the playing field for my own ends, prior to my resurrecting the cricket team, the playing field committee paid the district council £300 for six mows a year. I bought a tractor for £400 and mowed it twice a week during the growing season for free. In addition, I mowed and maintained the area round the children's play area, removing mountains of dog pooh in the process. I bought four mole traps and in the first few months caught eight moles that over time had reduced the outfield to the look of a ploughed field. Within a year, the mole problem had been eradicated.

The majority of the villagers said that the tidiness and general standard of the playing field had never been better and was a credit to the village. I personally paid for all petrol, diesel, fertiliser, weed killer, whitewash for marking the creases and boundaries, blanco for pads, disinfectants and cleaners for the showers and toilets, toilet rolls, etc., etc. Before we had raised sufficient funds for the club, I paid for a set of stumps, two bats, pads and numerous cricket balls.

To sum up, I was the honorary groundsman, kit maintenance man and pavilion cleaner. Sylvia, for her part, prepared the teas for both teams and spectators, often without assistance. This was after she had been on the go since early morning and would be working again during the evening. Sometimes we paid a member of our staff to assist her. It would have been easy to become disillusioned with the sniping and called a halt to it, but I was determined to provide the facilities the village deserved.

One year I organised a tour to the West Country. I placed an advert in the *Western Morning News* for opponents with no success. Not to be daunted, some 16 players and supporters complete with kit, set out for the Webbington Country Club near Weston-super-Mare for a hilarious weekend. Although we didn't play any cricket, the team scored in more ways than one. We certainly left our mark in the watering holes of the town. Were I to give a full report of the weekend's activities, I would lay myself open to charges of defamation of character; suffice to say we had a most enjoyable and entertaining "Cricket Tour".

I had been appointed skipper since the team was formed and after six years relinquished the position to Jim Wallis. I was hoping that Jim, as captain, would take some of the workload off me but it didn't materialize, even though he lived next to the ground. Jim's view was that in providing the roller he had done his share towards the club. I pointed out that though we were very grateful to have the use of the roller, someone had to operate it and if no one was prepared to do the physical work, the club would fold.

Jim and I had been good friends for a number of years and, together with David Powell and Rob Cockerill, had shared many experiences together; I think it was true that he had purposely moved to Blakesley to be nearer my pub. It was therefore with extreme sadness that the impasse over how much work he should be responsible for as captain of the club, led ultimately to our falling out. Although we would be in each other's company on odd occasions away from the pub, he never entered The Bart Arms again until the day of Rob's funeral.

Brian Smith took over the captaincy of the club and was a most able skipper until, sadly, a heart attack brought to an early end his cricketing career. He and his lovely wife Jean eventually took a pub in a village near Cambridge for a few years before Jean's early death brought that to a tragic end. Brian remained a good friend and visited us in Cornwall each year until a series of heart attacks finally claimed his life in his early 50s.

Richard Heritage, then in his early 20s, took over the captaincy and being of a similar age to the rest of the team seemed the ideal choice. Most of the original players, including myself, had retired from the game and the average age of the players was late teens. Richard was badly let down by a number of the very young players, both in their style of dress and their behaviour on the field. He lacked the ability to "whip them into line" which a more senior captain would have done.

Because of the "win at all cost" attitude adopted by the team, quite a few of the old opponents dropped us from their fixture list. John Ivens who had been the club President for a number of years and a regular spectator, told me he was disgusted with the team's bad language and objected to players turning out in jeans with shirts hanging out. One player had pink hair! Consequently he resigned from his post.

I had continued to prepare the ground for matches but other commitments meant that I did not have the time to devote myself fully to it. Richard assisted me but no other players offered any help. When I didn't prepare the wicket, they used an old strip rather than mark out a new one. Eventually I became more and more disillusioned with the state of affairs and called a special meeting of the players to sort things out.

When I stated that I would no longer be able to work on the field I was staggered to be asked if I would run raffles in the pub to pay for a groundsman! At that time, some 20 youngsters were involved in the club. That was the final straw and I told the meeting that I no longer wanted them to play under the name of the Bartholomew Arms CC and I would withdraw my financial support. The club had existed for 12 years and it was not a decision I took lightly but the team had become an embarrassment to me and a poor advertisement for the pub. So the club folded up.

The Bartholomew Arms societies

In addition to the cricket club, we had a pub football team playing in a very smart white strip with red shorts. Most of the team was on the wrong side of 30 but we made up for lack of mobility with a degree of cunning. Our defence, i.e. Peter and Doug Blake, David Powell, Jim Wallis and Frank Osborne, averaged 15 stone! I played in goal and had the good fortune to save three penalties in one game. Thereafter I was known as "The Cat". Tony Penny made a name for himself as our striker, quite what he struck we never found out but he scored a number of goals with his head.

Jim Wallis was also involved with me in forming and organising the Bart Arms Horticultural Society. It started as the largest pumpkin growing competition and progressed to competitions for the largest carrot, onion, marrow and runner bean. Jim invariably won the pumpkin competition having the advantage of growing some 20 plants in the corner of Eric Dickens's field. I won the prize for the heaviest onion one year with a weight of 3lb 12oz and should have won it again but for a tragic accident.

The night before the weigh-in I brought my heaviest onion into the bar, showing it off to customers, and unfortunately left it behind the counter after we closed. When Sylvia cleaned up in the morning she placed it out of the way in the kitchen.

Ann Broomfield, a young village girl who worked for us at weekends, was asked by Sylvia to make up a supply of filled rolls for sale that day. Cheese and onion was our best seller and my prize onion made 5 dozen rolls with some left over! Even the most cautious estimate of its weight put it in the 4 lb plus category. Poor Ann was beside herself with grief but everyone, bar me, saw the funny side of it. It was the main topic of conversation for a long time. Ann was such a lovely girl it was impossible to be cross with her.

In conjunction with the weigh-in, I went to St Neots produce market with Les and Joyce Shaw, and brought back loads of produce, which, together with the entries for the competitions, we auctioned off after the prize giving. The produce auction was always well attended and customers gave generously with the money raised going towards a Community Fund I had started, out of which we provided a Christmas dinner for our senior customers. Some 30 of the village elderly would sit down to a slap-up dinner in our upstairs function room. It was at one of these produce auctions that John Ivens was to have the first of his strokes which eventually led to his death.

When the room was turned into our private lounge the dinners carried on in the bars for a number of years but the produce auction was not as successful downstairs, simply because we were unable to display the produce properly. Eventually we handed over the running of the dinner to the local Darby and Joan Club but continued to raise money for it from raffles in the pub. After a number of years, when many of the village elders had died, it meant that members of the club from other villages outnumbered the OAPs from Blakesley. It was felt unacceptable that we were raising money from customers to entertain non-customers and, after some 12 years, it sadly ceased.

In the mid 1980s, our eldest son, Stephen, had been given a quiz game (Trivial Pursuit had not yet been invented) for Christmas and we spent an enjoyable evening playing it. Because of this experience, I thought it would be a good idea to hold a Quiz Evening in the pub. This was long before pub quiz leagues had been invented and we may well have been the instigators of what was to become a countrywide activity.

We held the quiz in the back room of the pub in that first year. I was the quizmaster; Derek Lucas was timekeeper and six teams of four entered. A team representing Woodend won the evening and afterwards it was agreed to make this a regular event. We decided to form a league within the pub, and hold a quiz on the first Thursday evening each month, from October to April.

Six teams of four regularly entered with such names as Bart's Bashers, Woodend Wallies, No Hopers, Know Alls, Greens Norton Gobsters and Soil Scratchers. In its second year, Derek Lucas took over as quizmaster with Lynda Maude as his assistant. Each team had three minutes to try and answer 20 questions with three rounds per team. We moved the action to the upstairs room with only the Question Master, assistant and team answering the questions present. This avoided having the answers given by spectators. Soon after I bought a video camera, installed it on a tripod in the room, and relayed pictures to a large TV set in the bar. This way, the other teams could hear the questions and answers and watch the antics of the competitors. I think this was another first for the Bart Arms.

Quiz night turned what would have been a quiet winter evening into a very busy night. We provided quite substantial snacks for the teams and at the end of the season; trophies were presented to the winners. I derived great satisfaction that the quiz evenings continued after we left the Bart.

Another event I started, which proved very popular, was the Annual Easter Egg Hunt.

I first organised it in 1977, an event open to children from the village aged 10 years and under and, with the assistance of sons Stephen and Timothy; we hid 200 gaily painted hard-boiled eggs in the hedgerows surrounding the playing field. We hid a further 50 around the tennis courts to be found by the under-four-year-olds. In addition, a "Golden Egg" was hidden at each location. The child who found the most eggs in each group was awarded a prize, and a similar prize went to the children who found the Golden Eggs.

We always had a very good turn out with some 40 children taking part and much competition among the competitors. Some of the younger ones would spoil their chance of winning by eating any egg they found before the count! A press cutting from that first year tells me that 10-year-old James Burt won the senior event with 28 eggs and four-year-old Carl Webb the junior. Alison Smith and Leesa Penny won the prizes for the senior and junior Golden Eggs.

Over the years, the eggs changed from hard-boiled eggs to 500 chocolate eggs and then to 800 wrapped lollypops. Future winners came from practically every family in the village and, up to when I left the pub, early competitors, now parents themselves, brought their offspring along to take part. It was sad that the villagers allowed the lovely growing-up tradition in Blakesley to die out.

After we had been at the Bart a couple of years, I organised a fancy dress party each New Year's Eve. I applied for a 2 a.m. extension of hours, which, surprisingly, the magistrates always granted. Perhaps it was because I told them we would use the occasion to raise money for our OAP Christmas Party. We were the only pub in the Towcester district to have such an extension. Originally, we held the party in the upstairs room but, after the alterations, we held it in the bars. They were always well attended and, for two years, we had the added attraction of the village jazz band performing on the night.

Another seasonal attraction was the Boxing Day food that varied from a cold buffet to a selection of curries. A help-yourself do, it started at 3 p.m. and carried on through till closing time. It was intended as a way of saying "thank you" to our regulars for their custom throughout the year. Naturally, being a free do, there were some non-regulars who took advantage but most people played the game.

The new Bart Arms takes shape

Trade had increased considerably to such an extent that by 1981 we badly needed more space to accommodate everyone. We had given a lot of thought about moving on but I think it was true to say, though still in our late 40s, the ambition to reach the top in our profession had diminished. Blakesley was such a lovely peaceful village in which to live. Our eldest son, Stephen, had left home and was living in a neighbouring village; at the time he was working as an estate agent and would shortly marry Mary; Timothy was still at home and had a good job locally as an agricultural engineer; Michael was attending a school in Towcester.

Work on our long-awaited alterations started in 1982. This involved incorporating our private lounge into the public area, moving the existing bar counter to the other end of the bar and continuing the servery through into the new area. The staircase was removed and a new stairs created bringing back into use the stairs that Mrs Bolton had installed to give her access to the upstairs function room. The room, which had been a great asset for functions, dinners, etc., became our new private lounge.

The local farmers had used the room to hold their monthly show meetings. The Blakesley Show, inaugurated in 1873, is a very successful event, one of the few remaining village agricultural shows in the country. Held in August each year, it attracted large crowds of people from the surrounding area; the committee, some 20 strong, were rather a mixed blessing to the pub. Most of them only used the premises on show meeting nights, but they seemed to be of the opinion that they were God's gift to wherever they chose to patronise.

In common with so many farmers, they were extremely noisy and generally we found that other customers stayed away on meeting nights. I always attributed their noisiness to having their nearest neighbours some distance away, and needing to carry on a conversation at the top of their voices!

As we had experienced at Thrapston market, farmers could be divided into two camps, those that bought more than their share of drinks, and those who never bought any. The former tended to be our regular customers and the latter the noisy ones. They would wait with their empty glasses until someone was buying a round, at which stage they would all put their glasses up for replenishment. Serving them was a nightmare. Most drank half-pints, which meant that a new round was started before all had received their drink from the last round. Some, who had not emptied their glasses, would ask to be included in the new round, and you had to try and remember who had received their drink in that particular round and who had not. The person paying had no idea just who he was buying for, and would often think he had been overcharged.

What with the noise, was it any wonder that we had difficulty getting staff to work on meeting nights? Generally, our takings were always down on what a similar amount of regular customers would spend over the same period. We were hoping that they would look for another venue for their meetings, and, when we closed our function room, to our dismay, they asked to hold their meetings in the lounge bar. It was some years before they finally got the message and looked for another venue. It was rather significant that my good friend Rob Cockerill very rarely attended the meetings; he too was very critical of their behaviour.

It was about this time that Ken and Liz Vaughan moved into the village; Ken was to play a large role in our future life at Blakesley. He was converting a barn in the village into their home. His builder, helping with the structural work, often accompanied Ken to the Bart for liquid refreshment.

Tony Lucas, the builder, had spent his early working years as a carpenter at the Pinewood Film Studios. I soon realised he was the ideal person to convert the ideas I had for the Bart into reality. I did initially have problems with him sloping off to complete other jobs he had started, but after a good old-fashioned "bust up" he, with assistance from Phil Cowgill and myself acting as labourer, completed the job in record time. Les Shaw supplied some beautiful old oak beams from a barn he was demolishing and Tony fitted them so well that they looked part of the original fabric. During demolition of part of a wall to create a doorway, we found an old fireplace and we made its chimney into a feature.

It was during the alterations that Watneys ceased brewing Starlight Ale, extremely popular with the customers, and the head brewer reliably informed me that we had received the very last barrel to leave the brewery. I filled a pint bottle with the last of the beer and, with due ceremony, had it cemented into a cavity we had created in the wall of the lounge bar. Together with the bottle were photographs taken of the bars before the alterations, and a document containing the names of Tony and Phil and Sylvia, our sons and myself. The Falklands War had just started and before the walls were repapered, I invited customers to write anti Argentine slogans on the wall with felt pens. I often wonder what future generations will make of it.

I paid Phil and Tony by the hour and the job came out some £1,000 under the projected budget of £9,000. Three men from a local *"Jesus Army"* commune carried out the decorating.

This organisation started life as a breakaway group from a chapel in the village of Bugbrook. Its members had to hand over all their worldly goods to the concern. They had grown to become one of the largest building supplies and contractors in the area. The men, mainly reformed drug and alcohol addicts, received free board and lodgings at the commune, and all the money they earned went to a central fund from which they were given £5 wages a week.

Phil and Tony questioned them about the rumours circulating that the commune was involved in free love. Had they received confirmation of their suspicions, I think both of them would have suddenly become religious fanatics and joined. At lunchtime, all three sat in their vehicle and read passages from the Bible to each other. They were very professional in their work and I was very pleased with the end result. We spent a lot on carpets, curtaining and extra furniture.

The kitchen was refitted with new stainless steel equipment including a large eight burner cooker, fryer, griddle, 6-pot bain marie, salamander and hot cupboards. A large walk-in pantry led off the kitchen and this contained, apart from dry goods, fridges and an electric bacon slicer.

We'd always had a sizeable collection of artefacts in all our pubs, but now set about buying even more. When we had finished, it was impossible to put your hand on the wall without touching an object. We had six ships in glass cases, stuffed fish and birds in cases, numerous ships artefacts including a magnificent Engine Room Telegraph.

One of the ships was a remarkable model of the *Cutty Sark*. It was made by Jack Humphreys who had been my first brewery representative when I took the Brave Old Oak. He had spent eight years building it and it was still not quite finished when he died. He had told his widow that he wanted me to have it as he had always admired my collection when visiting the Bart. I got Dick Foster, our local policeman, to finish it off for me and case it. Dick was a very good model maker and I bought quite a lot of ships and artefacts from him.

We had numerous old autographed cricket bats; the oldest sported a silver plaque stating it was presented to a Jake Chisholm in 1856. The best one was signed by all the 1934 Australian Test Team and included the signature of Don Bradman. In the inglenook were six hams that I had cured years previously. It was Fred Roberts, my butcher from Woodford, who taught me how to cure them. Also in the inglenook was a large collection of copperware, an old knife cleaner, stuffed foxes, a giant tortoise shell and six very old stone jars.

The beams were covered with ancient flintlock guns and swords. We had lots of old clocks including two fine grandfather clocks and an old National Time Recorder clocking in machine. I displayed crests from the seven ships on which I had served, and the torpedo room clock from the submarine *HMS Sidon*. Numerous displayed photographs and newspaper cuttings told the story of how in 1955 the *Sidon* sank in Portland Harbour with the tragic loss of 18 lives following an explosion in the torpedo room.

Where any space existed, pictures of many subjects including naval, cricket, hunting and rugby filled the gaps. In a lobby at the top of the stairs leading to the ladies' toilet, was a wheelchair that had once belonged to Mistinguett the famous French music hall artist who had been the mistress of Maurice Chevalier. It was unique with slender wooden carriage wheels and deep leather upholstery. Mounted high on the walls, outstanding in their majesty, were two large stags' heads.

The foot of the stairs was guarded by a carved figure 4 ft high depicting an old peg-legged seaman bearing an Alms Box with the lettering, "Give a Penny to the Seaman's Home". It was surprising how many ladies placed coins in the box on their way to the toilet. We bought the figure and the wheelchair in Ringwood, Hants, from an antique shop run by Martin & Judith Miller who went on to produce *Millers Antiques Guide*.

One resident said it took him three visits to take in all the items on display.

Some village characters

A lot of our other artefacts came from Joe Jefferson. Joe was a local institution, a farmer and *Dealer in Collectables* who, together with Bob Patterson, was our most regular morning customer. Most days Joe would either produce an object from his pocket with the comment "I don't know what this is worth?" or ask you to go and look at items in the boot of his car. He was an extremely knowledgeable and shrewd dealer in "objects d'art" and, in spite of acting unsure, knew the true value of every item. Sylvia must have been his best customer and even today our house is full of items she bought from him. His prices were usually very fair and we have re-sold many pieces at a good profit.

One day he brought a plate into the pub, for which he was asking £70. Very elaborately decorated, he said it was part of a dinner service belonging to the Emperor Napoleon Bonaparte. I slipped out into the kitchen and brought back a cheap dinner plate, which I hid under my pullover. I asked Joe if I could look at his plate and swapped the plates over, letting the hidden one drop to the floor where it broke with a loud crash. Poor Joe was beside himself with shock and with difficulty croaked, "You'll have to pay – you'll have to pay." Having turned a bright purple and worried he might have a fit; I admitted what I had done. Joe never let me handle anything breakable again. His death, after a long illness, robbed the community of a great character.

A contemporary of Joe's was Eric Broomfield, also a farmer.

Eric's main claim to fame was playing for Northampton Rugby Club. A hooker, he played for the club on 52 occasions between 1945-1954. He was the father of Mark, our son Timothy's best friend, Paul, Tim and Ann. They were all very well mannered nice children. Eric's lesser fame was his reluctance to part with money for a round of drinks.

Another trick I played which is still talked about by customers, involved my good friend Fred Dixon, one of our original Southfield GGGC members. Having relinquished the position of landlord of the Pirates Den, Fred and his wife Val moved into one of Rob Cockerill's farm cottages at Southfields. We had a very heavy snowfall one winter in the '70s, the village was cut off for four days. Val had recently given birth to young Fred and was desperate for provisions, including eggs for the baby's lunch.

Fred set off with a shovel and after a long treacherous journey finally arrived in the village and bought the required supplies from the village shop. He then decided he could not face the return journey without some form of sustenance and entered the pub, putting his supplies on a table. Five or six pints later, with many mutterings that, "Val will kill me if I don't get back with the eggs," Fred finally set out for the journey home. Due to the slippery conditions, and possibly the beer, he fell down many times but conscious of saving the baby's lunch held the eggs high above his head.

On arriving at the house, Val let Fred know in no uncertain manner that she was "aggrieved" for the time it had taken him. Fred was upset that Val did not appreciate the hazardous conditions he had battled through and the fact that in spite of the falls had delivered the eggs intact. It was therefore with some degree of astonishment that when Val went to crack the eggs they were solid. Fred's first thought was they must have frozen during the journey but this was dispelled when Val showed them to him. At some stage during Fred's pause for refreshment, I had taken the eggs into the kitchen and, for a joke, hard-boiled them. It was with a degree of sad pride that a couple of years ago at Fred's funeral, his lovely daughter, Louise, recounted this story to the very large congregation. During the same winter, Fred was party to another amusing happening.

I was sitting with Fred in the bar when I received a telephone call from a farmer in the nearby village of Preston Capes, asking if we could accommodate ten soldiers. The farmer had one of the largest farms in the area and was very high tech with radio telephone receivers fitted in all his vehicles. Portable telephones had not yet been invented.

An unexpected blizzard hit the area and suddenly, to his amazement, three helicopters landed in his field close by his Land Rover. He was equally surprised when a soldier wearing a grey beret emerged from one of them and ran over to him. The soldier, in turn, was surprised that a farmer should have such up to date technology installed in his vehicle and was able to telephone us to enquire about accommodation. Anyway, I said that we should be delighted to accommodate them and returned to Fred in the bar.

Fred was then working at the Crossroads Hotel, Weedon, owned by Richard Amos, another of our shooting crowd. Although the Crossroads was a much larger concern, Fred and I had an ongoing rivalry regarding which of our two establishments was the more exclusive.

Suddenly we heard the sound of the helicopters circling the village and Fred asked why were they flying so low. I told him they were probably customers, I said, unlike the Crossroads, a lot of our customers arrived by helicopter. Fred accused me of "bullshitting" and I told him to just wait and see. Minutes later they hovered before landing in a field opposite the pub. We then saw a soldier climb over the gate and walk towards the pub. I greeted him at the door and he asked, "I believe you have some rooms booked for us?" I looked at Fred, his eyes were popping out with amazement.

The helicopters were en-route from Lee-on-Solent, where the Royal Navy serviced them, to Catterick Camp in Yorkshire. While they were in the air a sergeant, the senior pilot was in charge.

Once they landed, one of two majors was then in charge and he obtained authorisation from Catterick to have all accommodation, food and drink on credit. They stayed a couple of days until the weather improved, and the locals had two most enjoyable evenings drinking with them.

When they came to leave, one of the helicopters refused to start despite the soldiers holding burning newspaper to the fuel lines. They decided that two helicopters would leave and the other would remain at Blakesley awaiting a repair crew. It was then that an argument took place between the major and sergeant about who should stay behind with the disabled machine. It was obvious each one wanted to enjoy another evening of our hospitality. The major argued that as the senior rank it was his decision, whereas the sergeant said it was a flying matter and therefore his. They ended up returning to the pub and throwing three darts each, the one with the higher score stayed.

We had a lovely surprise some two months later when the two majors and sergeant came to the pub and presented us with an Army Flying Corps plaque. They said their stay was an unforgettable experience. I thought to myself the same applied to Fred Dixon.

During that same winter, the village grit boxes, used for salting the roads, had emptied. I telephoned the council and was told that no more salt was available due to cutbacks. In the pub that lunchtime, we hatched a plot to shame the council into providing more road salt for the village.

We studied a map of Russia and picked out a town in Siberia named Verkoyansk. John Matthews rang the local paper and told them that some time back, Blakesley had sent flour to a town in Russia when they were facing a famine. We had since twinned with the town, Verkoyansk, and they, having heard we had no salt, were sending us a delivery with their mayor. The paper agreed to report our story and sent a reporter and photographer for the ceremony. Their report was as follows: -

RED ALERT ON VILLAGE ROADS

"Villagers in Blakesley stared in fascination as a shiny black limousine drew up outside the local pub carrying a Russian mayor, an interpreter and a KGB security man.

Vladimir Timov, mayor of Verkoyansk in Siberia, famous for all its salt, was there to commiserate with Blakesley over the state of their slippery roads.

Before enjoying a glass of vodka with Parish Council Chairman, Charlie Burbridge, the mayor spoke, with the help of an interpreter, saying that he had heard that we were so poor in England that we couldn't afford to repair our roads and so needed salt. He had hurried over here as soon as he could with his present of a year's supply."

John Matthews played the part of the mayor and Ken Vaughan the interpreter. A photograph showing John and Charlie spreading the salt, with Ken looking on, accompanied the article.

Prior to "the mayor" arriving, we had erected a Union Jack and Russian Hammer and Sickle flag on poles each side of the bin. When the limousine arrived, driven by Peter Blake dressed in a black leather jacket, beret and wearing dark sunglasses, I played the Russian national anthem from two loud speakers mounted in the pub upstairs windows. John Matthews, wearing a fur coat and hat, stepped out of the car and was greeted by Charlie Burbridge. Ken Vaughan, looking like a typical Foreign Office official in his morning suit, acted as an interpreter. The mayor stepped forward and with a silver spade – one we had covered in tinfoil – scattered some salt on the road. Sylvia then approached the group with glasses of vodka which after drinking, they threw the empty glasses against the salt bin. It was surprising how many villagers, who watched the ceremony, thought it was genuine.

The day after the report was published, the council sent a lorry and filled our salt bins.

Characters make village and pub life. Here are some others I recall.

Albert Kelcher came from an old Blakesley family and was semi-retired when we moved to the village. He was an asset to the pub in the way he would quickly engage strangers in conversation. In no time he would learn who they were, what brought them to the pub, and, if they had moved to the village, where their interests lay. He would then steer them towards locals with similar interests and leave the two to converse. Some might class it as nosiness but Albert was a naturally inquisitive person. His direct approach soon made people feel at ease and, in the case of new villagers, he welcomed them into the community.

He was a widower in his late 70s living on his own, and with the Bart his second home it was natural that he was always one of the last customers to leave each evening. It was one such night when a few of the "late nighters" had stayed on to celebrate Sylvia's birthday. At about 2 a.m. Albert, by then a little unsteady on his feet, fell backwards and caught his head on the corner of a dado rail. In spite of Sylvia's efforts with wet towels, the wound bled profusely and eventually we decided it best to call an ambulance. Albert vigorously protested saying he did not want to go but when the ambulance men saw the wound, they convinced him hospital was the best place. Sylvia followed the ambulance to the hospital and, after twelve stitches to the wound, brought him back. Poor Albert was so embarrassed, entirely unnecessarily, that he never came into the pub again in spite of John Sheppard's best attempts to get him there.

Of a similar age was Cyril "Tiddler" King. He lived in the village with his sister Dolly and his somewhat eccentric behaviour came to life when, without warning, he would recite a poem or sing a song. His demeanour would fluctuate between being an entertainer or dammed nuisance depending on whether he was taking his tablets. I clearly remember an instance, when watching the cricket, he thought our bowlers were incapable of taking a wicket so he strode onto the pitch wanting to bowl. I had to explain to him that as he hadn't been selected to play that week he would be unable to bowl. After threatening to report me to the MCC, he was escorted off the field. Apparently in his day, he had been a very good cricketer and footballer.

Reg Reynolds, one of three sporting brothers, was the first umpire for the Barts CC. Reg, a chauffeur for Plessey, delivered many visitors to the Brave Old Oak. Always having a good word to say about everyone, together with his wife Mary they were very good friends, as were his brothers Ray and Jim.

Although much younger than the others, George Powell was every one's idea of the perfect modern day villager. When we first arrived in the village, he was mortgage manager for the Anglia Building Society. Together with his lovely wife Angela, they lived opposite the pub and the paddock at the rear of their house was a mini farm. They kept goats, sheep, chickens, ducks, geese, rabbits and umpteen hamsters. Most of them had full use of the house together with their two dogs. One day the children from the village school went to George's house to see the animals as part of their studies. When they opened the door to his yard they were faced with numerous dead hamsters all minus their heads. It transpired that my Jack Russell dog, Gippy, had got under their gate, made a beeline for the hamster pens which he knocked over releasing the hamsters. Gippy then proceeded to nip their heads off before laying them out in a neat row. We offered to replace them but George pleaded, "Please don't, Tony, I never could stand the sight of the bloody things!"

George was a very talented person, he wrote the scripts for the village pantomimes as well as directing and acting in them. He loved dressing up and specialised in "drag queen – grand dame" type roles. I hasten to add that George and Angela had four children – all boys.

He took early retirement from his job with the building society and became the village postmaster, turning a room in his house into the post office. In this new role, he played an even greater part in village life. It was a big blow to the village when, his children having grown up and left home, George and Angela retired to Devon.

I first met Les Shaw, Rob Cockerill's father-in-law, through clay shooting. At the time, he lived with his wife Joyce at Greens Norton Hall, a magnificent house where I was to spend many happy hours playing him at snooker in his impressive snooker room.

At the time Les was a director of a local building firm Atkins & Shaw that later became Bacal Construction. Les had his critics but he was a good friend to both Sylvia and myself. After the war, in which he spent time as a POW, he worked as a bricklayer for Valerie Dixon's father, before teaming up with his future partner Eric Atkins. The business grew quickly and, as to be expected with such success, enemies were made. Les and Joyce were generous benefactors in their village and it was with much sadness that because of the collapse of Bacal, they had to move from their lovely home at Greens Norton.

After a series of moves, they settled at Southfields having converted Fred Dixon's cottage and the adjacent one into a single house. In no time, Les and Joyce set about making the gardens a picture and involving themselves in pub activities. After an all too short time in their new home, Joyce died in 1995 following a long illness. Sylvia and I always thought that Les was never the same afterwards and he died a few years later. We count ourselves fortunate that we were able to visit him at his nursing home some weeks before his death.

Nothing like the number of celebrities visited the Bart that visited the Brave Old Oak. We did, however, have the author Kingsley Amis as a customer on numerous occasions. What brought him to the pub, we never found out. We had a surprise one day when Mick Jagger, the pop star, walked in. The barmaids nearly swooned but I told them not to ask him for his autograph. This had always been my policy at the Brave Old Oak. I feel that celebrities should be free to walk into a pub and relax without being pestered. A large farm on the outskirts of the village was on the market and we think that Jagger had perhaps come to view it. It was also rumoured at the time that Princess Margaret was interested in buying it.

Peter Newcombe the internationally acclaimed artist and his girlfriend Jackie, were regular customers. Peter once painted a series of countryside scenes that were used by the Royal Mail on a set of postage stamps.

Another celebrity to use the pub was Michael French who, at the time, was appearing in the soap opera *East Enders*. He played the part of Pat Butcher's long lost son, David.

The actress Susan George and her actor husband Simon McCorquodale lived in the next village and were regular customers for a time.

Stanley Unwin the gobbledygook man also lived in a neighbouring village and would occasionally pop in for a ploughman's lunch and a pint of "Keggyflade"!

The National Hunt champion jockey, Richard Dunwoody was another regular caller when visiting the nearby racing stables of Terry Casey. Terry, himself an ex-jockey, lived with us for four months when he first arrived from Ireland. He trained many NH winners but the Grand National somehow always eluded him.

During our early years at Blakesley, a regular customer was Michael Batchelor. Micky was a steeplechase jockey of some repute. As a result, of his wife dying tragically giving birth, Micky took to the bottle and went off the rails. Following an incident at a nightclub in Coventry, he was robbed and hit over the head with a car jack handle. In this vicious attack, Micky lost an eye and from then on wore a glass one.

One day on leaving the pub he fell down and came back into the bar saying his glass eye had fallen out and he couldn't find it. With the help of a couple of the customers, we spent ages on our knees looking for his eye without success. I even lifted a storm drain cover to see if the eye had fallen down there. Micky left minus his eye and returned home. I received a phone call from him some time later to say he had found his eye. He had come out without it!

Of the many organisations who used the Bart Arms, none were more unusual than "The Green Friends of the Banbury Lanes", a walking group founded in 1981 by Lou Warwick and incorporating "The Strollers" which had come into being following a meeting at Joe Burgess's house in 1971.

Lou was editor of the *Northampton & County Independent,* a monthly glossy magazine. The members included Joe Burgess, Douglas Gibbs, Geoff Adington, Charlie Robinson, Roger Tyler, Reg Jones and Harry Gilby, all original Strollers, plus Tony Dutton, Stanley Joyce, Geoff Day, Ron Tookey, Stanley Welsh, Ron Tompkin and Mike Rigby. Lou gave everyone a title, e.g. Chief Slasher, Writer of the Ballads, Dawn Patroller etc.

When Sylvia, the first woman member, was enrolled in the group, she was given the title of Happy Serving Wench. For her initiation, she was led blindfolded along the lane until they came to a pond in "The Muddy Glade", whereupon she knelt down and had the "muddy hand" laid on her. Lou played the Last Post on his trumpet and she was duly elected to the secret society, as member No.19.

They had their own password, "DAGTITLA". What it stood for I never knew. Lou regularly delivered green envelopes to the pub. The contents for Sylvia's eyes only. His communications were typed on an old battered typewriter whose type had long since gone past its sell-by date. As a non-member I was not privy to their goings-on, the information I gleaned was by listening to audiotapes Lou had sent to Sylvia (she didn't know how to operate the tape player), and through the odd bits of ritual she told me of. Sometimes Lou talked to Sylvia in a strange tongue reminding me of the late Stanley Unwin.

Lou formed the group to pressurise local farmers and landowners to keep open the Banbury Lane, part of the ancient Welsh Lane, an old path used by Welsh drovers getting their sheep from Wales to the English markets. The lane had become overgrown, in places impassable. They were the instigators in having it restored to be used once again by walkers.

They assembled at the pub and, after breakfast and ample liquid refreshment, set off on a long distance walk. I had lunch prepared for them on their return and they then ate and drank until late evening. We felt greatly honoured to host their annual dinners.

Lou was a most gifted person, his poems and odes were hilarious, and he had a very vivid imagination in the manner of Spike Milligan. An author of some repute, he wrote many books about the theatre and music. An accomplished musician, he played various instruments, the trumpet was his favourite. He was very well-known in music circles and his friends included John Dankworth, the Jazz saxophonist, and the composer Malcolm Arnold.

Each year since his death, the remaining members take part in a night walk on the eve of Lou's birthday. In 1996, a large contingent of them came to Cornwall and spent a most enjoyable weekend with us.

Joe Burgess and his lovely wife Gertie, moved to Sticklepath, Devon, in the late 1980s to be near their daughter Libby and husband Mike. Joe soon made his mark on the local pub community and Sylvia and I spent a most enjoyable weekend there celebrating his 80th birthday.

In honour of Joe, the village blacksmith carried out an ancient ceremony which involved packing a newly cast anvil with gunpowder and igniting it. If the anvil split it was considered faulty. This one leapt 20 feet into the air and was pronounced A1. Joe and Gertie died in their mid 80s – a wonderful loving couple.

Bartholomew Arms staffing

The alterations proved a great success and the extra serving space was much appreciated by staff.

Janet Bull, who came with us from The Brave Old Oak, had put up with the previous cramped conditions in her usual indomitable spirit. We had employed numerous bar staff but, without wishing to diminish any of the others, Janet was the tops. She had a ready smile for all, never got flustered, and, most important of all, never let us down. We were immensely grateful to her long-suffering husband, Graham, for letting us occupy so much of her life.

Janet liked a drink, albeit in a moderate way, so it was with great consternation on our part when she announced she could no longer run the risk of being breathalysed on her way home which involved driving through Towcester. Losing Janet was like losing one of our family; we owed her a great debt for all the sacrifices she made for us at both The Brave Old Oak and Blakesley.

We were fortunate in having so many good friends to call on for bar work, Felicity Clarke, the effervescent Trish York, who was to be partially crippled following a tragic riding accident, Janet Blake, Valerie Dixon and daughter Louise, Helen Hallett, who together with husband Mel, now own a cake shop in Torquay, John Miller, Jan Dalziel, Brenda Scrafton who also worked for us at the Oak and now lives in Australia, Gill Slight, Colin King's girlfriend, Julie, and Terry and Tony, live-together partners but good barmen.

Later on, we employed many young girls from Blakesley and the surrounding villages including the sisters Nicky and Zoë Batchelor, Louise Bird, Kate Chidwick, Alison Smith, Debbie Clements, Laura Jones, Leesa Penny, Holly Wisner and her sister Alice, Andrea Hatton, Sara Burn, Emma Bragg, Sophie Lucas, the identical twins Kirsten and Ingrid Weaver and Louise from Greens Norton, who was the image of Zola Budd, the long distance runner.

In the early days, Ann Broomfield worked for us in the kitchen while still at school, as did Debby Callow and Mandy Webb. The latter two, together with Louise Bird, eventually married American servicemen and emigrated to the USA. Ann was extremely efficient and we had no qualms about leaving her in charge when we went away. She thrived on responsibility in spite of her tender age.

Our mainstay in the kitchen in later years was the lovely Jackie Bodily. Never flustered, in the space of an hour she could carry 80 meals up to the lawn on her own and still serve additional meals in the bar. Jackie was an invaluable member of the staff, often helping with residents and cleaning when the need arose.

Her partner, Alan, played a major role in assisting in the life of The Bart.

For the majority of our latter time at Blakesley we were fortunate to have the services of Barbara Welch, a "Brummie" girl with a lovely personality. Barbara, and husband Les, lived in the nearby village of Greens Norton. In spite of having a top sales job that involved long hours with the German company Bosch, Les brought Barbara to work at 6.30 a.m. each day, Monday to Friday. She cleaned the bars and assisted Sylvia with the residents' breakfasts, then moving on to clean the bedrooms. Barbara also worked behind the bar and her smart appearance and friendly personality were an added attraction at the Bart. Barbara went with us on our cruise to France, and her "enquiring" manner kept us all amused during the trip. She also acquired a good understanding of the French language.

For a period, Thea Packman assisted Barbara in her duties. Thea also lived in Greens Norton with husband Alan. She was a German lady who had met and married Alan when he was serving in the army there. Their son Frank was an outstanding wing-three-quarter for Northampton RFC and should, in my opinion, have been selected for England. He scored 284 tries between 1983 and 1993 for "The Saints".

We were indeed fortunate in having a near neighbour and friend in Lee Penny. Lee, the wife of my friend Tony from Brave Old Oak days, was a gem. A trained nurse, she had a soothing patient manner that no doubt she acquired from years of marriage to Tony. Lee helped out behind the bar whenever needed and we valued her assistance and friendship immensely. Her beautiful daughter Leesa, who fortunately took after Lee, helped in the kitchen as a schoolgirl. She went on to become a beautician working for Virgin Airlines.

Dee Lucas was an enigma. She lived in the neighbouring village of Woodend with husband Derek, a child psychiatrist. When Dee first started working for us, she was in the latter stage of her "hippy" phase. She came to work with beads in her multi coloured hair, wearing long skirts, flowing scarves and open sandals. If she was only 15 minutes late she would come ready dressed but if later would finish her breakfast and dressing in the wash-up area. The usual reason for her lateness was having problems with her daughter Sophie's horse. Dee should have been a stable hand; she held the record for how many straw bales you could get in a Skoda car and still be able to see out of the window. Her clothes were usually covered in straw and, when not in hippy gear, consisted of muddy jeans with even muddier wellies. Apart from the horse, Dee owned numerous cats and three uncontrollable dogs that ate floorboards. It was a good job husband Derek had a very laid back nature.

Dee was a good conversationalist and customers soon learnt not to interrupt her with requests for service. Many wives had cause to be thankful, for on the evenings when Dee was on duty, their husbands invariably returned home more sober than usual. Having to wait for Dee to finish her conversations before being served meant you were limited in the amount of alcohol you consumed in an evening.

Barmaid Jackie Stanbridge was a four feet something bundle of energy. She involved herself in all activities in the village ranging from being a fairy in the village pantomime to running the play school and Brownies. Together with husband Colin, they were good friends and Colin shared my love of cricket.

We always prided ourselves on the quality of the Christmas trees we erected at the front of the pub. Standing 20 foot tall with coloured lights, they could be seen from miles away.

One year, a group of customers showed great initiative when they decided to provide the tree themselves. They were led by a character with the initials PB! It was only after Christmas was over and the tree, all of 30 foot tall, was disposed of that I discovered from where it came.

Apparently five of them, on a dark evening, visited a local wood and selected a suitable specimen that they proceeded to chop down; they then covered the stump with mud to disguise their illegal act. Having satisfied themselves their crime would not be discovered, they started back, carrying their booty all the three miles to the pub.

On the way, they had to traverse a stream that had steep sides and was almost at flood level. Wading across was out of the question and it was a further mile to the nearest bridge, but I did say they had initiative. They stood the tree on its base and let it gradually fall across the stream. This done they then proceeded to walk across the tree and when all were safely across, they dragged the tree over to their side. Many people asked where I had obtained such a fine tree. I just told them, "It was on my doorstep when I opened up in the morning, and I decided it must be a gift from the Forestry Commission."

In 1984, we bought a Grand Bank type motor yacht named *C Symphony*. We had owned *Jonquil* at Woodford, a speedboat and various small cabin cruisers but this was a proper "Blue Water" boat. 40 foot long, 12 foot beam, it was beautifully fitted out with teak interior woodwork and teak decks.

We made many trips across the channel in her, usually accompanied by Doug Blake, Ken & Liz Vaughan and Derek Lucas. On one cruise to Salcombe, we had a crew of nine, but four plus Sylvia and myself was the usual complement.

On longer voyages, Sylvia spent a lot of time knitting and she made very nice thick sweaters for us all, with the boat's name embroidered across the chest. It was only when a crew photograph was taken that we realized, with arms folded, all you could see of the name was "ympho" which was rather embarrassing for the ladies.

Later on during a rather bumpy trip between Alderney and Guernsey whilst we were struggling to make eight knots, a beautiful boat passed us travelling at about 15 knots with no sign of rolling or pitching. After inspecting it at its mooring in Guernsey Marina, we learnt this type of boat was a "Nelson". From further research we discovered that Nelsons were widely used throughout the world as police, customs and pilot launches. They were renowned for their good sea-keeping qualities– when other boats sheltered in harbour, Nelsons would stay at sea.

The hunt was then on to find one for sale and eventually, after inspecting a few unsatisfactory ones, we discovered our dreamboat moored on the River Thames at Hampton Court. We sold *C Symphony* for £20,000 more than we paid for her and completed the purchase of *Bold Lancer* a seven-berth 40 foot "Weymouth" version of the famous Nelson design. Her two 250hp Sabre turbo charged engines gave a top speed of 18 knots. She was extremely well fitted out with a commercial radar, autopilot and echo sounder.

Not wanting to bring her round to Poole in the winter, we moored her in Chelsea harbour for four months. Chelsea harbour was in the early stages of being converted from old gasworks wharfs into a luxury development, with flats and town houses inhabited by millionaires and famous show business stars. Princess Diana was a regular visitor to the Fitness Suite situated in the main complex. Lord Snowden and Viscount Linley, Michael Caine, Jane Asher, Susan Hampshire and Shirley Bassey could often be seen walking round the harbour-sides. We were one of only 10 boats in the harbour and felt very privileged.

Eventually we brought her round to Poole harbour and moored at Cobbs Quay Marina where we had kept *C Symphony*. We had made some wonderful friends in the marina and visits to our boat were looked forward to with increasing eagerness. Particular good friends were Brian and Avril Toop, Bob Ames, Basil "Monty" Mountfort, John Keeley, Royston Dyer, Tony Emmett and Alan Hall.

After one of our more extended trips away on the boat, Sylvia and I arrived back in Blakesley to find that a golf society had been formed in the Pub. It had adopted the name "BAGS", the Bart Arms Golf Society.

I immediately pointed out that, since I was the owner of the establishment, I should be in charge of anything with the pub's name in its title. The locals retaliated with the argument that I was always gallivanting off on the boat and was in no position to hold such an important post. Accordingly, I set up a rival society called the "OBAGS", the Official Bart Arms Golf Society and arranged my own tournament. There was much heated discussion and negotiation over the next few days and a few dozen pints but we eventually merged the two but kept my title.

The OBAGS rules were loosely based on the Stapleford system except that we had our own handicapping system which had no upper limit, was relative to the "best" player and did not necessarily reflect the standard of golfing ability. We played once a month or so on various local courses, always moving on so as to avoid being refused a return fixture. We always ended up in a local hostelry and had a meal and a prize-giving ceremony. I got John Weekley to build a mahogany glass fronted display case containing my favourite putter with an engraved plaque stating "This putter was presented to the Official Bart Arms Golf Society by their President Tony Jacklin". The "President's Putter" was presented to the golfer who won the most competitions during the year. One of the more treasured prizes was the "Golden Peg," a gold-coloured (plastic) tee mounted on a solid metal block. This was awarded for the most ridiculous shot of the day and was always keenly contested.

From memory, apart from myself, the membership included Ken Vaughan, Shaw Cockerill, Bob Pickering, Bob Saunders, Doug Blake, David Bailey, John Matthews, Ian Ledingham, Dougie Harry, Freddie Dixon, Tony Penny, Andy Hunter, Bob Wainwright, Colin Stanbridge, Derek Lucas, Peter Conway, Tony Perry, Steve Coles, Ian Gillooly and Andy Slater.

Blakesley achieves international recognition

In 1978 the Formula 1 racing driver, Gunnar Nilsson, was dying of cancer and a research fund was established in his memory. Public houses throughout the country were raising money for this worthwhile charity and whilst in conversation with Doug and Peter Blake, it was decided that we should do something to contribute to the cause. The question was, what to do? Pubs traditionally staged wheelbarrow races, bed pushes, tug-of-wars, raft races etc to raise money for charities. All these old favourites were considered but ruled out for various reasons.

The village is built on a slope with an 80 ft fall from top to bottom. I suggested we should make use of this slope and hold a Soapbox Derby starting at the top of the village and finishing outside The Bart. Doug and Peter thought this was a good idea.

It had to be organised in quick time and we started co-opting customers onto an organising committee. To ensure we had the support of the village, we asked John Ivens to be the chairman, making the event "respectable" and deterring any accusations that the pub was using the village for its own benefit.

The committee that organised that first event consisted of John Ivens, myself, Doug & Peter Blake, Felicity Clarke, Rob Cockerill, Peter Tanswell, Eric Broomfield, John Sheppard Snr, Janet Keefe, George Powell, Graham Jones, Derek Lucas, John Matthews, David Bailey, Alan Rudge, Alan Bell and Martin Ball.

We had posters printed and a large banner made that stretched across the main street of the village. We also made use of the pennants last erected for the Jubilee celebrations. Because we were raising money for such a well-known charity, we found it easy to get publicity for the event. Felicity Clarke worked for Radio Northampton and was able to use her position to obtain us good media coverage.

The construction rules were very straightforward with no weight or size restrictions. It was assumed that most entrants would use pram wheels and build a simple timber chassis, but we failed to reckon with the engineering skills of some of the entrants. They varied from simple wooden frames with skateboard wheels to Rob Cockerill's monster built from scaffolding poles, lorry wheels filled with water and weighing over a ton. Martin Ball built a replica of the car used by TV character "Noddy", Phil Cowgill a fire engine, Plessey a super engineered box using an aluminium chassis and racing cycle wheels. I built a replica of a brewery dray, complete with wooden beer barrel on the back. Entries came from a wide area with the local bus company building a miniature double-decker bus. On the day, entries totalled 36.

We had planned the course with care using Peter Tanswell's

garage forecourt as the pits area. The course was 730 yards long with the start by the first house at the top of the hill. It then carried on down to, and round the village green and on down the main street to a finishing line outside the pub.

A week before the event, Rob Cockerill was testing his entry and came to me with the news that the hill wasn't steep enough. He had found that the hill at the top of the village had insufficient slope to get up enough speed to compensate for a level stretch before the village green. This was a disaster; we had assumed that the boxes would pick up speed all the way down the course. A hurried meeting was called and the outcome was we had to build a ramp to start from. Phil and Brian Cowgill hastily constructed this from scaffolding and Rob positioned his forklift truck with a platform fitted to raise the boxes to the top.

Having no idea the speed the entries would achieve, we placed straw bales at vulnerable spectator points and hoped this would stop any accidents. A local car club offered to marshal the event, which was a big help until the pub opened, after which they were a bit thin on the ground. We were also fortunate in having an offer of loudspeakers to cover the course with the operator supplying the commentary.

We had intended to use a klaxon to alert the timekeeper at the finish when the soapboxes started their run. On the day, this proved useless due to the volume of noise generated by the spectators. In desperation, I telephoned the house by the start from the pub, and by running an extension to the timekeeper and keeping the line open all day, was able to overcome this problem. My telephone bill was somewhat inflated after eight hours of continual use, but it worked. We had forgotten to mark out a finish line so a drum of "Vim" was hastily brought into use for this purpose.

On the day, we had expected a crowd of some 300 whereas in reality some 1,500 turned up. We hadn't arranged any parking facilities or toilets thinking none would be needed. We had marshals stationed at roads leading on to the course, and their job was to ask motorists to stop whilst a soapbox went past. Most cooperated willingly but the odd ones were incensed that their "right of way" was impeded and drove through the village at great risk to the spectators and competitors.

We hadn't officially informed the police in case we were doing something illegal so we had no help from the law in this respect. Looking back, it was remarkable the day was a complete success and no accidents occurred involving spectators. Peter Blake fell while pushing an entry and broke his collarbone and a couple of drivers suffered scrapes and bruises following collisions.

The Towcester Carnival Queen, Jenny Rhodes, presented the prizes to the winning drivers. Her fiancé, Norman Dabell, a reporter for the local paper, ensured us good press coverage. He is now the BBC golf correspondent.

Rob Cockerill easily won the overall event with the fastest time. Most constructors built their machines as light as possible with narrow wheels. Rob had run down the course late at night with his lorry in neutral and then the same with his car. He had timed the runs and the lorry won hands down. On this evidence, he built his entry as heavy as possible. In common with most soapboxes, he used foot and rope steering, and because of its weight, needed a brakeman to control the lever that operated a simple brake pad. This additional person added even more weight to his machine.

The following article that appeared in the *Northampton Echo* perhaps best sums up Rob's achievement: -

> Local farmer Rob Cockerill won the first Blakesley Soap Box Grand Prix on Saturday – 27 years after an accident had apparently wrecked his 'career'.
>
> At 12 years of age, Rob was one of the district's most promising soapbox starlets. Then one day, his kart collided with a car while he was practising on the A5. A future, it seemed, lay in splinters by the roadside. Rob returned

home and eventually became a farmer, still nurturing faint hopes of making his name on four (probably pram) wheels.

Nothing happened. Seasons passed. New sports emerged as national favourites but there was no sign of the soapbox. Then came news of the Blakesley Grand Prix. At 40, he wondered if his reactions were swift enough, if his nerves had not frayed by that A5 ordeal of yesteryear. He took no chances.

With one week to go he signed up his son Shaw (co-driver) and Tim Martin (co-designer) as members of the Southfield's Racing Stables.

Rumblings at dead of night wakened residents of Blakesley as the trio uncovered their prototype for top secret testing down the main street Thoroughness was rewarded. Their revolutionary water-weighted "Chicken Run" scurried along the 700 metre course in 54.8 seconds for the fastest time of the day and an average speed of 26 m.p.h.

Plessey won the class for Business Firms, Towcester Round Table won the Pubs and Clubs class and Shaw Cockerill won the Junior Class.

Stan Bindley, a local cine enthusiast captured the event on film, which he later copied onto a new medium called "video" Unfortunately the transfer from one to the other was not entirely successful and ended up very grainy.

The day raised a total of £1000 for the fund, which was later presented to Lord Hesketh. The opinion of all competitors and spectators was that the day was an unqualified success and the race should become an annual event.

We learnt many lessons that first year and were able to draw on this experience when we again staged the event in 1979. The event was still low key but we managed to raise £2,500 to buy a baby resuscitator for Northampton General Hospital.

Since its inception, the event had started to receive recognition by the public and the media as an event far more serious than the average "Soapbox Derby". The regional TV companies, BBC and ITV, were now covering the event, so we decided to call ourselves "The Blakesley National Soap Box Grand Prix". We had been approached by Alcester (Warwickshire) Round Table to assist them in staging an event at Ragley Hall, so we felt justified in calling our event "National". Much of the publicity referred to our close proximity to Silverstone, so Grand Prix seemed appropriate.

We were contacted by the organisers of a children's soapbox event held in the village of Long Itchington in Warwickshire. They asked if they could compete in our event, the result was we gained some 10 entries. An added bonus was we had the services of their organiser, Alan Hickling, who was a most competent commentator. Alan helped to make our event more professional.

A major change for 1980 was that we were able to obtain permission from the local council to close the roads through the village during the event. The local police provided a bobby to enforce the order and for the first time we laid on car parks and portable toilets.

The committee had grown and we were now handpicking people for their job influence that we could use to our advantage. Through illness, John Ivens had had to take a less active role so he became President and I took over as Chairman and Clerk of the Course. Felicity Clarke was Joint Secretary with Janet Keefe, George Powell, Treasurer, and Doug Blake was in charge of Entertainments, Peter Blake, Course Construction, Peter Tanswell, Technical, David Bailey, Car Parks, Derek Lucas. Start Controller, Eric Broomfield, Chief Scrutinizer. Phil Giles, Timekeeper, John Mathews, Press and Publicity, Alan Rudge, "Gofer", and Charlie Burbridge, Towing Marshal.

For the first time we had strict construction specifications drawn up by Phil Giles. Soapboxes were built to enter one of four classes.

Formula 1 for boxes up to 10cwt in weight
Formula 2 for boxes up to 5cwt
Formula 3 for boxes up to 3cwt driven by a person under 15 years.
Formula 4 for Novelty boxes.

All entrants had to have efficient brakes and Formula 1 & 2 had to have wheel steering and foot operated brakes.

The quality of entrants had become very sophisticated and now totalled 52. We had an entry from Hesketh Racing that took 250 hours to build. It contained the rack and pinion steering system that had been used on James Hunt's winning car at the 1975 Dutch Grand Prix. Another famous entry "Bloodshed" made its first appearance that year, entered by Gordon Townsend. Rolls Royce Apprentices Derby, Barclaycard, Blackwood Hodge, British Timken, Wolverton Railway Works and Avon Cosmetics also entered. My entry was a replica of a 12ft Carlsberg Lager bottle called "Probably the Best Soapbox in the World".

The *Towcester & Brackley Advertiser* reported the event as follows: -

> Winners again at the first attempt. That's the Hesketh stable of Towcester, whose famous racing colours were fastest past the chequered flag in Sunday's Blakesley Village National SB Grand Prix. Driven by Dave Morris the Hesketh entry beat all rivals by setting a new course record of 45.8 seconds (28.6 m.p.h.). But there was a worry too, about shortcomings in the design and with good reason; rivals were chasing so hard that, in the final, Hesketh's actually fell behind. Gordon Townsend's "Bloodshed" clocked 46.1 seconds and this was so fast it seemed he might gain compensation for an earlier accident. Four thousand spectators came alive with interest as Hesketh's made their final bid – and scurried home by a mere .3 of a second.

That year saw the first major accident when an entry from The Air Training Corps crashed and a following soapbox went over the top of the driver. He was taken to hospital and had 25 stitches put in a gash in his backside! I bet he proudly showed off his "racing scar" to his schoolmates!

Another first was having sideshows and a craft fair in a marquee on the playing fields. This addition was not without its own drama. The marquee had been erected the day before the event, and late that evening a gale force wind blew it down and practically into the next village. We had to hurriedly drive vehicles up to the playing field and onto the flattened marquee to stop it blowing away. We could well have done without another arduous task. The event raised £2,500 for the Jimmy Saville Stoke Mandeville Hospital appeal.

The history of Soapbox racing at Blakesley warrants a whole book to itself, so I shall restrict myself to the highlights of our events. 1981 saw our biggest publicity coupe to date.

Byron Rogers a freelance journalist whose articles appeared in the *Sunday Telegraph, Sunday Express, Evening Standard* and numerous periodicals had recently taken up residence in the village. Byron came to me one day and said he would like to do an article on the forthcoming event. I was in the process of converting last year's "Beer bottle" entry into a "Space Rocket". He asked me how fast I thought it would go and I told him, "If we had enough slope it would touch 70 m.p.h." Imagine my surprise and delight when the *Sunday Express,* which was published on race day, had a half page article with the headline, *"Where they will be doing close to 70 m.p.h. today in a soapbox."*

Dominating the page was a picture of my entry looking like a sleek jet fighter plane, complete with traffic cone as a nose. We had put the cone on for the purpose of the photograph. It looked fabulous but was illegal making the entry 15 feet long, 3 feet longer than the permitted length.

The organisation was coming on in leaps and bounds. Our technical department, Phil Giles, and Peter Tanswell, had worked overtime.

We now had electronic timing to 1/1000th of a second, and electronic release mechanism that operated at the same time as the timing equipment. In a small way, I could take some credit for the latter.

Phil explained that we wanted a system that would release two soapboxes simultaneously. Any delay between them gave one an unfair advantage by starting earlier. I remembered that during my time in the Royal Navy, ships whalers (and lifeboats in the Merchant Navy) were released by a piece of equipment called "Robinson's patent disengaging gear".

My old *Naval Ratings Handbook* explains it as follows:

> "It is essential when lowering a sea boat, and when the ship has way on her, that both falls should be disengaged from the boat simultaneously, so that the boat can be slipped above the level of the waves. To effect this all ships' boats in the Royal Navy are fitted with Robinson's disengaging gear."

To explain it further in layman's terms, the boat is suspended from davits (cranes) just above the waves by ropes (falls) attached to a RPDG at each end of the boat. At the order, "Out pins," the two crewmen responsible withdraw the safety pins that hold the jaws of the RPDG in a locked position. A chain joins the two RPDGs and at the right moment when a wave is rising, the coxswain (steerer) pulls a slip lever and the RPDGs open simultaneously, releasing the boat, which drops to the water. Clear? If only one fall released or was delayed, the boat would tip and the occupants would end up in the water. Mr Robinson's invention has saved thousands of lives.

I wrote to the Admiralty explaining what we wanted and asked them if they could let me have a schematic drawing of a RPDG so we could get them made. They duly obliged and Plessey made us two, with the lever opening by a solenoid run from a 12-volt battery.

Each entry had to be weighed and, in previous years, we had

used a pig-weighing machine. With his connections in the engineering industry, Graham Jones had a sophisticated platform made that worked on pressure pads connected to a digital display.

All marshals and officials were now equipped with walkie-talkies, compliments of Plessey security section. The public address for the commentary, given so professionally by Alan Hickling, now had state of the art equipment with double the amount of speakers.

For our first three events, we had made do with straw bales protecting spectators. This year we had proper insurance cover and one of the requirements was that we provided "Substantial spectator safety". We enquired about hiring barriers but the quotation was astronomical. Fortunately, help was at hand in the shape of Silverstone Circuit. They offered us – free of charge – all the barriers we needed. With tremendous enthusiasm, Towcester Round Table supplied the labour, an articulated lorry and collected some 300 interlocking metal barriers from the circuit. The entries were becoming more and more sophisticated and with that sophistication speeds increased. Accidents were becoming more numerous so we, and the drivers, were thankful for the added protection.

Since our second event, we had received good support and coverage from BBC Anglia TV. This year they sent along their top presenter, Graham Bell, to cover the event, and we arranged for him to present the trophies. Graham was a lovely chap and we became good friends. Together with Sylvia and his lovely wife Sue, we spent many happy hours on my boat in Poole harbour. Graham became part of the soapbox scene and, after John Ivens's death, took over the Presidency. Sadly Graham himself died in 1994 at a very early age, I do not think he ever fully recovered from the injuries he received in a serious car accident.

The reason we had a record crowd of 6,000 was probably due in no small part to Byron's article. After our ever-increasing bills were paid, we presented a cheque for £5,000 to Northampton Hospital premature baby unit.

A further spin off from Byron's article was that alarm bells rang at the Police HQ when a senior officer saw the 70m.p.h speed quoted. For this year, and all future events, we had a Police Mobile Incident unit in attendance together with an inspector, two sergeants and up to ten constables!

Byron once again came good in 1982, in an even more outstanding coup. He told me he was thinking of doing an article on soapbox racing for the *Sunday Telegraph* and asked if I would make my soapbox available for some photographs. I had painted the "Rocket" a bright red colour and it looked evil. The photographer phoned, made an appointment and I talked the drivers, my son Timothy and his friend Mark Broomfield, to take a day off work. The photographer duly arrived complete with an assortment of cameras. His name was Richard Olivier and, in conversation, we discovered he was the son of Sir Laurence, later Lord Olivier.

We spent the whole day pushing the soapbox round the village for him, getting the shots he wanted. It was a sunny day and he said it would be good if he could create a shimmering effect on the road, like a jet plane taking off. I suggested we get a can of petrol, pour in on the road and ignite it. This we did and pushed the soapbox down a slope for it to run over the flames. Unfortunately, we hadn't allowed for the fact that there was no bottom in the Rocket, and, as luck would have it, the soapbox stopped in the middle of the flames. Mark was driving and let out such a shriek we quickly ran through the flames and pushed it away.

Richard took ten rolls of films that day and when we asked if he could make it pay he told us if his picture was chosen for publication, it could be worth £1,000 to him. He then asked if he could come back very early the next day, as the light was especially good in the early morning. Tim and Mark agreed as long as it was early enough for them to get to work afterwards. Richard took two further rolls of film between 7 and 7.30 a.m. and departed.

On Sunday 12th September 1982, the week before that year's

event, a picture of my soapbox, together with Tim, Mark and myself, appeared in glorious colour on the front cover of the *Sunday Telegraph* magazine! It was one of the pictures Richard had taken early in the morning. Both Tim and Mark looked rather glum, neither of them being at their best that time in the morning. Inside was a five-page article on soapbox racing written by Byron, surpassing his previous article in the *Sunday Express*.

By the time we staged the 1982 event we had already helped to organise events at Bournemouth, Alcester and at the Prescott Hill Climb circuit near Cheltenham. It was during that year that I received a telephone call from the Isle of Man asking if I would organise an event on the Island. The caller, Sir Dudley Cunliffe-Owen, a Bobsleigh champion in the 1950s, said they were prepared to offer our drivers £5,000 in prize money to compete there. I contacted some of our stalwart entrants and the general view was that if they paid travelling expenses instead of prize money, they would be interested.

I got back to Sir Dudley with this proposition but he said the money was being put up by the Tourist Board and a couple of sponsors and could only be for prizes. My old friend David Powell was living on the island at the time and I would have welcomed having a few jars with him.

I was also contacted by an organisation in Holland who wanted us to organise an event on a length of disused motorway near Rotterdam. It transpired that this flyover had been constructed only for the motorway to take a different direction making it obsolete!

We had owned a flat in Bournemouth for some years, and one day by the swimming pool, I got talking to our neighbour, Andy Hepburn, a retired ship surveyor. He was the chairman of the Bournemouth Lions Club and was looking for new ideas to raise monies for charity. I told him about our soapbox event and he arranged for me to give a talk to his members. The talk went well and the seeds were sown.

I was aware at the meeting that the members seemed to be

rather on the aged side, but assumed that as they were mainly local businessmen they could call upon employees, etc. to assist. This was not the case and we soon found they had more chiefs than Indians. There was a lot of influence in the club but no one wanted to do the hard physical work. After the first run, I had to take over the running of the pits and starting organisation with the assistance of the drivers. The course, through a local park, was neither long nor steep enough. I felt sorry for the entrants who had travelled a long distance to get there. One had travelled from Sheffield and another from Cheshire. As it was in the middle of the holiday season, a good crowd attended but I didn't think they had their money's worth. However, two good things came about as a result of that event.

First, one of the Lions Club members was involved with TVS, the south coast's main independent television company. As a result of my talk to the Lions, they produced a most professional, entertaining half hour programme on soapbox racing called *"The Race is On"* which was screened nationally, two weeks before our event.

The programme centred round a soapbox built by a Bournemouth entrant, Paul Brown. He had entered our event the previous year and had constructed a most magnificent machine for this year's series, resembling a vintage car. The other entry that featured prominently was Blakesley's Paul Broomfield. He drove his soapbox, shaped like a block of cheese; he and his wife dressed in mouse outfits.

The film started with interviews with Jimmy Greaves the footballer, the comedian Max Bygraves and Paul Shane and Su Pollard, stars of the popular *Hi di Hi* television series. They gave very interesting accounts of their soapbox experiences as children. After showing scenes of Blakesley, including an interview with me inside the Bart Arms, the film moved on to Easton Neston Hall, the home of Lord Hesketh.

He gave a very amusing account of how I had persuaded him to enter our event and how much his entry had cost him. He praised our organisation for its professionalism, and added that our trophies were better than those he had won in Formula 1.

The action then moved on to the Prescott Hill Climb event. The soapboxes descended the course, and its steepness led to some very good racing with spectacular crashes. One soapbox turned completely over in front of the cameras and travelled 20 yards upside down.

In our wildest dreams, we could not have hoped for such splendid national publicity. I spent a week with the film team, shuttling them round the county, and by the end was exhausted. I received a cheque for £300 which I donated to our funds.

The other good thing to come out of the Bournemouth event was the participation of Frizzells Insurance and their major client, the Civil Service Motoring Association.

The CSMA marshalled the event very professionally and I talked them into officiating at Blakesley. Their chairman, Tony Richardson, joined our committee and it was the start of a long, successful relationship.

The meeting at Prescott's was organised by the owners of the circuit, the "Bugatti Owners Club". They were restricted in the amount of hill climb meetings they could hold each year because of the noise factor. People living in the neighbouring village of Bishop Cleeve complained about the sound of cars revving hard to climb the hill. Some of the larger ones had Formula 1 engines. The committee thought a silent event like soapbox racing would provide an alternative source of spectator interest.

They had an excellent course, as one would expect for an old established circuit. Very little had to be done to prepare for this new medium, apart from protecting some of the hairpin bends with straw bales.

The event was well attended and efficiently run with some 30 of the national entries taking part, but we did have problems with one or two of their officials. They were after all "The Bugatti Owners Club" with each of their cars costing a fortune. Some of the cravat and peaked cap brigade looked upon us as an "inferior species".

It was a bit like Cowes regatta holding races for jet skis! The trophies they presented were sandblasted BOC wine glasses retailing at £2 in the club shop.

Celebrities do us proud

The chosen charity for our 1982 event was the Royal National Lifeboat Institution.

In April that year, I was drinking in a yacht club bar at Poole and spotted a tall gentleman who I was certain I had met during my time in the Royal Navy. I went to the toilet and on my return saw Sylvia talking to him. I joined them and the reason I thought I knew him soon became apparent.

A couple of years previously the BBC had produced a 10-part television documentary about life onboard HMS *Ark Royal*. Rod Stewart singing the theme song, "*We are sailing*", had made the series more memorable. The gentleman with the familiar face had been the ship's captain who featured prominently in each episode. He was now Rear Admiral Sir Wilfred Graham, Director General of the RNLI. whose HQ was in Poole.

We discussed our service in the Royal Navy, and the *Ark Royal* TV programme. Eventually the conversation got round to the work of the RNLI.

I had been a lifetime supporter of the charity and knew they were always short of funds. I told him about our soapbox events and he asked if I would consider raising money for the RNLI. He said they would do all our printing at their HQ, supply lots of publicity material and arrange for a celebrity to attend. I put this to the committee at our next meeting and the RNLI was adopted as our 1982 charity.

True to his word, the institution arranged for Ernie Wise, half of the Morecambe and Wise comedy duo, to be our guest celebrity. We were over the moon at such a famous star attending our event.

On the race day, Ernie did everything we asked. He started a race, went down the course in a soapbox, drove down the course in an open topped car stopping to chat to spectators, and presented the trophies at the end. He worked tirelessly to ensure we had the best ever event, raising £8,500 for the RNLI. The estimate of the crowd attending, quoted in local papers, ranged from 8,500 to 10,000, due largely to Ernie Wise.

Mathew Clark, the company that marketed, amongst other products, Martell Brandy, invited us to present the cheque to Admiral Graham at their hospitality suite in London. Every lifeboat carries a bottle of Martell onboard to give to survivors and, if used, is replenished on return.

Wilfred Graham was a very nice chap and both he and his charming wife called to see us at the pub whenever they were passing through the area.

The soapbox event ran successfully for a further seven years. Each year had its highlights and large sums of money were raised for various charities.

John Matthews, our press and publicity committee member was doing a great job. He had been interviewed many times on local radio and early in 1983 was asked to go to London and be interviewed by Derek Jameson live on the national BBC Radio 2 morning show. This was a splendid start to our new season; the programme had a listening audience of around three million.

In 1989 Murray Walker, the famous motor racing commentator, produced a half hour radio programme entitled *Mad dogs and Englishmen,* about unusual sporting events throughout the country. Murray attended our 1988 event and actually drove a soapbox down the course whilst commentating on his progress. He interviewed me for 10 minutes and I am the proud possessor of an audiotape recorded from the programme when it went out on air. Murray was a national institution and Mr Grand Prix racing since his first commentary in 1949. He spent 50 years with the BBC before moving to ITV in 1997 finally retiring in 2001. During his career, he commentated on 350 Grand Prix events.

Murray published his autobiography in 2002 and I was overjoyed that he had given our humble little event a mention, quote: -

> ...as was my epic drive at the Blakesley Soapbox Grand Prix later the same year. Blakesley is a village close to Silverstone and the course starts on a man-made ramp at the top of a hill and plunges past the friendly Bartholomew Arms, where I had been known to take a beer or two. I was there to do a piece for a BBC Radio Four programme called *Mad Dogs and Englishmen* about the potty things the English do. 'Have a go, Murray,' they said. 'We'll put you in "Bloodshed".' It's a Formula 1 soapbox which holds the hill record and if you've got big enough balls you can't help doing well because if you take a deep breath it'll just go round corners without braking.
>
> The things I do for England. I frightened the life out of myself but they were right. I kept right off the stoppers and we fairly flew down the hill – 54.62 seconds compared with the winner, speed king Eddie Edwards' 52.79. Not bad, great fun and as I recorded commentary all the way down we got a cracking piece for the programme. An action photo of my sensational debut (and finale) was still hanging in the Bartholomew Arms the last time I was there.

His book contains a photograph of him sitting in "Bloodshed" on the start ramp.

Other celebrities who attended our events included the comedian Don MacLean, TV presenter Leslie Crowther, Ken Bailey the England Cheerleader best known for using his England flag to cover the ample proportions of Erica Rowe when she streaked topless at Twickenham, and Tom Arnold, Walter Gabriel of *The Archers* fame.

I must make extra mention of Leslie Crowther. When we first learnt of his wish to attend, we were overjoyed; he was a very high profile TV star. We were raising money that year for the Spastics Society. Leslie was part of a voluntary body called SOS – Stars Organisation for Spastics.

We had his name printed on our posters and the media had given great prominence to his appearing. Imagine our dismay when his agent informed us that he was performing at Blackpool on the Saturday evening and would be unable to drive down in time on the Sunday.

Phillip Purser, who lived in the village, was the television critic for the *Daily Telegraph*. Phillip and his charming wife Anne had been part of our organising team and each year placed their lovely house at our disposal as a hospitality suite. Phillip tried to use his influence to get Leslie Crowther to change his mind, and John Matthews threatened to contact all the national press to tell them of his late withdrawal, but to no avail.

Whilst discussing the problem in the pub, Tony Penny said he was prepared to fly to Blackpool on Sunday morning in his light aeroplane and bring him to Blakesley, returning him after the event. We put this to his agent and, after much deliberation, he reluctantly agreed with this arrangement.

On the Sunday morning just as Tony was about to leave for the airport, we received a telephone call that Leslie Crowther was on his way down by car! I personally felt like telling him not to bother

Anyway, he duly arrived in his Rolls Royce and I have to give him credit, he was magnificent and, just like Ernie Wise previously, did everything with great enthusiasm. He was a real star turn. It was with sadness that we later discovered he was an alcoholic and, after a terrible car accident, faded from the entertainment scene until his early death. He gained a lot of fans that day at Blakesley.

By contrast, Don McLean, whose trademark is his grin, was a picture of misery all day, and seemed as though he couldn't get away quickly enough.

Each year our fame was spreading and we started getting international recognition. In 1985, a crew from the American TV Company, CBS, filmed the whole event and, in 1986, Japanese TV Company filmed us.

Peter Tanswell, while on holiday in Spain, picked up a magazine in his hotel room. Imagine his surprise to see an article in Spanish on the Blakesley Soapbox Grand Prix!

Changes to improve the running of the event were always being undertaken. The ramp was now a 16ft high monster, resembling a ski slope. This was organised by one of our new committee members, Len Burchill. Rob Cockerill, in his resourceful style had built an electric winch, complete with remote control for hoisting the boxes to the top.

We now had three separate commentary boxes on the course and marshal's telephone communications, courtesy of British Telecom arranged by Charlie Burbridge. Charlie also organised a fleet of vintage tractors to tow the machines back to the start, a big added attraction for the spectators.

Doug Blake had expanded the events on the playing field, making it a show in its own right. This continued expanding in future years, with such attractions as the Avon Cosmetics Model Aeroplane flying display, Tiger Moth aerobatics, Jazz Bands, Exhibition by the Mary Rose Trust, Static Engine displays, Clowns, Bouncy Castles, Dog Displays and numerous trade stalls. Every year Doug surprised us with something new, more spectacular than before.

One year we had a very large marquee erected, in which we staged a barbecue the evening before the event and an Antiques Fair on race day. We now had teams, officials and spectators camping, and caravanning in the village on the Friday and Saturday nights prior to the event; resulting in 350 people attending the event.

Alan Tebutt had joined the committee and was responsible for the car parks. Under Alan's very efficient supervision, the various youth organisations offered from within their ranks attendants who worked diligently, and the car parks, at last, produced the takings we always believed possible.

Ken Vaughan and his fiancée Liz had moved into the village. Both of them were involved in marketing and their talents were soon being put to good use. Ken obtained advertising for our programmes from such prominent firms as Johnson's Wax, General Foods, Marstons Brewery, Maxwell House, Britannia Rescue, Flopak, Rank Xerox, Volvo, British Timken, Royal Mail, Ford Motor Company, GPO Telecommunications Nottingham, William Younger Brewery and Anglia Television, plus local firms. The revenue created practically covered our major expenses in advance of the day. He and Liz also organised raffles.

During the life of the Blakesley event, we had the services of numerous secretaries, Felicity Clarke, Janet Keefe, Pat Patterson, Marion Austin and Lynda Maude. Their job was the most important and arduous of all the organising committee.

We started with George Powell as our treasurer. His position with Anglia Building Society, made him an ideal person for the job. When the work started taking up too much of his time we approached John Coward, my bank manager at the local National Westminster Bank. John carried out the duties with zeal and became an enthusiastic member of the committee. George became one of our team of very professional commentators.

Colin King, our local butcher, was in charge of weighing the soapboxes, the ideal man for dealing with the many drivers who might try and cheat the system.

Derek Lucas was our long-serving start controller. His work involved getting the drivers to the start in the correct order, making sure they had been weighed, scrutinized and were running in the correct formula.

After Phil Giles, who had been one of our stalwarts, moved away from the village, Colin Stanbridge took over his timekeeping role and performed with his usual thoroughness.

Bob Pickering (Pickers) was chief paddock marshal. He ensured that drivers were waiting in the correct order for their turn to ascend the ramp. Many years later, Bob and his wife Andrea moved to Market Harborough where he sadly died shortly after the move. Bob and Andrea were both enthusiastic participants in our quiz evenings.

David Bailey, a county roads surveyor, was our chief course builder and in this role liased with Towcester Round Table for the collection and return of barriers to the Silverstone Circuit. David did a vital job and having spent many Mondays with him cleaning the streets after the event, I have first-hand knowledge of his efforts.

The Soapbox event goes national

We had formed a National Soapbox Committee to run separately from our own and be responsible for the national events. I had the honour of being the first chairman and we were extremely fortunate in having two excellent officials in Martin Slevin and Bill Barby. They had been two of our early Blakesley entries and their enthusiasm ensured the growth of the national circuit. Lord Hesketh became president of the National body and thereafter, always presented the National trophies at Blakesley.

The National Committee together with our own team assisted in events at Melbourne in Derbyshire, Belvoir Castle and Sylvia's home village of Foxton both in Leicestershire, Harlaxton in Lincolnshire, Cricket St Thomas in Somerset, Norfolk Park in Sheffield and at a venue in Kent.

It has to be said that most of these events, usually run by Round Tables and the like, start with lots of enthusiasm. Their organising committees would attend our events at Blakesley gaining an insight. The problem was they then assumed that because our event worked like clockwork with, so it seemed, little effort, they thought running an event was a piece of cake. Nothing could be further from the truth.

When they fully realised the amount of people, organisation and hard graft involved, they tried to cut corners. When this involved spectators' safety, it had alarming far-reaching effects. The event at Foxton was a typical case in point.

They had put together a very capable and enthusiastic committee. On the day, though, I was surprised that not enough thought and preparation had been spent on course construction and safety. A popular spectator point on a tight bend was left completely unprotected. In the third round, the inevitable happened. A heavy F1 soapbox clipped the kerb, flew through the air, and landed amongst the crowd that included many children.

I was videoing the event from a high platform so had a bird's eye view of the incident. My first thought was there had been a fatality. Two children's shoes were seen lying in the road and the screams were deafening. Fortunately, the ambulance was soon on the scene and the badly injured taken to hospital and the less injured treated on the spot. I was particularly annoyed because I had twice asked the chief organiser to protect that corner with straw bales.

I had captured the whole incident on video and the next day was approached by the local TV company for a copy of the tape. To protect future events, I denied having taken any film of the accident.

I never did discover the full extent of the injuries to those involved, but I do know that the insurance company contacted me. I was asked to attend an on-site meeting at Foxton with their representative. He could see that the steep hill through the village would enable entrants to build up considerable speed, making it difficult to negotiate the corner in question. He was dismayed the organisers had taken no precautions to protect the spectators.

All events had been using the same insurance policy with a very reasonable premium. Because of this accident and the assessor's report, the premiums doubled with the insurers imposing much stricter safety conditions for all future events. Because of one organising committee's shortcomings, we were all penalised. As a result, we revised the rules for organisers, and gave national officials the right to suspend racing if safety rules were not being strictly adhered to.

In all, we raised almost £100,000 for our selected charities during the 10 years we held soapbox racing at Blakesley. For me personally the highlight was in 1984 when we raised £10,000 for the RNLI. This was not the largest sum we were to raise but that year, at the London Boat Show, we presented the cheque to TV personality Raymond Baxter.

I had been a great admirer of Raymond Baxter from his days presenting *Tomorrow's World* and commentating at air shows, Motor Racing and other events involving speed. He was then communications director for the British Motor Corporation and commodore of the Dunkirk Little Ships Flotilla, an organisation close to my heart. The whole committee went to London for the presentation and a most impressive occasion it was.

At a signal, we all walked out on a pontoon to the middle of the indoor harbour, where Raymond Baxter was waiting for us. With a fanfare of trumpets, the spotlights shone down on us and I presented the cheque to him. Raymond made a speech praising the fact that a village in the heart of England, with a population of just 600, could raise so much for the RNLI. Together with the proceeds of two previous years, we had raised £25,000 in total for them. We left the arena with applause echoing all round the Earls Court Exhibition Centre: a most memorable day, one that made all our efforts worthwhile.

In 1988, we made our largest presentation to the RNLI at their HQ in Poole. In conjunction with the CSMA, we took part in a competition throughout the year and with the money raised on the day we presented a cheque for £19,443. The money was used to buy a "D" Class Inshore Lifeboat, which was named *Blakesley Village/CSMA*. For quite a few years afterwards, we received a six monthly report from the RNLI showing where the craft was stationed and how many lives it had saved.

A return to the sea is imminent

I was spending a lot more time on our boat at Poole and enjoying every minute of it. Sylvia and I made many trips to Cherbourg and the Channel Islands, usually in company with Doug Blake and Ken & Liz Vaughan, but felt the need to do something more challenging.

The licensed trade entails keeping late hours in an environment not conducive to healthy living. As if this wasn't bad enough, I smoked heavily and liked a regular supply of alcoholic beverage. I suffered from high blood pressure and, in common with my sister Paddy, seemed to have inherited my mother's arthritic knees – although years of kicking rugby and soccer balls when they were made from thick cow hide did not help either.

At the age of 30, when at Woodford, I had taken out a small retirement policy to mature at 55. In 1964, it seemed incomprehensible that in 25 years' time, people would still be required to work until the age of 65 to draw their pension, especially if they left school at 14, as Sylvia and I had. 51 years spent working is a large chunk out of a person's life. I had forecast that by the time I was 55 years old in 1989 all people would be retiring at that age.

Many incidents had taken place that made me think about my future. I had discussed what we would do in retirement with my good friend Ivor Denny on many occasions. We were both of the opinion that, after spending many years in the trade, we would retire at as early an age as possible. The fact that Ivor never lasted long enough for him to enjoy his well-earned retirement had a considerable effect on me. When another good friend, Jimmy Hunter, also died in his early 50s I started to take stock of my life, and which way I wanted it to go. In 1990 I was 56, had spent 31 years in the trade and had outlived Ivor and Jimmy by a number of years.

The "pull of the sea" was getting stronger and stronger and that year I read two books that fired my longing for an extended period away on my boat. The first was Roger Pilkington's book *Small Boat on the Lower Rhine* and the other was a book that my eldest son Stephen gave me for my 55th birthday, Bill & Laurel Cooper's *Watersteps through France*. Both describe their voyages through the waterways of Europe.

Another incident that fuelled my sense of urgency happened at Cobb's Quay Marina, Poole where I moored my boat.

On the opposite berth to mine, was moored a beautiful small sailing vessel, with highly varnished woodwork. I often chatted to the owner, Richard, and he told me he had four years to go before retirement, then he was off on his boat to the Mediterranean. The boat was his pride and joy and he worked tirelessly on her every weekend. I became concerned one spring when I hadn't seen Richard for some time and his boat was beginning to look the worse for wear. I enquired at the marina office and learnt that his boat was up for sale.

I saw Richard later that spring and he told me he had developed severe arthritis in his wrists and could no longer maintain or sail his boat, and had been forced to put her up for sale. His dream had ended and his retirement was no longer eagerly awaited. This convinced me I should do all that I wanted to with my boat while I was still able.

Sylvia, whilst sharing my love of boating, was still very contented running the pub, and I was consequently spending a lot of time onboard on my own. Our trade had reached eight barrels of beer a week with wine and spirits still increasing. Although it reduced our net profit considerably, we decided to engage a manager, enabling us to spend more time away from the pub and assisting Sylvia when she was in residence.

We employed a variety of managers but the first one to make his mark was Russell who had a very pleasant laid-back manner. Sylvia was a very hard taskmaster but she and Russell worked very well together with next to no friction between them. Russell was 6' 3" tall and came from Nottingham. Initially he was very conscientious and wasn't bothered about not having time off.

He eventually met a young lady, Maria, who was an officer in the American Air Force. They became engaged and he then wanted as much time off as possible. We were beginning to find that when he returned from being with her, he was morose for days. It was not the carefree Russell we originally engaged as our manager. He eventually left to get married.

After Russell came Harry who was working as assistant manager at a large public house in Winchester. I went there to interview him and the owner of the pub spoke highly of him. I suppose the first time we became concerned about Harry was when he returned from a short holiday spent in Hamburg. He told us he'd met a Polish ballerina who had a daughter with only one kidney and that was diseased. He was quite emphatic he was going to donate one of his kidneys to her. He showed us a photograph of the lady and it was instantly obvious she was "on the game". You may ask, "How did I know she was on the game?" Even though I had been out of the Royal Navy for some 30 odd years, I still had vivid memories of the type of female who inhabits the waterfronts in areas like Hamburg. In the photograph, the "lady" wore a white fur shortie jacket, hot pants and long white boots. If this was not enough to convince me, the pose she adopted said it all.

Harry showed staff and customers jewellery he bought for her and toys for the daughter. He went back to Hamburg a month later and, this time on his return, told us he was going to marry her. I tried to suggest to Harry that he was being taken for a ride but it was obvious he was madly in love with her. Even speaking her name brought tears to his eyes. He returned to Hamburg to fix up the wedding but returned two days earlier than expected. It transpired that he had looked in a drawer and found numerous letters from other English "clients". All had been promised matrimony and sent money for the daughter's "transplant". When Harry tackled her about the letters she just laughed and threw him out of the flat.

We excused Harry's behaviour as the actions of a lonely man, but we were beginning to have doubts regarding his suitability to run our business. Our fears were realized when after a weekend visit to his hometown of Whitby, he returned to say he was getting married. When I asked him how long he had known his future wife, he said they were at school together, but admitted he hadn't seen her since leaving. As Harry was in his late 40s, it seemed rather a long time to be parted from the woman he loved. I told

Harry we could no longer employ him after his marriage and he accepted the situation.

Harry gave his notice and got married in Whitby a couple of weeks later. A few of our customers travelled up for the wedding, including Cyril "Tiddler" King. As they were going into church, Harry asked Cyril if he could lend him £200 until he could get to the bank. It was a well-known fact that Cyril always carried large sums of money with him. Cyril duly obliged and, after the wedding, never saw Harry or his money again.

We had suffered three stocktaking deficits during Harry's last few months, but none were large enough to be alarmed about. Compared with some of the deficits incurred by future managers, Harry's was insignificant.

In 1989, we had a very good manager in Andy Hunter. Andy, a Liverpool University graduate, had a very easy manner and was well liked by the customers. I felt confident in Andy's ability to run the business in our absence so with this in mind, I decided it was now or never. Having spent considerable time that winter planning a cruise on the French canals, I broke the news to Sylvia in early spring.

We always held our first soapbox meeting early in the year, and it was at this meeting that I announced my wish to stand down as chairman, to spend more time on my boat. There were three people who I thought might take on the role of chairman; and I was therefore dismayed that the general feeling of the committee was if I finished, so would they.

Looking back, the ten years in which I helped to organised soapbox racing at Blakesley was probably the most taxing yet enjoyable period I had spent in the licensed trade. However, because we had achieved so much continuous success, the pressure on all the committee to surpass the previous year's fund-raising put a great strain on us all. Any reduction was looked upon as a failure, and I think we were running out of new ideas.

I hastily contacted the parish clerk, John Weekley, to call a village meeting to break the news and invite the village to take on the role of organisers.

Over the years the various village organisations i.e., Church, Playing Field, Village Hall, Play School and PTA had each raised a large amount of money for their concerns on Soapbox Sunday. I think it was true to say that, for many, it had been their main source of income. The Church in particular had raised a considerable amount of money with little effort on their part. We had undertaken all the organisation, planning, advertising, financial risk taking, and physical work in staging the event. All the village organisations had to do was man a stall or sell teas to raise money.

I am sure I speak for all our committee who attended that meeting when I say the response from the organisations represented was pathetic. I think they had made so much money from our events, they felt they could sit back and wait for the pub customers to organise something else for them. The village parson was particularly vocal saying that the villagers would probably relish an opportunity to have a quiet year. It was typical of a man who had done nothing but ensure he had a quiet time since he first arrived in the village.

So that was it: what had been an exciting part of village life for a decade had ended. At least, Doug, Peter Blake and I had the satisfaction of knowing that an idea we hatched over a pint in the Bart Arms had raised almost £100,000 for good causes and, who knows, may have been responsible for saving lives. All those enthusiastic members of the committee and other helpers, who had given so much of their time and commitment over the years, could be happy in the knowledge they had been part of a unique organisation.

Although I think I have mentioned them all before I would like to record their names one more time:

Doug Blake, Peter Blake, Rob Cockerill, George Powell, Felicity Clarke, Janet Keefe, Alan Bell, Phil Giles, Peter Tanswell, John Ivens, John Sheppard, Eric Broomfield, Phil Cowgill, Brian Cowgill, Martin Ball, Alan Rudge, Ken & Liz Vaughan, John Matthews, John Sheppard Jnr, David

Bailey, Derek Lucas, Alan Tebutt, Colin King, Bob and Pat Patterson, Marion Austin, Len Birchall, Lynda Maude, John Coward, Tony Richardson, John Harrington, Colin Stanbridge, Bob Pickering, Gill Slight, Alan Hickling, Charlie Burbridge, Mick Gulliman, Steve Nunn, Graham Hill, Peter Huntly, Tony Penny, Phillip and Ann Purser, Martin Slevin and Bill Barby, the members of Towcester Round Table and CSMA Marshals.

I take my hat off to them all and thank them most sincerely for their support in staging what was, after all, a pub-inspired event. Looking at that list again and thinking about the apathy in the village, reminded me that almost a third of those mentioned lived outside of the village!

In addition, I would personally like to pay tribute to the late Graham Bell and Lord Alexander Hesketh for their patronage and support over the years. I must also not forget that right from the early days, David Knighton obtained generous sponsorship for us from his employers Carlsberg Brewery.

The national association carried on organising events at various venues round the country, but without the jewel in the crown, Blakesley, the drivers and constructors soon lost interest.

A couple of years later an unconnected event was held in the village of Silverstone with tragic consequences. The local newspaper reported the accident as follows: -

"A kart with bald tyres and below par brakes was given the go ahead to compete in the Silverstone Soap Box Derby.

But the fun day out ended in tragedy when the kart crashed into a barrier and landed on teacher John Tyler, who was killed instantly, an inquest in Northampton heard.

The accident happened as 41-year-old Mr Tyler walked along a footpath near the fastest part of the course.

Police vehicle examiner, Stuart Cutmore described the 600lb vehicle as crude with three of its tyres having no tread. It seems the car was driving too fast for the attempted turn and the driver lost control."

When I read the report, I was instantly made aware just how close we came to the same tragic consequences at Foxton.

Because of this incident, the insurance company no longer provided cover for events and they ceased.

Europe, here we come

On the 9th April 1990 at 11.30 a.m. *Bold Lancer* with Sylvia, Barbara the barmaid, Ken Vaughan, Derek Lucas and yours truly onboard, sailed out of Poole harbour bound for France.

On the 28th August 1990 at 6.30 p.m. and 3,285 miles later, *Bold Lancer* with Sylvia and myself onboard, set sail from St Valery-sur-Somme, France, for the return trip to Brighton and then home to Poole.

During our cruise, which took us through France, Belgium, Germany and Holland, Sylvia kept a diary and I wrote regular letters to Ken with tales of our travels. The two accounts were later put in book form and distributed amongst friends and interested parties.

Ken wrote a foreword to the book that I think best sums up the adventure.

> "Blakesley is a small, relatively unspoilt village near Towcester in South Northamptonshire and is therefore situated virtually as far from any coastal water as it is possible to be within Britain. Not ideally placed for the keen offshore sailing enthusiast, you might think.
>
> Tony Hackett is the landlord of the only pub in the village, The Bartholomew Arms ('Bart Arms') and is a man who is not easily deflected by such misdemeanours of

geography. He is an avid motor yacht sailor, with a vessel berthed at Cobb's Quay boatyard, Poole.

With his long-suffering wife, Sylvia, he hatched a plan to take an extended holiday in the spring/summer of 1990 and tour the canals of France. Given that Tony was a self confessed xenophobe (the French were particularly singled out) this came as a big surprise to the regular clientele at the pub. Nevertheless, armed with pictures of Jesus in case of unchristian natives, and ample supplies of boiled sweets in case of unfriendly lockkeepers children, in April the great adventure began.

The following pages represent an account of that voyage as seen through the pages of Sylvia's exhaustive and meticulously kept diary, interspersed with Tony's more expansive description of the same events as contained in sporadic letters to me.

For those who enjoy a good yarn, it is just that; but it is more. For anyone contemplating a similar trip, it is a rich insight into what might be expected and what could easily be avoided.

Conversely, for those looking for the deeper meaning of things, a brief profile of the characters involved might be helpful. For instance, there is Tony Hackett himself who is, politically, significantly to the right of Genghis Khan, likes the odd drink, sports a full ginger beard, smokes heavily and runs a very successful business. His stated reason for that success is that he does all the thinking and leaves the work to Sylvia, she is the perfect foil for this strategy."

Ken, Barbara and Derek left us in Paris and returned to England. Brian and Avril Toop from Poole joined us for a week followed shortly afterwards by our youngest son, Michael, with his fiancée Claire and two friends for a few days. Later on Brian and Avril again joined us together with John and Chris Keeley for a week's cruise that ended in Strasbourg. It was great to have them with us – albeit for just a brief spell – to share our experiences. Apart from these visits, we were on our own for the rest of the cruise.

The trip was an unqualified success and thoroughly enjoyed by us both. We returned to England for two weeks in July to attend our son Timothy's wedding, then back to Amsterdam to continue meandering through the waterways of Holland and France.

Byron Rogers in his weekly column in the *Sunday Telegraph* wrote at some length about our experiences and some feature in his book *The Green Lane to Nowhere*.

As we were halfway across the English Channel on our way home, we had a rude awakening when at midnight Andy, our manager, phoned to say he wanted to give his notice as he had found a better position. This was the first call we had received on our portable phone for six months! Seconds later we nearly ran down a small yacht that suddenly appeared in the darkness.

Andy had been a good manager and friend and we were sorry to lose him, but fully understood his reasons. He later got married to Sara one of our barmaids, a nice Australian girl, and eventually they emigrated to Australia.

We return to Cornwall after 40 years

Steven, our next manager, was a nice lad but lacked the confidence and the ability of Andy. He had previously been employed as a chef at a golf club in Worcestershire. In spite of his shortcomings, we felt confident enough to plan another cruise for 1992. This time the cruising ground was to be the West Coast of Scotland.

We left Poole in April with Ken Vaughan and Derek Lucas as crew and headed for Scotland via, Hope Cove, where the crew disembarked, Plymouth, Penzance, Padstow, Milford Haven, Fishguard, Portdinorwic, St Mary's IOM, and Carrickfergus Northern Ireland.

We experienced very rough weather between Penzance and

Padstow, and spent two weeks sheltering in Padstow harbour waiting for better conditions. This was our first real experience of Cornwall since 1952 when we toured the county in Sylvia's 1931 Morris Minor two-seater.

One night in a pub, I met a local estate agent and we became friends. Donald Weekes had his office in St Columb Major and each night he brought me details of properties in the area.

Following a fabulous cruise that took us as far north as Ullapool and the Isle of Skye, we returned four months later, and again holed up in Padstow due to bad weather. This gave me another opportunity to renew my acquaintance with Donald.

The cost of mooring the boat at Padstow was much less that at Cobbs Quay, so I decided to keep *Bold Lancer* there for the remainder of the year. We fell in love with the town and I arranged to have our car brought down to make us more mobile.

Donald was still plying us with details of properties and, mainly out of curiosity; we started viewing some of them. After looking at about 20 properties, we saw this lovely traditionally built little cottage in St Columb Major and instantly fell in love with it. We paid a deposit and within a month were the proud owners of a Cornish retreat.

I kept my boat at Padstow for 18 months before moving her to Falmouth, which gave us a much greater choice of cruising grounds. However, I missed my friends at Poole greatly and although we had a few long distance cruises from Falmouth, it was never the same. We still keep in touch with our Poole friends and are comforted in the knowledge that they miss us as much as we miss them

Managerial problems plague us

Steven had been with us for three years and, although lacking any real personality, he was loyal and tried hard. In some ways, he was a strange person. Although in his early 30s, he still went on holiday with his elderly parents. He was very much a loner and, during his time at Blakesley, never made any real friends. His stock results started to deteriorate and I had to read the riot act to him on a number of occasions. I think he realized the writing was on the wall when he left to take a job with Unwins, a chain of off-licence shops. During the next few years, we spent more and more time in Cornwall, mainly returning to Blakesley to dismiss staff!

On one of these occasions, Sylvia went up to Northants with Burtie.

I first met "Burtie", Ian Burton, in my local, The Airways Hotel at St Mawgan. He was a 31-year-old Yorkshire man and sported numerous tattoos, had a crewcut hairstyle and wore earrings. In short, everything I detested in a man. Over time, though, I got to like him better and after, at my request, he removed his earrings and wore a long-sleeved shirt to cover his tattoos, we played golf together. He had numerous talents and golf was one of them.

Burtie had been a miner in Yorkshire and during the national miners strike in 1984, had returned to work, in common with a lot of young miners who had large mortgages to repay. As a result, he was ostracised by the older miners and eventually forced to move out of the village where he had lived all his life. He had worked as a double-glazing fitter, a roofer and a barman since then but could turn his hand to practically any task.

I had got him to do odd jobs for me in Cornwall and when he heard Sylvia was going to Northamptonshire, he asked to go with her. Burtie was a nomad. I had strong reservations about how he would be received in Blakesley which was about as conservative as any place could be. The only males wearing earrings and tattoos in the village were bulls. I need not have worried. After a cautious start, the locals took to him in a big way. He did a lot of maintenance work on the outside of the pub and passers-by would stop and chat to him. Burt was a very good talker. Quite a few villagers got him to carry out jobs for them, as a handyman in a sentence he was a godsend to the village.

It would probably be unfair, and possibly libellous, to reveal all the problems we had with umpteen managers during our last few years at Blakesley. Suffice to say, I never realised there was so many con artists, criminals and inefficient persons passing themselves off as experienced staff. In one short spell, we sacked three managers in as many weeks.

To give an example of the problems we experienced, we engaged a manager who took up his position at midday. That evening I said he could have an early night and leave cashing up the tills till the morning. After he left for bed, Sylvia and I checked the tills and they balanced exactly. Before putting the takings in the safe, I put a marked £10 note in with the money and marked all the remaining £10 notes.

In the morning, I asked him to check the previous evening's takings and he reported them being correct. Minutes later I told him I had received a telephone call from a regular customer to say he had just realized that during the previous evening he had been given change for a £10 note when in fact he had paid with a £20 note. I said the customer was the manager of a local bank and I had no reason to doubt his word, therefore the tills should be £10 up. He insisted the tills had been exactly right and the customer must have been mistaken. I asked him to turn out his pockets and the only money they contained was a single £10 note. Needless to say, it was one I had previously marked. He held the record as the shortest serving manager of the Bart Arms.

Another manager came with excellent references provided by a well-known politician-author and his wife a college lecturer, who lived in a village near Cambridge where he worked as manager of the local pub. He had two further references, both from University dons who also used the pub.

We thought that Ian, aged about 50, would fit in very well at Blakesley, as it was a very similar village to his previous place. At the interview, he wore well-tailored smart tweeds and was very articulate. In all respects, he seemed the answer to our prayers.

After he had settled in, we returned to Cornwall, confident in his ability to manage The Bart to our satisfaction. The next day we received a telephone call from son Timothy to say that Barbara had arrived for work in the morning and found Ian lying behind the bar in a comatose state surrounded with empty supermarket vintage cider bottles.

We immediately drove back up to Blakesley and confronted him about his behaviour. It transpired that he left his last position after a disagreement with the female owner which had affected his nerves quite badly. He said that as soon as we left the pub, he suffered a bad attack of nerves and turned to alcohol. He left the next day with the intention of checking into a clinic.

Not having a lot of success with managers, we thought we would try our luck with a manageress.

Jane was from the North Country, a bit of a rough diamond but seemed quite popular with the customers. After she had been in charge for a few weeks, I received a telephone call from a member of staff to say a man had moved in with her. It turned out he was a tarmac layer whom she had just met and was working locally. Each evening after work, he would return to the pub, have a bath and Jane would cook him a meal. He would sleep in her room and, in the morning, he had breakfast while she packed him up a lunchbox.

Returning to the pub I asked her if what I had heard was correct and she confirmed it was. Jane could see no harm in this arrangement, neither did she think my concern that he was using our business as a free lodging was justified. When I pointed out that she knew very little about his character and I did not want a stranger having free access to my business, she thought I was being unreasonable. A few weeks after she left, we heard that he had taken all her money and left her.

In the past we had considered employing a couple but, as this would mean giving up our bedroom and lounge to them, we decided against it. However, with our record of unsatisfactory managers, we thought we would give it a try.

The first couple came from Northamptonshire. He had run a pub with his ex-wife and was now living with a much younger girl. Peter was in his early 50s and Jane mid 20s. She was a very attractive girl and it was obvious from the start he was jealous of the attention she received from our younger customers. Staff said they could hear them constantly rowing in their room. After a couple of weeks, matters came to a head and he left her. She asked to be allowed to run the pub on her own but, in our opinion, she was too immature and "flirty".

Another couple we employed were caught selling their own food, and started telling the customers and staff that they were buying the pub from us. Other issues we discovered suggested they were far from honest. We had to return from Cornwall unannounced to make sure they did not take our belongings with them when they left.

You may wonder why we had so many disasters. We wondered too. We usually advertised in the *Lady* and the *Hotel & Caterer* magazines and in the *Morning Advertiser,* the licensed trade newspaper. We always had plenty of enquiries and would select two or three to come for an interview, an expensive exercise as we always paid their travelling and other expenses.

First impressions at the interview played a big part in our selection process. It was staggering the number of applicants that turned up unsuitably dressed or with long hair and dirty fingernails. One applicant, who had good references and sounded ideal over the telephone, turned up in torn jeans, a garish T-shirt and wore numerous earrings in both ears.

The actual selection was usually a compromise between those who had the best references and experience, and those who presented themselves best on the day. We were both of the opinion that the standard of applicants deteriorated as the years went by. Some might say that we demanded too high a standard from our managers. However, we knew the way we wanted the Bart to be run, a formula that we had developed successfully over the years and we were not going to reduce our standards.

Sylvia and I both had difficulty in trying to remember just how many managers we did employ. We had to turn to our friend Doug Blake for help and he sent us a list, which totalled 16 in all. He gave them all a "nickname" which, though humorous, I must resist the temptation to quote for fear of libel!

In 1988 when I was 54 years old, a multiple licensee asked if we would sell him the Bart Arms. He offered £450.000. At that time, if we had sold we would have been subject to considerable Capital Gains Tax, which meant paying tax on the difference between what we had paid for the business and the price we were selling it for. The age limit for exemption was then 60 – by 1996, this had been changed to 55; also at that time we had no wish to sell.

A lot of people thought we had wanted to sell for a number of years. These rumours seemed to be prevalent in the trade once publicans reached the age of 60; I was then 62 and still hadn't decided to call it a day. In spite of our problems with managers, we were able to spend some time at our cottage and the business still provided us with an income, albeit a reduced one.

It would have been even less, except that a few years previously I joined a buying consortium, a collection of inns whose owners joined together to negotiate a bulk-buying discount from selected brewers. Membership had the advantage of instead of my paying £26 free trade price for a 10 gallon keg of Carlsberg Lager, I was able to buy it for £19. This worked out at 23p per pint. The selling price of a pint that year, 1994, was 1.40p, not a bad profit percentage. Buying consortiums had been in operation for a number of years but it was only in 1990 I discovered we qualified for membership.

Brewery tenants had always complained – quite rightly – about the price gap between what the free trade and tied trade paid for their beers. The advent of buying groups only exacerbated this position. The breweries' explanation for their price differentials was always the same; they did not have any capital tied up in bricks and mortar with free houses. This, they argued, enabled them to offer their beers at a reduced price. With the astronomical rents breweries were now charging their tenants, it was difficult to see how they could justify this argument.

When Rex Groombridge retired from his pub in 2000 he was paying the brewery £26,000 a year rent. Although his pub was on the main A5, Fosters Booth was a hamlet and the pub had limited potential. I once worked out with Rex that if The Bart had been a tied tenancy, on the volume of trade we were achieving the rent would have been £50,000.

It was only after three disastrous managers in quick succession, that we decided to sell at the right price. The turnover of managers was having a detrimental effect on the customers and the takings were starting to drop off considerably. After receiving some speculative inquiries, we received a genuine one and the buyers were prepared to pay the asking price. (This was less that the £450,000 previously offered!)

Without wishing to discredit the buyers, I often wondered afterwards if they had really given proper thought to the whole enterprise. Entering the licensed trade is a big step.

From the very start problems developed, with the sale fluctuating on and off from day to day. Having got past that stage, a huge problem arose when the buyers indicated, with 10 days to go, that they didn't want to take over the artefacts in the pub. I had paid £1,000 for an established firm of valuers to draw up an inventory, which they valued at £18,000. As far as we were concerned, the items were part of the business, and had been for many years.

To sell the pub without the artefacts would be like selling a dog without its pedigree! We were devastated. The buyers indicated odd pieces which they wanted but declined to take the greater part. I told them this was unsatisfactory. This late decision by the buyers left us with just 10 days in which to organise the sale.

I had recently bumped into Dick Foster, our ex-village policemen from who I had bought a lot of guns and ships in the past. He told me his wife was working for a firm of auctioneers who specialised in selling antiques and collectables. I contacted Dick and told him the problem I faced, and he arranged for the firm to organise the sale.

Because of the number of items involved, it was impossible to hold the sale on the premises. Had I had more time, I would have hired a marquee and held the sale on the lawn of the pub. As it was, we had to make do with the village hall, which, because of its size, was far from satisfactory. It meant the buyers would have to bid on the strength of what they had seen in the pub and the description in the catalogue. This is never a satisfactory way and can lead to buyers making mistakes by bidding for the wrong lot. The notices of the auction were printed six days before the event, and the catalogues prepared with just three days to go.

The hammer falls

On Saturday 14th December 1996, our 37-year collection of pub artefacts went under the hammer. We had withdrawn a few pieces to take to Cornwall, but the remaining 278 items realised £28,036.75 – £10,000 more than they would have cost the purchasers of the pub had they agreed to buy! In spite of this unexpected windfall, I still think it was a tragedy they hadn't remained where they belonged.

Buyers came from all over the country plus some Japanese and Americans. The auctioneers said had they been given more time to advertise the sale, they could have doubled the number attending, which, almost certainly, would have meant even higher prices. In spite of all the problems, certain items fetched far more than we expected.

Mistinguett's Bath Chair made £600, the peg-legged seaman £2,000, a Naval Cutlass £180, Brown Bess flintlock gun £600, Flintlock pistol £580, Cavalry Sword £290 and Don Bradman cricket bat £270. A clocking-in machine £320 and the clock from HMS *Sidon* £460. Two Grandfather clocks were both bought by a Japanese buyer, one for £920 and the other £1500. A stuffed fish fetched £280 and a stuffed fox £60, a Turtle shell sold for £90 and two Stags heads £140, a Press-gang truncheon £230 and two 1 Penny Sweet dispensers for £560, an oil painting of a Stage Coach £580 and an oil Portrait of a Young Lady £310 and one of a Young Man £410. An Engine Room Telegraph made £310, a Ship's Bell £320 and a model of a Scottish Puffer boat £300. A Copper Samovar £350, a Copper Urn £150 and a copper Gunpowder Magazine Lantern £105. An antique Baby's High Chair £210 and an Office Desk £420. The Home Cured Hams averaged £20 each.

A lot of strangers came up to me and asked if we were sad at parting with our collection, I gave them all the same answer. We had enjoyed seeking out the items, buying and displaying them; we just hoped other people would derive the same pleasure from them. That said it was a sad occasion for a lot of people present to see the break-up of the collection.

On the following Monday we transferred the licence to the new owners, for the first time in 37 years, we were no longer the holders of a Justice's Licence and my name ceased to be over a pub door. An era was over.

REFLECTIONS

Looking back over those years we had seen many changes in the licensed trade, very few for the better. I deplore the drop in standards. A licence holder no longer has to be a person of impeccable character; even people with drink-driving convictions are getting licences. As for the reduced age of licence holders, how can a girl of 21 be expected to deal with a group of drunken yobbos spoiling for a fight? Is it any wonder pubs no longer hold their attraction for mature drinkers when landlords actively encourage foul-mouthed kids into their establishments?

It was with some regret that soon after moving to Blakesley I ceased to take an active part in my local LVA. I had always been very much involved in all the district associations, none more so than Towcester. But I was becoming greatly concerned by the type of persons who were becoming licensees, so much so that I rarely told people I was a publican when asked what I did for a living, I would most times say "catering trade".

Get-rich-quick merchants, completely lacking in personality and intelligence, had devalued what had once been a proud dignified profession. Once upon a time the licensed trade was a lifetime career but recently it has become a stop-gap position for the likes of redundant car and double-glazing salesmen. Five years as a licensee now seems to qualify you for a gold watch.

Good "old fashioned" landlords were more than just dispensers of beer. They, and more importantly, the wife, were marriage, bereavement and financial counsellors, therapists, mentors, admonishers, arbiters and friends to all their customers. Were their skills available to customers today, the government and health service could do away with thousands of highly paid "ologists". Today's publicans are more likely to have a degree in Microwave Technology than Psychology.

During our 21 years at the Bart, a tenanted pub in a neighbouring village changed hands eight times. At LVA meetings these newcomers invariably spoke with the loudest voices, often making it clear to all assembled that they intended to apply professional techniques to take the trade away from a bunch of well-meaning amateurs. Their wives were always "professionally trained" in catering, which usually means they were awarded an "A" grade for Domestic Science at school. One character from a pub, in the next village, even had the audacity to apologise to me in advance for taking my trade away! Less than a year later, he was bankrupt.

Standard dress for landlords and wives now appears to be tracksuits, often worn with a replica of their favourite soccer teams shirt, and trainers. Should the wife be overweight – which is often the case – ultra tight leggings seem to be popular attire behind the bar. The days when landladies were pictures of sartorial elegance have gone. The typical modern publican has often invested in a gallery of tattoos, earrings, a plentiful array of gold chains and an obligatory ponytail.

I saw such a publican being interviewed on local television the other evening. He was behind the bar of a lovely old pub in a village on the edge of Dartmoor. When asked a question, he was incapable of stringing together a single intelligent sentence. The interviewer was asking whether the road works under discussion had affected his trade. His replies were littered with expressions like "At the end of the day, at this moment in time, basically yes, if you know what I mean". Years ago that pub would have had a real jovial local character as a landlord, this one had a strong Essex accent, an outsider – and it showed.

Invariably, if the couple have children, they will be running amok in the bars and avoiding falling over their array of toys is an achievement. At other establishments, you have to keep a nervous eye on the landlord's ferocious dog. The drop in standards is not restricted to publicans and their wives. The quality of modern bar staff leaves a lot to be desired.

Increased problems with arthritis led us to sell *Bold Lancer* in 1997 which meant we were without a boat for the first time since buying *Jonquil* at Woodford in 1966. After a few months, the thought of being permanently "shore bound" was getting to me and we decided to purchase a narrow boat for use on the canals. When we lived at Foxton – which stands astride the Grand Union canal – we enjoyed many trips on narrow boats so had some experience of them.

In 1999 we decided to travel by *Emma Hamilton* to London, to spend the Millennium New Year's Eve in the London Docks. We cruised down the Grand Union canal to Limehouse Docks, and then the short distance on the River Thames to the West India Docks. It was a memorable occasion not least when I fell in the dock on New Year's day.

For the return journey we travelled the 15 miles down the Thames to Teddington Lock which took us under Tower Bridge, past the Houses of Parliament and the new London Eye. After going through the lock we continued up river and one evening moored for the night in the lovely village of Clifton Hampden. My thirst soon took me to the Barley Mow a famous waterside Inn where Jerome K Jerome wrote *Three Men in a Boat* in the 19th century.

The barman who served me wore a smart white shirt and bow tie. I asked, "Could I have a pint of real ale please?" he grunted, "What sort, mate?" indicating with his hand the pump handles – he obviously was unable to remember the names of the two on offer. I checked the pump badges and made my choice. Passing me my beer, the barman told me the price, again adding the word "mate". He gave me my change with the remark, "There you go then, mate."

Being unable to contain my anger any longer I said, "Excuse me, would you think I am old enough to be your grandfather?"

He looked surprised and answered, "I suppose so, mate." I then asked him, " Well, if that is so, why do you think it appropriate to address me as mate?" The lad looked amazed and said, "What do you want me to call you?" I replied, "Would you think sir was out of order?" He muttered, "I suppose so," and wandered away.

I should have told him I objected to a barman passing me my drink, with his fingers wrapped round the rim of the glass from where I have to drink. I decided this extra advice was too much for him to digest in one day.

After a long day on the water, I was ready for a pint. The pub had a nice fire, was clean and welcoming, the barman was smartly dressed but I'm afraid his disrespectful approach annoyed me intensely. I finished my drink and left.

In all the establishments we have run, staff were always instructed to address customers as Sir, Madam or Mr and Mrs, unless familiar with them. It seems to be a form of address fast becoming extinct in the service industry.

Some serving and ex-publicans blame the licensed trade for all their ills, including their children going off the rails and their marriages ending on the rocks. Our answer is, "It undoubtedly would have happened anyway." Certainly the pub trade puts great stresses on marriages and family life, but so does being a sales representative away from home all week and what about the Armed Forces and their long separations? When our children came home from school, we were both there to greet them and Sylvia would have a meal ready. If anything, I think I sometimes saw too much of my children.

Our three sons were brought up in the trade with two of them born whilst we were licensees. None of them have ever been in trouble with the law, taken drugs, been in major debt, or suffered from the many other defects of modern young society. They all have good responsible jobs, Stephen is a senior manager with a major power distribution company, Tim is a director of a large agricultural engineering business and Michael has his own electrical and alarm installation company. Even more important, they all have good, lasting marriages. This is not due to any magic formula, just old-fashioned standards. For a bonus, we have five lovely grandchildren who would be a credit to any family.

When we first started in the trade in 1959, it was to be 10 years before we took our children away on holiday, not by choice but circumstances. We could neither afford the time nor money. When they were old enough they went with their grandparents and, in no way, did they feel deprived. Today, if publicans don't go out for a meal with friends at least once a week, and take their children to the "Costa del Bomb" twice a year, they feel disadvantaged. In our opinion if young publicans spent more time looking after their customers and less on themselves and their families, they would be better landlords and reap richer rewards later in their careers.

Both Sylvia and I are convinced there is still a place for the old fashioned pub, one which welcomes mature people, provides good company, good conversation and good drink, without having to compete against loud bar staff, loud music, loud kids and the air reeking of frying food.

We deprecate too the way that food is taking preference in pubs at the expense of drink. There is a demand for food in public houses, but we find it unacceptable when we enter a pub to discover all the tables in the public bar laid up with cutlery and place mats. If all you want is a drink, it makes you feel you have entered under false pretences.

We see nothing wrong with *good, honest* value for money "Pub Grub" which we prided ourselves on serving, and had a reputation for, at The Dukes Arms, The Bartholomew Arms and in the buffet bar at The Brave Old Oak. What does annoy us is when a pub offers a large range of elaborate starters, followed by an even larger selection of exotic main courses which, by their very composition, tells everyone but the dimmest that they are bought in pre-prepared dishes. They don't even have the intelligence to stick to the masquerade by describing the odd dish as "home made" which confirms your suspicion that the rest are "imported".

In the larger establishments the food is often brought to you by unenthusiastic, clueless Australian backpackers disguised as waiters.

For many years while at Blakesley, Captain Dickie Hawkins MFH and his charming wife Anne frequently came with friends for a bar snack, up until his death. The Hawkins lived at Everdon Hall whose parkland sported a superb private cricket ground. Teams of celebrities travelled from all over the country to play Dickie Hawkins XI. I assumed that included amongst the Hall staff was at least a cook, if not a chef, and yet when they came to eat at the Bart, they always chose ham, egg and chips! We prided ourselves on the quality of our ham and they, like so many others, obviously enjoyed good honest simple food. It was probably through eating shepherds pie at the Brave Old Oak that Lord Jeffery Archer became addicted to it!

On television a few nights ago, a well known London chef was sent to a bar in a small Yorkshire town to sort out its catering problems.

The bar's 21-year-old head chef had visions of grandeur, and an ambition to be a television chef himself. His speciality dish of black pudding, scallops and hollandaise sauce looked disgusting.

The celebrity chef cooked a steak and kidney pie and they took both dishes onto the streets, asking passers by to taste them and give their verdict on which they preferred. Everyone picked the steak and kidney, proving that good honest simple food usually wins hands down.

When the young chef was asked to make an omelette, he admitted he had never made one before! At the end of the programme it stated he had left the bar and got a job as a chef at a nearby pub. God help the customers.

The morning after the programme was screened, the 21 year old chef was quoted in the press as saying, "He made me look like the biggest idiot in Britain." Few would disagree with him.

Within a few years of our leaving The Bart Arms, the new owners sub-let the catering to an Indian gentleman. We were told the smell of curry wafted far up the village street. In a conservation village in Northamptonshire! Is nothing sacred?

A couple of years ago whilst cruising in our boat on the River's Severn and Avon and Stratford-on-Avon canal, we noticed a lot of pubs were offering "Lamb Shanks" as the "Dish of the Day". This intrigued us as we hadn't come across this before, and all identically described it as "Lamb Shanks served in a Mint Jus" or "served in a Red Wine Jus".

A visit to our local Cash & Carry, some months later, revealed all. There on the meat counter were boxes of the ubiquitous lamb shanks. Our curiosity got the better of us and we bought a box. Urgh! Each plastic pouch contained a very small shank, more bone than meat, and a disgusting sticky liquid.

Coincidentally, after offering them unsuccessfully to our dog, we still have some of them left. If you wonder why, when son Stephen comes to stay, his Labrador loves them! I have one in front of me.

Quote, "Product of Australia" "Ingredients: Lamb, Thickener (1422), Maltodextrin, Red Wine Extract, Wheat Flour, Vegetable Powders, Salt, Food Acids (262,330), Herbs, Vegetable Gums (415, 412), Yeast Extracts, Colour (150), Sugar, Spice, Flavour Enhancer (612), Emulsifier (433), Flavour, Water Added." "Reheat in Microwave for 7 minutes."

Most of the pubs we visited, offering the dish on their menu, described it as *"Homemade* Special Dish of the Day!" I rest my case.

You continually hear the argument that pubs have to provide food to survive: this is rubbish. In the old days, it was possible to have a good business when you were lucky to achieve a gross profit percentage on drink of just 15 per cent. Today the profit on a range of drinks can be as high as 250 per cent, especially on some of these trendy Alco pops. Whoever thought the day would come when you paid 19/- (95p) for a small bottle of tonic water that the landlord buys for 18p or would pay £1 for a glass of water? It takes far less effort, involves less overheads to make £10 profit on drink than it does on food.

Wastage on food can be very high; on drink, it is negligible. In 1996 a good barman or barmaid could take £100 in an hour for which they were paid £4. To take the same amount on food required paying preparation staff, chef/cook, waitress, washer-up and expensive equipment to store, cook and present it. *Good* kitchen staff do not come cheaply.

Whilst not in anyway suggesting that our policy for running pubs was always correct, our success, in terms of finance and reputation, indicates that our formula was not too wide of the mark.

Last orders, please

Since listing our original customers at the beginning of the Bartholomew Arms era, lots of new people moved into Blakesley and surrounding villages, and many, but by no means all, used the Bart. A considerable number have already been mentioned as original customers, or through being involved in the cricket or soapbox events so I will not mention them again. At the risk of missing anyone out, I will attempt to list other regulars, or I should say friends, who graced us with their custom during our many happy years at the Bart. In compiling this list, I must pay tribute to the assistance received from Lee Penny, Barbara Welch, Ken Vaughan and Doug Blake.

> Harry Butter and sister Thora, Bob & Pat Patterson, Major Hugh Merreck, Bob & Annie Wainwright, Peter, Maxine & Julie Conway, Pat Blake, Linda Jefferson, Chris Halliday, Graham & Christine Hill, Ron & Sue Parker, Arthur & Barbara Bradley, Bob & Val Saunders, John & Ann Weekley, Dennis & Joan Bailey, John & Margaret Bourne, Nick & Rosemary Bromwich, Don, Janet, Nancy & Ashley Boone, Gerald Chidwick, Robin & Rodney Webb, Ann Cunningham, Bob Hatton, Steve & Jill Nunn, Tim Martin, Mickey Laughran, Ian Leddingham, Phil Kingston, Byron

Rogers, Jack Salmons, Tiny Howkins, Brian & Sue Lucarotti, Tony & Henny Perry, Phil & Sue Bates, John & Veronica Miller, Mike and Anne Scott, Sarah Payne, Bruce Hatton, Doug Evans, Alan Saunders, Adrian (Eggy) Williams, John Jnr, Jenny, Peter, Skip and Emma Sheppard, Roger Duckworth, Anthony Penny, Rick East, Nick & Chris Green, Mary & Nick Penn, Shaw and Ander Cockerill, Mathew & James Wallis jnr, Dudley Smith. John & Helen Leeson, Norman Cox, Tom Wills, The "other" David Powell (Towcester RDC), Alan Nunn, Ellen Robinson, Peter Donger, Roy & Rita Wilson, Capt & Mrs Dickie Hawkins, Graham Weaver, Mick Sheppard, Claire Sheppard, David Oliver, Andrew Oliver, Ron Roberts, Bill & Sheila Tremelow, Eric & Lorna Steele, John and Bill Lee, Jeff & Sheila Smithson, John & Pat Oliver, Peter Warner, John Callow, Linda Callow, Doctors Tim Reynolds, Vince Sanger & Richard Wallace, Austin Hutchison & Jeffery from down the lane, Ian Gulliman, Karen, Tracey & Debbie Neal, Christine Jackson, Colin Marriott, "Bristol John" Gardiner, Mary & Elaine Hillary, Carol Cook, Ken Bartlett, James Taylor, Nigel & Jill Felton, Andre & Tony Bodily, Janet & Heather Bodily, Sue, Richard & Hayley Brown, Stuart Reynolds, Rob Chilcott, Mathew Purser, Robin Powell, Noel Crane, Bernard Chester, Paul & Viki May. Brian Hitchcock, Tommy Tucker, Admiral & Mrs John Roberts, Colin Webster, Mike Buswell, Brian Gardiner, Ted Lock, Tom & Sara Burn, Peter Newcombe & Jackie, Martin Mills, John Mawle, Peter & Marlene Thornton, Austin Nightingale, Rev Alfred Ridley, Keith Downes & parents, John English, Ian Osborne, Chris & Sara Scott-Young, Nigel Jones, Peter Orton, Ian Vine & parents, Paul & Rosy Berry and Bill Gurney.

None came to play the juke box, pool table, game machines, karaoke, skittles, and darts or to watch Sky TV because there weren't any. Quite a few had bar snacks on occasions, but mainly they came for good beer, an argument with the landlord and to be in the company of other very nice people.

I apologise most sincerely to the many customers I have almost certainly missed. The memory is not what it used to be. Some listed have sadly died but I feel their names should still be recorded.

There were literally hundreds of others who came from near and far to drink at the Bart. We could not possibly remember them all so will not try, but I cannot close this book without mentioning Mike & Jenny Street from Langley in Cheshire, two of the nicest people you could ever hope to meet. Sadly, they both died within a few months of each other and were greatly missed by their many friends at the Bart.

Looking back, we have often wondered how our lives would have changed if back in 1959 I had joined the Leicestershire Police Force. We shall never know, but what we do know is we could never have made so many good friends, or had so many unforgettable experiences in any other line of business. Neither Sylvia nor I have any regrets.

If I was asked for one piece of advice for youngsters thinking of entering the licensed trade, I could do no better than echo Mr R O Baillon's question to us in 1959 and say, *"How strong is your marriage?"* If it isn't, *"Forget it."*

Ours was then, Mr Baillon, and what's more, still is.

"Time, ladies and gentlemen, please."

Cornwall 2004